Staking Out the Terrain

SUNY Series in Environmental Public Policy
Lester Milbrath, Editor

JEANNE NIENABER CLARKE
DANIEL McCOOL

Staking Out the Terrain

POWER DIFFERENTIALS AMONG NATURAL
RESOURCE MANAGEMENT AGENCIES

State University of New York Press
ALBANY

To Jim and Michael
(J.N.C.)
To Olivia and Jack McCool
(D.C.M.)

Published by
State University of New York Press, Albany

© 1985 State University of New York

For information, address State University of New York
Press, State University Plaza, Albany, N.Y., 12246

Library of Congress Cataloging in Publication Data

Clarke, Jeanne Nienaber, 1943-

Staking out the terrain.

(SUNY series in environmental public policy)

Bibliography: p.

Includes index.

1. Natural resources—Government policy—United
States. 2. Environmental policy—United States.
3. Administrative agencies—United States. 4. Bureaucracy—United States. I. McCool, Daniel. 1950-
II. Title.   III. Series.

HC103.7.C53 1985   33.7′0973   85-12663

ISBN 0-88706-020-X

ISBN 0-88706-02108 (pbk.)

10 9 8 7 6 5 4 3 2 1

Contents

ACKNOWLEDGEMENTS   vii

ONE   *Differentials in Agency Power*   1

TWO   *Bureaucratic Superstars: The Army Corps of Engineers and the U.S. Forest Service*   13

THREE   *Agencies that Muddle Through: The National Park Service, the Soil Conservation Service, and the U.S. Fish and Wildlife Service*   48

FOUR   *Organizational Shooting Stars: The Bureau of Reclamation and the Bureau of Land Management*   92

FIVE   *A Cross Validation of Agency Power: Budget, Personnel, and Status Rankings*   125

SIX   *Resource Management in the 1980s: Who Guards the Guardians?*   143

APPENDIX   151

NOTES   153

BIBLIOGRAPHY   175

INDEX   184

Acknowledgments

Many people as well as a few organizations have assisted in the preparation of this volume. Of the organizations, the senior author wishes to thank the Office of Water Research and Technology, in the Department of the Interior, for its 1976-77 financial assistance. She is also indebted to the Water Resources Research Center of the University of Arizona for insisting that the project be completed. Both authors are extremely grateful for the assistance given by personnel in the seven federal agencies included in the study. Their contributions, which must remain anonymous, are evident in chapter 6.

Several friends and colleagues have enlightened us over the years in which this study has evolved, and it is a pleasure to thank them for their assistance. We are especially grateful to Helen Ingram, who worked with us on an earlier version of this study and whose insights we hope are preserved in this present draft. Two graduate students, Milo Mecham and Carol Williams, provided important research assistance during the summer of 1977; their contributions are particularly evident in the histories of the agencies. Recently, we have been assisted by Randal Evans of Texas A & M University and Shih-kuan Chien of the University of Arizona. Several people read earlier drafts of this study and provided us with their critiques. They include: Richard Andrews, James Clarke, Hanna Cortner, Paul Culhane, Robert Dickens, Herbert Kaufman, Richard Liroff, and Aaron Wildavsky. Aaron made a particularly important contribution in suggesting the kind of typology of agency behavior which we subsequently developed.

Finally we wish to express our appreciation to the Department of Political Science at the University of Arizona, under the chairmanship of John Wahlke, for its material support of our research activities. Special thanks go to Mary Sue McQuown, the department's manuscript typist, for an excellent job in preparing this manuscript.

CHAPTER ONE

Differentials in Agency Power

INTRODUCTION

Much public attention has been focused over the last fifteen years on natural resources issues. In the late 1960s concern was directed toward what was labeled an environmental crisis: singular events such as off-shore spills, smog-producing temperature inversions, and tension-filled summers in the nation's overcrowded metropolitan centers suddenly became interconnected in the public mind. A pattern emerged. So did a political movement. Not since the days of Theodore Roosevelt did Americans evince such concern over environmental issues and act on that concern. From 1965 to 1975 — roughly the years spanning this second conservation movement[1] — many programs were enacted with the intent of protecting in one way or another the nation's environmental quality. For example, laws were passed to clean up our lakes, rivers, and coastal zones; to protect endangered species; to maintain and improve air quality; to regulate and monitor the disposal of hazardous wastes; and to create a national wilderness system. But probably the most celebrated of the numerous statutes passed during this time is the National Environmental Policy Act of 1969 (NEPA). This piece of legislation seemed to many to be the movement's crowning achievement because it forces federal resource managers to add environmental impact to their list of criteria for project and program evaluation. The act's philosophical intent was aimed at promoting better conservation practices throughout the federal government, but in particular it was intended to substantially modify the activities of agencies like the Army Corps of Engineers, the U.S. Forest Service, and the agencies of the Department of the Interior. How these agencies responded to NEPA is a central part of this study.

Public attention to any given issue is generally short-lived. As interest in environmental quality issues began to wane, a new, albeit related, issue came to the forefront of national attention. Uncertainty over the

1

adequacy of energy supplies was dramatically felt by many Americans during the winter of 1973-74, as we waited in long stationary lines at local gasoline stations. Familiar themes were reiterated during this latest crisis: Were we running out of oil and other valuable energy resources? Had our natural resources been grossly mismanaged, possibly squandered away by short-sighted entrepreneurs operating in both the public and private sectors? Was it necessary to devise more rational policies for the coming worldwide era of frugality? One presidential ship of state was largely wrecked on the shoals of the energy crisis, and another was swept into office by the tide of popular sentiment favoring fiscal conservatism—particularly as it pertained to the federal government. Scarcity and frugality were the key political concepts of the 1970s, and by the middle of the decade the environmental crisis had evolved almost imperceptibly into the energy crisis. As had been the case with the environmental issue, the federal government acted on the public's concern over energy shortages by passing several pieces of legislation designed to alleviate the energy crunch.[2] And again, resource-managing agencies found themselves the focus for much of this public attention.

Formulation of new public policies, through the legislative process and by executive order, is by no means the end of the story, however. In fact, the recent scholarly and journalistic attention accorded the implementation stage of policymaking makes it appear as though new federal legislation is virtually the beginning of the process rather than, as we used to think, its conclusion. In some respects this is so: how policies get twisted, changed, modified, distorted, and even at times successfully executed has become the subject matter of a flourishing subfield within the disciplines of political science and public administration. Even a single piece of legislation—for instance NEPA—is subjected to microscopic analysis by students of the policy process (It is possible to refer to oneself nowadays as an "NEPA specialist"). Finally, then, how a goal or objective is implemented in the policy process is at least as important a step as deciding on that goal.

When the focus is on implementation one is inevitably drawn into the milieu of the federal bureaucracy, for one or another bureaucratic organization is nearly always given the responsibility of executing federal laws.[3] In a book on the presidency Francis Rourke noted recently, "It is important also to remember that while the White House staff may be very good at designing broad-guage programs, these programs must be carried out by some bureaucratic organization."[4] Whether policies succeed or fail in their objectives is largely dependent upon the nature of the organization mandated to carry out those policies. And those natures differ. The flora and fauna of what is commonly referred to as "the federal bureaucracy" is actually rich in its diversity and complexity. Although it appears monolithic when viewed from the outside, or from a distance, that vast executive branch establishment headquartered in Washington, D.C., and its environs is actually a collection of hundreds of agencies, bureaus, departments, councils, and commissions. By one count, the executive branch is composed of something like eighteen hundred of these subunits.[5]

It is the thesis of this study that the characteristics that distinguish one organization from another in the federal bureaucracy can be as significant as those elements that they hold in common. By and large, the scholarship on bureaucracy has stressed, beginning with the seminal work of Max Weber, the common features of bureaucratic organizations. Without trying to minimize these important generalizations, this study will emphasize the idiosyncratic. We wish to examine what accounts for the performance differences that exist among certain federal agencies— for that which makes one agency rich, powerful, and influential in the governmental process and another one impoverished, impotent, and inconsequential. Our intention is thus to provide a detailed examination of what Rourke has called "differentials in agency power,"[6] and to discuss why these differentials are important in the policy process.

The scholarship on NEPA is a good illustration of how agency differences come into play in policymaking and policy implementation. As mentioned previously, NEPA rather quickly became a celebrated and much-studied piece of legislation. Because one of its principal intentions was to force agencies to change established patterns of behavior (through sec. 102(2) (c) of the act), the statute provided an uncommon opportunity for social scientists to observe the dynamics of organizational change. Several things were discovered. First, it was learned that the discipline lacked universal indicators of organizational change. A measurement problem surfaced. What yardsticks could be used to assess the extent of change within an organization? Many had to admit that such measures did not exist, so they had to be constructed. Observation thus became intertwined, as is inevitable in the social sciences, with evaluation. The result was that to a certain extent the units of measurement varied from study to study.

A second important discovery had to do with the fact that federal agencies did not respond in a uniform manner to the new NEPA goals and objectives. Notwithstanding a certain degree of imprecision, as we just mentioned, in the measurement techniques being used, most observers discerned rather clear differences among agencies with respect to their willingness to change. Some agencies simply responded more quickly, more effectively, and more thoroughly than did others. Many observers wondered why.

Third, and last, certain paradoxes emerged with respect to the bureaucratic response to NEPA. All who studied the act admitted that it contained a pro-environment, pro-conservation, and hence an anti-development or anti-public works bias. A good guess would have been that those agencies whose missions were most congruent with the basic philosophy of the act would have been the agencies with the best, or better, response records. Agencies like the National Park Service and the U.S. Fish and Wildlife Service ought to have responded more quickly to NEPA than, for example, pro-development agencies like the Corps of Engineers and the U.S. Forest Service. This was found not to be the case. In three separate studies on the implementation of NEPA, the researchers found little or no correlation between the nature of the agency's mission and its response to new environmental requirements. For example, Allen F. Wichelman, in his study of NEPA, found the Corps of Engineers to have as good a response record as the U.S. Forest Service, and a better track record than the National Park Service.[7] A study by Richard Andrews, *Environmental Policy and Administrative Change*, compared the Corps of Engineers with the Soil Conservation Service in the Agriculture Department;[8] the former agency comes out far ahead of the SCS. Finally, Richard Liroff's book evaluated the Corps of Engineers' implementation record and labeled it "extremely well" to "best of all."[9] Other agencies do not fare so well: The Bureau of Reclamation has done poorly, and the National Park Service and the Fish and Wildlife Service both have been "slow" to implement requirements that, ostensibly, fit in well with their existing programs and policies.

The point to be emphasized here is that there exist observable and significant differences in how federal resource managers perform under similar circumstances. This is seen in not only the implementation of NEPA, but in the way agencies have responded to a whole series of changes in their immediate external environments; for it must be remembered that the ecology movement not only produced NEPA and its environmental impact statement (EIS) requirements, but scores of other new requirements as well. The energy crisis of the 1970s, for instance, had several impacts on agency behavior, from stepped-up minerals exploration on the public lands to a renewed interest in and funding for the energy benefits derived from federal hydroelectric projects. We argue in this study that what accounts for these performance differences is a set of organizational and political conditions that have produced different types of agencies within the executive establishment. Consequently, these varying types of organizations manifest different patterns of response to essentially the same stimuli, and so a situation is produced wherein certain organizations have what amounts to "favored-agency status" relative to other agencies. The adage that nothing succeeds like success thus has a certain relevance and even poignancy to the world of bureaucratic politics, especially as that world has become more populated, more complex, and more differentiated in the twentieth century.[10]

What exactly are these political and organizational factors that act as sources of agency power? And what kinds of agencies have been produced as a result? In answer to the first question, the literature on bureaucratic behavior suggests that organizations have two primary sources of power. In *Bureaucracy, Politics, and Public Policy* Francis Rourke noted that agency resources include (1) the expertise, knowledge, and information an agency has at its disposal, and (2) the clientele and other external support an agency can muster in support of its programs.[11] The classic research by Weber stressed the element of expertise as the bureaucracy's primary source of power:

> Under normal conditions, the power position of a fully developed bureaucracy is always overtowering. The 'political master' finds himself in the role of the 'dilettante' who stands opposite the 'expert,' facing the trained official who stands within the management of administration. This holds whether the 'master' whom the bureaucracy serves is a 'people,' equipped with the weapons of 'legislative initiative,' the 'referendum,' and the right to remove officials, or a parliament, elected on a more aristocratic or more 'democratic' basis and equipped with the right to vote a lack of confidence. . . . It holds whether the master is an aristocratic, colleagiate body, legally or actually based on self-recruitment, or whether he is a popularly-elected president, a hereditary and 'absolute' or a 'constitutional' monarch.[12]

Our own research into the histories and behavior of seven federal resource agencies corroborates these analyses. The display of expertise and the mobilization of political support are crucial to an analysis of agency behavior. However, we also found that for purposes of comparing one agency's power base and performance with others, it is necessary to look at the several dimensions that go to make up expertise and political clout. In other words, these two resources can be broken down into their constituent parts. We thus see the first resource—expertise and the control of information—as being composed of: (1*a*) the nature of the mission originally given the agency; (2*a*) the extent to which the agency embodies a highly regarded profession; (3*a*) the degree to which the leadership of the agency can capitalize on the knowledge base of the organization; and (4*a*) whether a sense of esprit de corps permeates the organization. The second variable, political support, appears to include such characteristics as: (1*b*) the existence of an optimal-size constituency on which the agency generally can count; (2*b*) the extent to which the agency's mission is linked to identifiable economic interests in society; (3*b*) whether it is a service or a regulatory agency; and (4*b*) the organization's position vis-à-vis its executive branch superiors and the U.S. Congress. These characteristics are displayed in table 1-1.

Table 1-1 Sources of Agency Power

1. Expertise/Control of Information			
1a Nature of Mission	1b Dominant, Established Profession	1c Astute Leadership	1d Esprit de Corps
+pro-development; multiple-use; utilitarian values +created by an organic act +contains a mission that is expandable 0 age of organization —the product of executive orders or reorganizations —narrow or esoteric mission; dominant use; preservationist values	+scientific, military bases of expertise —interdisciplinary; melting pot or professions	+scientific or military leadership +a strong founder +recruitment from within —political appointments to head agency	+coherent public image +well-defined agency character +integrated organization —servile attitude; inferiority complex —lack of a competitive edge
2. Political/Constituency Support			
2a Constituency Size	2b Linkages to Majoritarian Interests	2c Service or Regulatory	2d Intra-governmental Support
+large; evenly distributed +well-educated, well-funded —narrow exotic interest —broad, amorphous interest	+concrete, economic interests +defense contractors —the poor; ethnic minorities	+service orientation —regulatory functions	+congressional support +presidential support

Note: + = positive influence or characteristic; — = negative influence or characteristic; 0 = no discernible effect

Each of these factors has been extensively studied elsewhere, so we wish here to simply summarize what is meant by each of them, why they are significant determinants of agency behavior, and how they relate to our seven-agency study. In the three chapters that follow, we expand upon the argument presented here by tracing the historical development of each of these seven resource-managing agencies, with emphasis on how each agency's power base has molded its subsequent behavior.

THE EXPERTISE FACTOR AND ITS CONSTITUENT PARTS

It is often observed that knowledge is power, and bureaucracies in the modern state are the acknowledged repositories of vast amounts of data and expertise. For Weber, as well as for more contemporary students of organizational behavior, collecting and using information is the sine qua non of all bureaucracies. (In some ways even our second broad variable, constituency support, can be viewed as flowing from the first.)

But not all agencies share equally in this power source. As sociological research has shown, some professions or areas of expertise are more valued by members of society than are others. Generally speaking, the most highly regarded professions today are those of science, engineering, medicine, and the law.[13] Hence, if an agency's mission substantially involves any of these areas, its advantage in the political process is enhanced. Rourke summarizes this point:

> As a source of power, expertise reaches its fullest development in those organizations which have skills related to the survival of society. Scientists and military officers, for example, are in a highly advantageous position today to command respect for their particular talents.[14]

The skills of a particular bureau are inextricably intertwined with its mission. Some organizations are blessed with having an original purpose (in most concrete terms, an "organic act") that is highly valued and/or in accord with dominant societal values. For example, both the Army Corps of Engineers and the U.S. Forest Service derive much of their potency from a multiple-use, utilitarian philosophy that allows them to contribute in a material way to the economic development of the nation. This kind of mission contrasts sharply with one so broad that it is supposed to control everything—for example, the mission of the Environmental Protection Agency[15]—or so narrow that it is perceived to be at best peripheral and at worst a hindrance to our national well-being. Such a mission has contributed to the modest performance of the U.S. Fish and Wildlife Service for a good part of its hundred-year history.

Linked to an agency's mission are the conditions surrounding its creation. For instance, was the agency originally set in motion by a legislative statute—an organic act—or through an executive order? One might think this distinction slight, but according to some of Kaufman's recent research a statutory base is a more secure foundation for an agency than is creation by departmental or executive order.[16] The latter can more easily be repealed. Also, some agencies do evolve from an executive order to a statutory base but often are the objects of several reorganizations along the way. Reorganization saps strength; whatever the benefits to presidents and congresspersons, there is little doubt that from an agency's point of view the costs of reorganization outweigh its benefits. Thus the evidence seems to favor, as we show in the succeeding chapters, agencies that are given a statutory base at the time of their creation, or shortly thereafter. Such a base tends to extend their longevity as well as enhance their influence in the political process by giving them a definite identity to work with and from.

Just as having Congress "present at the creation" is an advantage to an agency, so is having a mission that is flexible enough to allow the agency room to grow. Agencies that have grown powerful over the years are those that slowly but surely add new functions without sacrificing old ones. These organizations actively sniff out new opportunities to expand their missions by continuously monitoring their external environment, in hopes of finding problem areas that might conceivably fall under their original flexible purpose. Considerable criticism has been directed toward the concept of *multiple use* but from the organization's standpoint, it is a wonderfully flexible management philosophy. Other agencies may become trapped by a contradictory mission—one that is fulfilled in a relatively short time, or one that is so narrow that the organization finds little room for maneuvering in the bureaucratic jungle.

As Rourke noted above, deference is accorded to military and scientific experts in this society. Our research amplifies this observation by arguing that resource-managing agencies that have a dominant, scientifically based profession develop into stronger organizations. The classic illustration is the Army Corps of Engineers, an organization that is able to capitalize both on the military and engineering mystiques. Professional forestry also has served the Forest Service well. Agencies that are interdisciplinary—a melting pot of professions—generally encounter greater difficulties in developing into a cohesive organization. One may find our argument here somewhat contradictory in that we claim that a flexible mission leads to greater success while the dominance of a single profession within an agency also contributes to its stature. Though at first glance our argument might appear illogical, we believe that the historical records of our seven-agency sample bear out these assertions. A multiple-use mission, together with a well-established profession, is a potent combination.

Agencies that have a strong sense of their own identities and of their mission—often referred to as organizational zeal or esprit de corps— have an edge over those that do not. Just as we can sense when we are in the presence of a particularly strong, charismatic personality, so, too, are there agencies that know so well what they are about that they exude a sense of self-confidence in their relationships with others. Though it is a difficult factor to quantify, it is nonetheless a real source of power for an organization. For political power is as much a matter of reputation as it is of budget size, size of work force, and the like. The agency with esprit de corps can both better maintain the loyalty of its members and the support of its outside constituencies. Along these lines, much has been written recently comparing the U.S. automobile industry with that of the Japanese, and it is widely concluded that the latter's success can be attributed in great part to the community spirit actively cultivated by Toyota, Datsun, and other Japanese car manufacturers with respect to their labor forces. Governmental organizations are no different in this regard.

Finally, leadership of the organization must be considered as a part of its information base. Astute or farsighted leadership is never guaranteed to an agency throughout its existence, yet there do exist certain conditions pertaining to its top management that aid an agency rather than hinder it. Those agencies that can recruit their leaders from within the organization rather than have a political appointee thrust upon them have an advantage. Also some evidence suggests that a strong founder, who starts an agency off on the right foot, is a power source for the agency later on. Something like a founder's myth does exist and does give organizational benefits. For example, the exalted status of the Federal Bureau of Investigation, from its inception in the 1920s to the late 1960s, was due in large part to the leadership of its director, J. Edgar Hoover, during that period of time. Hoover was instrumental not only in creating the Bureau, but in capitalizing on the public's continual concern about crime control by fashioning and maintaining a cohesive organizational unit to combat a highly visible social ill.

THE SEVERAL DIMENSIONS OF CONSTITUENCY SUPPORT

Like expertise, political support can be conceived of as a composite of several factors. A review of the existing literature combined with our own research into the histories of these seven agencies yields four clusters of factors that are most important to understanding differentials in bureaucratic power in this area. They concern the size of the constituency, the nature of the interests clustering around the organization, the nature of the agency's mission, and the extent of intragovernmental support for the organization.

The simplest taxonomy of federal organizations divides them into two types: service and regulatory. Service-oriented agencies are those that generate "benefits rather than restrictions on the public";[17] regulatory agencies have the essentially thankless task of restricting some economic, social, or political activity. It is evident that service-oriented bureaus are advantaged vis-à-vis those agencies whose purpose in life frequently puts them in a position to incur the wrath of influential segments of the public as well as influential policymakers in Washington. Regulatory agencies thus face budget cuts, personnel reductions, and diminutions in their scope and authority more frequently than do their service-oriented cohorts. During the last seven or eight years we have witnessed an increase in the level of dissatisfaction with governmental regulation, both among the American public and our national leaders; the result is that several regulatory bureaus have fallen by the wayside in the Washington policymakers' effort to whittle down the power of the federal bureaucracy.

Regulators like the Environmental Protection Agency, the Federal Trade Commission, and the Occupational Safety and Health Administration must continuously face a hostile environment. Supporters, who are few, come from the general public (and hence the unorganized public). Among the agencies we discuss in this study none is of the pure regulatory variety, although some agencies are a mixture of both. In actuality, most federal agencies do some of both: they regulate certain activities, like the Corps' disposal permit program, while at the same time providing benefits to others—the design and construction of new municipal waste-water treatment facilities. The generalization still holds, however; the more regulating an organization does, the less popular it will be. Most organizations thus try to keep their regulatory activities to a minimum in order to avoid being perceived, as has been the case recently of the Fish and Wildlife Service, as a producer of bureaucratic red tape.

The size, nature, and type of interest group support are critical variables affecting an agency's power base. A broad-based, but organized, clientele is preferable either to a distinctly narrow constituency (historic preservationists, bird watchers) or to a constituency so broad that it cannot be mobilized easily. The fate of the nationwide consumers' movement is illustrative of what happens with an amorphous clientele. Because this movement presumably includes virtually everyone in American society, organizing either a permanent interest group or a bureaucracy around it has proven to be exceedingly difficult. To date, Congress has hesitated before launching a Consumer Protection Agency whose mandate conceivably would be broader, more abstract, and more open to administrative interpretation and discretion than are existing statutes that have created similar federal regulatory agencies.

But optimal size is only one factor to consider in measuring constituency support. What also must be considered is how evenly distributed, both in a geographic and a socioeconomic sense, is the agency's interest group support. Organizations that are spatially limited, like the Bureau of Reclamation, whose organic act allows it to operate only in the seventeen western states of the nation, find themselves competing with a handicap. This holds as well for those agencies like the now-defunct Office of Economic Opportunity, whose clientele consisted of the most economically disadvantaged groups in American society. Compared with the education lobby, for instance, or the forest-products industry, these more limited constituencies can offer an agency little real support. We turn again to Rourke to provide a summary of the ideal association from an agency's viewpoint:

it can be said that the ideal administrative constituency is large and well distributed throughout all strata of society or in every geographical section of the community. It should include devoted supporters who derive tangible benefits from the services an agency provides. However, an administrative agency should not be excessively dependent upon the support of any segment of its constituency, nor should it carry on activities that threaten the interests of substantial outside groups. Finally, the economic or social activities in which a constituency engages should be in accord with the most highly-ranked values in society.[18]

Federal agencies must not only cultivate interest group support for their activites, but they must jockey for position among the power centers in the nation's capitol. Like it or not, political executives must continuously seek congressional and/or presidential support for their programs in an increasingly competitive and populated bureaucratic milieu. For a variety of reasons, some agencies are better at this than are others, and so they have the budgets, work force, and prestige associated with intragovernmental support.

Generally speaking, agencies may look to the president, to Congress, or even sometimes to both for protection and assistance. There are some agencies that have been the darlings of presidents, like Kennedy's Peace Corps in the early 1960s, Johnson's Office of Economic Opportunity and Civil Rights Division in the Justice Department, and Reagan's Defense Department. When chief executives take a special interest in a particular organization it usually fares well in the policymaking and budget process; generally the Congress will defer, at least for a time, to the president's pet programs. However, the other side of the coin is that presidents come and go with greater frequency than do members of Congress, so being a favorite son or daughter of the president is a relatively less secure position than being a congressional favorite. Consider, for example, the fate of the Peace Corps and the OEO—organizations that were, for a while, in the limelight but which have since faded into obscurity or have been abolished. The OEO survived less than ten years.

Those tight little iron triangles that presidents and their top administrators rail against are, of course, an agency's best hedge against bad times. Former secretary of health, education, and welfare Joseph Califano called it "molecular government," and it is the bane of anyone wishing to make significant changes in the existing power structure. The three-cornered triangle of agency, congressional committee, and lobby proves highly resistant to intrusion and influence even from the president of the United States.

Of course the classic example of this relationship has been the Army Corps of Engineers, described by Arthur Maass in 1951 as the construction and engineering arm of the U.S. Congress.[19] The Corps' unusually close association with Congress allows it to fend off harsh criticism, bad publicity, and frequent attacks to its sovereignty by even presidents and Supreme Court Justices. And, as our research will show, the agency flourishes in the process.

SUMMARY

Our purpose in this chapter has been to discuss briefly the several sources of power that agencies can exploit, and further to suggest that, over time, different kinds of organizations have been produced as a result of this continuous interaction between the agency and its environment. Our research into the histories of seven federal resource-managing agencies has uncovered three fairly distinct types of organizations, each of which displays a characteristic mode of behavior. Our sample of agencies consists of: the U.S. Army Corps of Engineers, the Bureau of Land Management, the Bureau of Reclamation, the U.S. Fish and Wildlife Service, the U.S. Forest Service, the National Park Service, and the Soil Conservation Service. Four are Department of the Interior agencies, two are housed in the Department of Agriculture, and one is located in the Department of Defense. But their formal position in the executive branch is a less important determination in molding agency behavior than are the factors discussed above, with this important exception: None of the Interior Department agencies falls into our "most successful" category.

What are the types of agencies that this research has discovered? Basically, we posit three categories:[20] what we call bureaucratic superstars, agencies that muddle through, and organizational shooting stars. Two agencies, whose histories we discuss in chapter 2, fall into the first category. They are the Corps of Engineers and the Forest Service. Next, those agencies that have found a relatively secure niche in the bureaucratic environment and that show only modest variations in behavior from year to year are discussed in chapter 3. To borrow a concept from Lindblom, they "muddle through."[21] These agencies are the National Park Service, the Soil Conservation Service, and the Fish and Wildlife Service. Our third category includes the Bureau of Reclamation and the Bureau of Land Management—the shooting stars of the federal establishment. They are the agencies that burn brightly for a short period of time; they rise quickly only to face a relatively precarious future. We discuss them in chapter 4.

In the following three chapters, we expand upon the ideas and the model presented here. Chapter 5 presents further measures of agency power, and chapter 6 contains our conclusions concerning the relevance of this research to environmental issues of the 1980s.

CHAPTER TWO

Bureaucratic Superstars:
The Army Corps of Engineers
and the U.S. Forest Service

THE CORPS OF ENGINEERS

No civil function has been more important in the history of westward expansion than the development of an inland, water-based transportation system. For over a century, from the founding of the Republic in 1789 to the closing of the great American frontier in the 1890s, the United States was embarked upon the development and geographical expansion of its national economy. That expansion was dependent in turn upon transportation, of "the need to move people and goods to and from the ever-advancing frontier."[1] If ever an organization mirrored the economic history of a nation it is the Army Corps of Engineers. The nearly two-hundred-year history of the agency is thus inextricably intertwined with the political and economic development of the country. Small wonder, then, that the Corps of Engineers continues to enjoy in the 1980s an unparalleled reputation for power and influence among the federal establishment. It is among the oldest surviving organizations, and its record of achievements is perhaps unmatched by any other federal agency.

The Corps of Engineers was established by congressional statute on the 16th of March in the year 1802. There is nothing remarkable about the Corps' beginnings—nothing, in other words, that would presage its unusual development. Congress in 1802 simply stated:

> And be it further enacted, that the President of the United States is hereby authorized and empowered . . . to organize and establish a corps of engineers, to consist of one engineer, with the pay, rank and emoluments of a major; two assistant engineers, with the pay, rank and emoluments of captains; two other assistant engineers, with the pay, rank and emoluments of first lieutenants; two other assistant engineers, with the pay, rank and emoluments of second lieutenants, and ten cadets, with the pay of sixteen dollars per month,

and two rations per day: and the President of the United States is, in like manner, authorized . . . to make such promotions in the said corps . . . and so as that the number of the whole corps shall, at no time, exceed twenty officers and cadets.[2]

This ordinary beginning bears resemblance to the headwaters of a mighty river—the Missouri River, for instance, which begins as a small rivulet not more than fifteen feet wide in west-central Montana. As it makes its southeastern descent through the Rockies, flowing down through the Great Plains, it gains momentum and is fed by a number of tributaries that join the main stream. At some point the river, small and insignificant at its source, becomes an impressive natural force that dictates the patterns of habitation for the heartland of America. The river makes transportation, agriculture, and energy production possible.

The Corps' creation coincided with and complemented the nation's era of exploration. From its beginning, with some twenty army engineers, the agency assumed a central role in the protection and utilization of the U.S. waterways. The Army Engineers were also the principal agents of the federal government in locating viable wagon and railroad routes in the exploration of the West. It is no coincidence that the most famous expedition in U.S. history, the Lewis and Clark, commenced in 1803, one year after the Corps' inception. Trained in Illinois, just across the Mississippi River from St. Louis, the expedition set out on a three-year investigation of the western territories. In May 1804 they began their expedition up the Missouri River.

Throughout the nineteenth century, the Army Engineers distinguished themselves in the exploration of the continent: In 1815, Lieutenant Zebulon M. Pike (after whom Pike's Peak in Colorado is named) explored the Missouri Valley; later, Lieutenant John C. Frémont surveyed the Oregon Trail and parts of California; and other Corps survey parties helped to locate the transcontinental routes—which generally followed river routes—of the Santa Fe, Union Pacific, Northern and Southern Pacific railroads.

A significant expansion of the Corps' duties occurred in 1824 when Congress passed the first of what came to be called rivers-and-harbors bills—known to later critics as pork barrel bills. On May 24, 1824, the Eighteenth Congress of the United States authorized the Corps to investigate and improve navigation on the Mississippi and Ohio rivers, appropriating $75,000 to be used for that purpose:

And be it further enacted, that, for the purpose of improving the navigation of the Mississippi River, from the mouth of the Missouri to New Orleans, and of the Ohio River from Pittsburgh to its junction with the Mississippi, the President of the United States is hereby authorized to take prompt and effectual measures for the removal of all trees which may be fixed in the bed of said rivers; and, for this purpose, he is authorized to procure and provide, in that way which in his discretion may be most eligible, the requisite water craft, machinery, implements, and force, to raise all such trees, commonly called "planters, sawyers, or snags."[3]

The Corps' interest in navigational improvements persists to the present day in the form of channelization projects, dredge-and-fill activities, beach erosion control, and the like. Indeed, a major portion of the Corps' ongoing activities are connected with these so-called internal improvements. While there was considerable discussion as to the constitutionality of federal expenditures for the purpose when Congress first began the procedure, a historian of the conservation movement concludes:

> Despite the long series of learned questions about the constitutionality of federal expenditures for waterways, neither the Congress nor the executive ever forced a clear-cut court test; they simply accepted the responsibility gradually over the years.[4]

Constitutional or not, the function was so necessary to the economic development of the country that the Corps never really faced a serious attempt to halt these activities once they were set in motion. Though the Corps has been frequently criticized by environmentalists for the self-serving aspect of its programs, it has operated too much in the mainstream of America's overall objectives to be at risk of losing its functions. As a member of the Appropriations Subcommittee on Public Works said in 1974,

> We do not want the Corps to go out of business. In times like these, when unemployment is going up . . . a number of public works projects on the shelf ready to go into construction is a good thing to have.[5]

Early in the Corps' history it became apparent that this was to be a versatile organization rather than an agency dedicated to a single mission. The major dichotomy within the Army Engineers is between civil and military functions; the fact that the Corps today is still an agency directed by military engineers should not be minimized, for the military aura lent to all of its functions adds to the agency's prestige. Looking only at the civil functions of the agency, however, one is impressed by the wide array of activities engaged in by the Corps. Over the span of a hundred and fifty years, from 1824 to the present, this accretion of functions has been gradual, but complimentary, in nature. The Corps rarely turns down an opportunity to expand its horizons. Even when confronted by a direct challenge to its activities, such as the National Environmental Policy Act of 1969 and the impact statement requirement, the Corps manages to find a silver lining. As Andrews has shown in his comparison of the performances of the Corps and the Soil Conservation Service, unlike the Service, the Corps puts the best face on any new restrictions and requirements.[6] For example, despite considerable urging from numerous congressmen the Corps was never willing to openly state that it resented or felt hindered by NEPA requirements. On the contrary, the act was always discussed in public as a step forward; any difficulties the organization experienced from it were of no significance in the long run; the agency would, in fact, be better off for having been put to the test.

In 1850, Congress added another function to the Corps' growing repertoire. It authorized the agency to survey the Mississippi River valley to "determine the most practical plan" for flood prevention. In 1879 the Mississippi River Commission was established, with the Corps directing it, to investigate and improve both navigation and flood control aspects of the river basin. With the addition of these new responsibilities—flood control and intergovernmental coordination—the Corps became involved in the concept of river basin planning, a concept that became increasingly important to its mission in the twentieth century.

In 1909 still another responsibility was added to the agency's activities. That year's rivers-and-harbors bill authorized the Corps to consider among its project studies the development of hydroelectric power. By 1917, the notion of comprehensive water resources development was firmly established. Though the Corps was initially hesitant about the concept of multiple-purpose water development, it quickly moved to capture the program once Congress determined to pursue it. The authorization to construct flood control projects by the agency was extended beyond the Mississippi River valley, and Congress authorized the Corps to embark upon comprehensive water basin studies—including navigation, flood control, and hydroelectric power generation—wherever appropriate. The Flood Control Act of 1936, establishing a national flood control policy, simply gave the agency even greater authority to act in these areas of "national concern." As modified in 1938 and 1941, certain local participation and approval requirements were removed,[7] and the Corps was well on its way to becoming what Arthur Maass described in his 1951 classic study of the agency: the engineer consultants and contractors of the U.S. Congress.[8]

During the New Deal era and the post-world war period new concerns in the natural resources policy area surfaced. While the nation did not abandon its historic commitment to economic development, nevertheless concern grew over a possible deterioration in water quality, caused in part by the industrial and municipal practice of dumping untreated wastes into the nation's lakes, streams, rivers, and adjoining oceans. At this time, several bills were introduced in Congress (though none was enacted until the 1960s) to establish a National Water Quality Commission. In 1948, however, the federal interest in water pollution control was set out, albeit on a limited basis, "with enactment of a five-year program of grants to the states for pollution studies, and the establishment of a Public Health Service pollution research facility at Cincinnati."[9]

Responding to this shift in national concern, the Corps claimed that it too had a long-standing, though limited, interest in the area of pollution control. The 1899 Refuse Act had authorized the agency to detect, regulate, and/or prohibit the dumping of wastes into the navigable waterways of the United States. Also, its survey of water pollution in the Ohio River valley had been instrumental in the attempts to enact water quality legislation during this time. Nevertheless, not until the 1970s did the agency really capitalize on its pollution control function, primarily through a new urban studies program and an expanded permits program. In 1945, the Corps, evidencing unusual behavior, chose to take a back seat in this area. Testifying before the Rivers and Harbors Committee the deputy chief of engineers told Congress:

> as far as the Corps of Engineers is concerned we have no desire to enforce the regulations in regard to pollution. . . . It seems to us that the handling of this pollution business in streams is a matter for the Public Health Service.[10]

Despite some initial hesitancy in regard to enforcing the 1899 act, in 1969 the Corps nevertheless estimated that of a possible twenty to thirty thousand violations, the agency had been able to pin down and take action against three thousand such incidents. In addition, it assisted on the cleanup of spills whenever possible, although this was not part of its statutory duties.

Though there were attempts by both the Roosevelt and Truman administrations to gain greater executive control over the strong and independent agency,[11] the Corps, together with its congressional supporters, succeeded in keeping the agency away from control by the Interior Department. Thus, by 1950 the Corps' duties had not only not been diminished, they actually had been broadened. For example, in 1944 the Corps was authorized to develop "public use" facilities at its projects, thus giving the agency a role in the creation of recreational facilities throughout the nation. By 1964, the Corps estimated that it spent nearly 2 percent of its construction budget on recreation facilities and calculated that, in comparison with the National Park Service's 94 million visitors in 1964, the Corps' visitor-use days amounted to 147 million. The 1946 Fish and Wildlife Act also affected the Corps, requiring it to cooperate with the U.S. Fish and Wildlife Service and the various states in preventing and/or mitigating damage to these resources. (In 1958 this act was amended to provide that "full consideration" be given to the preservation and enhancement of fish and wildlife in the agency's project planning.)

The more recent history of the agency, from 1950 to the present, shows the same pattern of behavior: the Corps rarely turns down an opportunity to expand its areas of responsibility. It even takes challenges to its developmental orientation as opportunities to demonstrate its responsiveness to changing public values. The Corps' response to the environmental movement of the 1960s and 1970s is further demonstration of the agency's flexible, even innovative, style. Several analysts of the Corps' response to NEPA generally reach the same conclusion: the agency's response was sincere, swift, and impressive.[12] It incorporated the environmental issue in a manner that forced the grudging respect of even its most strident critics. Its response record was often better than that of federal agencies with a more overtly conservationist orientation. The authors of one such book on the Corps thus conclude:

> The Corps is noteworthy for managing to go through a change cycle while reconciling or at least juggling seemingly irreconcilable demands for water resource development, environmental protection, and open planning. After making a decision to change, the agency moved expeditiously and rather successfully to accommodate itself to a changing social and political environment. Thus, this study serves as a classic illustration of the process of mutual accommodation that occurs between an agency and its attentive publics in a changing world. In observing this particular example of change, one cannot help but note also that the Army Corps of Engineers has once again proved to be a most politically astute organization.[13]

Due to the incorporation of so many new responsibilities and the continued expansion of traditional ones, the Corps' budget skyrocketed in the late 1970s. The 1980 budget estimate of $3.2 billion included $1.7 billion for the construction of over two hundred projects, including river and harbor improvements, locks, dams and canals, intercoastal waterways, flood protection, reservoirs, and hydroelectric power production. The Corps also planned to spend $31 million in 1980 on the construction of recreational amenities in order to prepare for an estimated 523 million recreation days of use at these sites. In addition, after the Teton Dam disaster the Corps was given the responsibility to inspect approximately 6,400 dams for possible safety violations. To accomplish all of these tasks, the Corps employed an army of over 28,000 permanent employees.[14]

Recent attempts to alter the politics of water allocation have left the

Corps relatively unscathed. Traditionally, water projects such as dams, canals, and flood control are suported by a strong tripartite alliance that consists of congresspersons (especially members of the Public Works and Appropriations committees), the federal agencies that build and maintain water projects, and water-user constituency groups. This iron triangle of symbiotic interests has often been accused of authorizing pork barrel projects, and while these projects may be of questionable value in terms of cost-benefit ratios or environmental impacts, there is no question that they solidify constituent support for incumbents in Congress. A result of this powerful political alliance is the emphasis on structural rather than nonstructural solutions to the country's water problems.

The federal agencies authorized to build or manage water control structures are the Tennessee Valley Authority, the Corps of Engineers, the Bureau of Reclamation, and the Soil Conservation Service. These agencies ally themselves with the dozens of congressional committees and subcommittees that deal with water development, as well as with interest groups such as the National Water Resources Association and the Western States Water Council. The failure of recent attempts to reform traditional water policy attests to the strength of this alliance. The Corps of Engineers is often cited as the premier example of an agency that has successfully functioned within this tripartite alliance. Its continuing ability to accept and incorporate new responsibilities while resisting significant diminution of its traditional activities is quite evident in the recent political struggle over water policy reform, a subject we discuss next.

A challenge to "water politics as usual" came in 1977 when newly elected President Jimmy Carter announced that he was cutting federal funds for some 18 ongoing water projects. This action quickly produced a storm of protest from western governors and powerful southern and western congresspersons. The president responded by expanding, by one, what came to be known as the "hit list." If left unfunded, this action would have amounted to about a $289 million cut in the 1978 budget. In addition, Carter ordered the review of 320 other public works projects and stressed that they would be evaluated in terms of economics, environment, and safety. Eleven of the 19 projects slated for termination were being built by the Corps of Engineers.[15]

The initial congressional response to Carter's proposed reforms came as something of a surprise since, just a week earlier, seventy four members of Congress had sent a letter to Carter expressing their "support for your efforts to reform the water resources programs of the Army Corps of Engineers and the Bureau of Reclamation."[16] It appeared that Carter—a newcomer to Washington—did not totally appreciate what he was up against. Philip Fradkin describes some of the opposition:

there were certain interests at work within the government that were not in sympathy with what the President wanted. They were the bureaucrats in the Corps of Engineers and Bureau of Reclamation whose long careers had been molded by the structural concept of water development.[17]

The difficulties that the Carter administration experienced challenging traditional water policy were exacerbated by three factors. First, the president failed to discuss the proposed cuts with relevant congresspersons and governors; the specific cuts therefore came as a surprise to them. Second, all of the projects on Carter's list were projects already underway, that is, a substantial amount of money had already been spent on the projects. After the cuts were announced, the seventy four congresspersons who wrote to Carter explained that they had intended to support Carter in resisting any *new* project starts, but that they did not intend to de-authorize existing projects.[18] Third, 1976 and 1977 were severe drought years in the West, so the interest in water development was substantial.

Despite congressional opposition, on March 23, 1977, Carter announced that 14 more projects would be reviewed, 10 of which were Corps of Engineers projects. But on that same date he reinstated funding for 3 Corps projects that were on the original cut list.[19] A month later Carter created a revised list of 29 projects; full funding was restored for 8 of these projects (5 of them Corps projects), 5 projects were partially funded (2 Corps projects), and 14 projects—11 of them being built by the Corps of Engineers—were still slated for termination.[20]

By early May the battle over the water projects reached a new plateau. The Congress—always a stronghold of support for water development— vehemently resisted the administration's cuts. The House Appropriations Subcommittee on Public Works voted to fund 17 of the 18 projects on the original cut list. The previous week a resolution passed by the full House called for full funding of all ongoing projects.[21] In June the Senate attempted a compromise by voting to cut funding for half of the 18 projects in question. Of the 9 projects approved by the Senate, 8 of them were in states whose senators were on the Appropriations Committee, and 7 of them were in states whose senators were on the Appropriations Subcommittee on Public Works.

The political power of the Corps of Engineers becomes evident when the membership of relevant committees is compared to the list of Corps projects judged by the Carter administration to be superfluous. As tables 2-1 and 2-2 show, a significant overlap exists between states that are represented on the House and Senate Appropriations committees, and states where the Corps' most controversial, and possibly most marginal, projects are located.

Table 2-1 Senate Committee on Appropriations Membership compared with Corps of Engineers Projects Reviewed or Cut, 1977

Senators from States with Reviewed/Cut Projects	Projects on Review/Cut list in Senator's State
Stennis (Miss.) Chairman, Public Works	Tennessee Tombigbee Waterway
Hollings (S. C.)	Richard B. Russell Project
Johnston (La.)	Tensas Basin Bayou Bodcau Mississippi River, Gulf Outlet Red River Waterway Atchafalaya—Bayous Beouf, Chene and Block
McCellan (Ark.) Chairman, Appropriations	Tensas Basin Cache Basin
Huddleston (Ky.)	Dayton Yatesville Lake Paintsville
Proxmire (Wis.)	La Farge Lake
Eagleton (Mo.)	Meramec Lake
Schweiker (Pa.)	Tyrone
Bellmon (Okla.)	Lukfata Lake
Hatfield (Oreg.)	Applegate Lake
TOTAL: 10 out of 25 senators	TOTAL: 17 out of 22 projects

Note: These projects include those that appeared on the original cut list of 19 projects as well as 14 additional projects Mr. Carter chose for extensive riview in March 1977.

As is evident from the tables, both the Senate and House Committee on Appropriations and their respective Public Works subcommittees were chaired by southerners during this skirmish with the president—ironically, himself a southerner. These legislators, grown powerful by their seniority, obtained a disproportionate share of the Corps projects (some 9 out of a total of 22) that were considered questionable by President Carter. But it must be kept in mind that the Corps' support comes from all of the members of the Appropriations committees, regardless of region. Of the 22 Corps projects reviewed or cut by the administration, 20 of them were located in states that had legislators on one of the two Appropriations committees. Clearly, the Corps has many friends in high places. As a region, our research shows that the South does not receive a disproportionate share of water development projects; but to the Carter administration it did have an overabundance of projects of questionable value. Perhaps this was due to the fact that Carter was a southerner and therefore especially familiar with the local controversies surrounding the projects. We return to this issue of regional bias when examining President Reagan's proposals to change water politics.

Carter was not the only voice speaking out against pork barrel politics in the late 1970s, however. The Coalition for Water Project Review was

Table 2-2   House Committee on Appropriations Membership Compared with
Corps of Engineers Projects Reviewed or Cut, 1977

Congresspersons from Districts with Reviewed/Cut Projects	Projects on Review/Cut List in Congressperson's State
Bevill (Ala.) Chairman, Public Works Edwards (Ala.)	Tennessee Tombigbee Waterway
Whitten (Miss.)	Tennessee Tombigbee Waterway Tallahala Creek Inlet
Boggs (La.)	Tensas Basin Bayou Bodcau Mississippi River, Gulf Outlet Red River Waterway Atchafalaya—Bayous Beouf, Chene and Block
Flynt (Ga.)	Richard B. Russell Project
Natchee (Ky.)	Dayton Yatesville Paintsville
Steed (Okla.)	Lukfata Lake
Flood (Pa.) Murtha (Pa.) McDade (Pa.) Coughlin (Pa.)	Tyrone
Shipley (Ill.) Yates (Ill.) Michell (Ill.) O'Brien (Ill.)	Fulton Freeport
Obey (Wis.)	La Farge Lake
Burlison (Mo.)	Meramec Lake
Alexander (Ark.)	Tensas Basin Cache Basin

Duncan (Oreg.)
    TOTAL: 10 out of 25 senators
	Applegate Lake
	    TOTAL: 17 out of 22 projects

Note: These projects include those that appeared on the original cut list of 19 projects
as well as 14 additional projects Mr. Carter chose for extensive review in March 1977.

formed by more than twenty environmental groups that opposed the
construction programs of the Corps. These groups no longer limited
their objections to environmental factors. By 1977 they had begun to
challenge the projects on the basis of economics. Moreover, the environmentalists were joined in this tactic by such money-conscious groups as
the National Taxpayers Union as well as by public interest lobbies like
Common Cause and the League of Women Voters.[22] A good example of
this economic-oriented strategy is found in the lawsuit filed by the
Environmental Defense Fund and a railroad company against the
Tennessee-Tombigbee Waterway. The suit claimed that the Corps of
Engineers' cost-benefit analysis was calculated to make it appear that
the project would result in a net economic gain. According to the suit,

the project would benefit a small group of private barge operators and would in the process destroy 30,000 acres of forests and 17,000 acres of farmland.[23]

The Carter strategy also placed great emphasis on the economics of water projects, although the administration did not neglect environmental considerations. The president's press release of April 18, 1977, stated that "activities which are wasteful, unsafe, or economically or environmentally unsound simply cannot be pursued. The water resource development programs of the Corps of Engineers, the Bureau of Reclamation, and the Tennessee Valley Authority are a case in point."[24] The press release went on to summarize the costs and benefits of each project, and reached the following conclusions regarding three of the most marginal projects: First, the Meramec Lake project would inundate 12,600 acres in order to provide total flood protection for 11,900 acres and additional recreational benefits for the area—these latter accounting for 25 percent of the project's total benefits. Second, the Atchafalaya project would benefit two oil rig companies at a cost of $20.3 million and would cause the inundation of 7,500 acres. Third, the Bayou Bodcau project would benefit sixty families at a cost of $240,000 per family.[25]

Much of the criticism directed at the Corps' cost-benefit formula concerns interest rates. The law required that an interest rate of 3.25 percent be applied to any project authorized before 1969, even though funds for the project might not actually be appropriated until a later date when interest rates would be higher. In 1974 the rate was boosted to 6.37 percent. Carter wanted to raise it to 10 percent.[26] His April 18, 1977 press release states: "Many of the projects I reviewed were authorized at such low rates that even though we are building them today, we are pretending that the cost of capital is still the same as it was many years ago."[27] By changing the interest rate from 3.25 percent to 6.37 percent five Corps projects on Carter's cut list lost their favorable cost-benefit ratio.[28]

In addition to revamping cost-benefit formulas, Carter's proposed water policy called for five additional reforms: 1) greater emphasis on environmental protection, 2) increased dam safety, 3) more attention paid to water conservation, 4) increased cost sharing among states and the federal government, and 5) a redirected public works program.[29] The first three reforms posed little threat to the Corps of Engineers. Quite the contrary, the agency readily incorporated all three functions into its expanding repertoire of responsibilities. However, the latter two reforms presented a significant challenge to the Corps' traditional functions.

Carter's cost-sharing provision would require users of water projects to help pay for them. As he said, "I will work with the Congress to develop a system to recoup the costs from the beneficiaries."[30] But much of the agency's strength has derived from the fact that it has practiced the politics of distribution for most of its two-hundred-year history. For example, a dam that directly benefits a specific area is paid for largely by the nation as a whole. It is precisely this characteristic that makes such projects so appealing to Congress and to the well-organized recipients who, in Carter's words, "pay nothing for their construction or maintenance."[31]

The absence of a requirement for payback or cost-sharing is one of the most important factors that distinguishes the Corps from the Bureau of Reclamation. A case in point is the Applegate Lake project in Oregon. The dam was to be planned and constructed by the Corps, and the Bureau of Reclamation would then operate the resulting Applegate irrigation system. When President Carter ordered a review of the project, the Corps quickly completed its study, while the Bureau became bogged down in calculating repayment schedules. During appropriations hearings a Corps spokesman explained why the Bureau of Reclamation was behind schedule:

> responsibility for repayment of irrigation costs [*i.e., the Bureau of Reclamation's part of the project*] rests with the Department of Interior pursuant to Federal laws. . . . the project will not be operated for irrigation purposes until the Secretary of the Interior makes necessary arrangements with non-Federal interests to recover the costs, in accordance with Federal reclamation law."[32]

Later Carter expanded his cost-sharing plan to include state governments. Secretary of the Interior Cecil Andrus predicted that the proposal would be accepted by "those states that do have good projects and are willing to put their money where their mouth is."[33] Carter suggested that the states pay 5 to 10 percent of project costs. This modest proposal, like the idea of users fees, evoked a strong response from Congress. None of the cost-sharing proposals became law.

The other controversial reform proposed by President Carter was what was termed a "redirected public works program." This proposal involved nothing less than a total turnaround in our concept of water development. Margot Hornblower of the *Washington Post* wrote:

> The new water policy . . . will be an effort to reverse the historic tide of massive structural waterworks, providing billions of dollars in federal subsidies for selected areas and economic interests. . . . Such changes would amount to a revolution in water policy, challenging the historic American faith in technology as the answer to all water problems.[34]

The success or failure of Carter's attempt to "revolutionize" water policy can be measured by the number of structural projects that continued to be funded in the ensuing years. The public works iron triangle battled the president at every turn, so that by the fall of 1977 the president's reforms were in disarray. In an effort to salvage something out of his original lofty goals, Carter signed a compromise FY 1978 public works bill that provided $2.8 billion for the Corps—$150 million over his earlier request—and a total public works appropriation of $10.9 billion. In an effort to meet Congress halfway, Carter agreed to fund half of the projects that were on the original cut list. The president called the bill "a precedent setting first step." Environmentalists called it a sellout. And the Congress promised to renew the fight to fund the nine projects that went unfunded, but not de-authorized, in FY 1978.[35]

Over the following three years of his administration, Carter fought for water policy reform but met with not a great deal more success than he had had in 1977, his first year in the presidency. Throughout 1978 Carter battled the Congress on two fronts: project authorization bills and the annual appropriation bills for the Corps and the Bureau of Reclamation. The House wanted to authorize as many as 125 new projects while the president had his own list of 36 new projects that met his new criteria.[36] Ultimately none of the authorization bills became law.[37] Carter also objected to the level of funding proposed by Congress, and vetoed the FY 1979 appropriation bill for public works. But the final compromise bill that Carter signed into law cut little funding from ongoing water projects; the total appropriation was just slightly less than the original House bill. The president did extract one concession, however; the Congress agreed to temporarily delete 6 of the 8 projects that had been deleted the previous year.[38]

In 1979 Carter announced two new proposals aimed directly at reducing the power and independence of the Corps of Engineers. In early February he made public a plan to create a Department of Natural Resources. The new department would include most agencies presently housed in the Department of the Interior, plus the Corps of Engineers. This reorganization was intended to increase the president's control over that particular agency by reducing its autonomy, and with it attenuate its strong alliance with Congress. The idea of a Natural Resources Department is of course nothing new. A generation ago the Hoover Commission recommended that all agencies involved with public works— including the Corps—should be placed in the Department of the Interior.[39] Former President Richard Nixon also proposed a Department of Natural Resources that would have complete control over planning and policy for civil works.[40] All of these proposals threatened the status quo and all of them failed. A southern senator reportedly told Carter: "You're going to get your nose bloodied on this one—why take on one you're sure to lose?"[41] Carter's plan died a quiet death.

The other proposal that presented a significant threat to the Corps of Engineers concerned President Carter's view of an enlarged role for the Water Resources Council. Under his plan, the council would be the final arbiter in determining which projects would be recommended to Congress for funding. Both houses of Congress voted down the plan.[42]

Carter continued his fight to decrease the public works budget throughout 1979. During congressional hearings Representative Bevill of Alabama provided a precise summary of Carter's proposed budget:

> there is 183 or 184 projects either deleted or slowed down. To be more specific, 56 ongoing studies deleted, 15 advanced engineering and design projects deleted, 59 studies and advanced engineering and design projects and 46 construction projects that have been stretched out, and no new starts.[43]

Congress's only significant concession to Carter was to defer funding for two projects: the Yatesville Dam, which would have required the relocation of 93 cemeteries, 213 dwellings, 6 churches, and 4 commercial buildings, with a primary benefit of "flatwater recreation;" and Bayou Bodcau, which would have benefitted 60 landowners at a cost of $240,000 each.[44]

After three long years of feuding and some minor victories, Carter clung tenaciously to his policy reforms. During the first month of 1980 the president informed the Congress that he wanted 125 projects cut from the 1981 budget.[45] But the $12.1 billion public works he signed later that year restored nearly all of those 125 projects, at an estimated cost of $111 million. For instance, the bill included funding for the Yatesville Dam, and it appropriated $212 million to continue the construction of the Corps' most ambitious and most expensive project, the controversial Tennessee-Tombigbee Waterway. (Total cost for this one project has been estimated at $1.4 billion, with a cost-benefit ratio of .87 calculated at 6⅜ percent interest.)

Reviewing Carter's four-year crusade against the Corps of Engineers in particular and public works in general, we find that the agency emerged basically intact and unreformed. The president was unable to change the cost-sharing provisions that have helped to make the Corps so powerful. He failed to create a Department of Natural Resources. The mandate of the National Water Resources Council was not enlarged. The president also failed to turn America away from the so-called structural approach to solving our water problems, as is evident in more recent budget proposals. His attempt to terminate questionable projects was only temporarily successful, as Congress eventually funded most of them, and the savings that Carter managed to eke out of the Congress were only a small percentage of the total expenditures for water projects in these four years. During the Carter presidency, the Corps' budget increased by about $600 million, approximately a 24 percent increase in four years.

One quite significant change was wrought by Carter, however. He succeeded in imposing a "no-new-starts" policy on the Corps of Engineers. This worried numerous congresspersons who were afraid the Corps would run out of business. But the agency, in a characteristic mode of behavior, appeared calm; it never publicly questioned administration policy, preferring to wait for the political winds to change.[46] To further insure future activity, the Corps earmarked a considerable amount of money in the 1981 budget (with Carter's approval) for thirteen new "pre-authorization studies," two new dam safety assurance projects, and five new major rehabilitation projects.[47] This obviously left the door open for a great deal of future work, a no-new-starts policy notwithstanding.

The Carter reforms detailed here were the most aggressive attempt in forty years to increase presidential control over the Corps of Engineers. Yet the agency emerged from this confrontation no worse off than previously. Its relationship with Congress and its position in the executive branch were not modified, and its budget was larger in 1980 than in 1976. Moreover, the agency actually expanded its operations into several new areas. Continuing a long tradition, the Corps managed to convert political challenges into bureaucratic oportunities. For example, when Carter ordered a review of all federal water projects the Corps promptly screened all of its 292 projects planned for work in 1978. The agency's review concluded that 19 of those projects needed further study. The 19 projects were dubbed a hit list when Carter announced he would indeed study them further, and possibly exclude them from the budget. The point is that the president had to rely on the Corps to do a review of its own projects.[48] A month after the first cut list was announced, the Corps made public a list of 38 additional projects to be reviewed. This document was released at the same time that a congressional backlash against the president's proposals was gathering momentum. This newest list further provoked the Hill, but resentment was aimed at Carter rather than the Corps which was, of course, only doing what the president had bidden.

The agency made other astute moves as well. In response to increased public concern about environmental degradation, the Corps established in the mid seventies an Environmental Effects Laboratory that "gives evidence of changing with the changing times."[49] Other additions to the Corps' responsibilities were actually initiated by President Carter. In 1977, the White House requested that the Corps of Engineers begin a safety inspection program of nonfederal dams. The inspection of 9,000 "high hazard" dams in fifty states ultimately required until 1981 to complete. The Bureau of Reclamation was not asked to do any of the inspections.[50]

The dam safety program was not the only instance where President Carter expressed a preference for the Corps of Engineers over the Bureau of Reclamation. In his reorganization plan to create a Department of Natural Resources, he recommended the transfer of all Bureau of Reclamation construction and maintenance responsibilities to the Corps.[51] Had this proposal been adopted, it would have meant the demise of the Bureau.

The Corps' budget also received a boost from Mother Nature. In 1980, two natural disasters—the Mt. St. Helens eruption and Hurricane Allen—resulted in a substantial increase in disaster relief funds. In the case of Mt. St. Helens, the Corps came to the rescue with $172 million for cleanup activity.[52]

The 1982 budget that Carter sent to Congress proposed a 12 percent increase in the Corps of Engineers' budget, pushing their total outlay to an impressive $3.365 billion. The budget for operations and maintenance alone was $1.085 billion, a 20 percent increase that the Corps considered to be "austere funding." But the 1982 Carter budget never went beyond congressional hearings. One of President Reagan's first acts was to throw out the Carter budget and substitute his own, which was designed to "stretch out" capital investment in the civil works program.

The proposed Reagan budget reduced the Corps' funding increase by $230 million. This amounted to about a 7 percent reduction from the Carter proposal; still it was a 5 percent increase over the Corps' budget for the previous year. President Reagan thus proposed a budget of $3.135 billion for the Corps in fiscal year 1982. More than two-thirds of the Republican administration's proposed cuts were made in the agency's construction program, and more than two-thirds of the total reduction can be attributed to three projects—the Red River Waterway, the Big South Fork National River and Recreation Area, and Yatesville Lake.[54] The first 2 projects were slated for a gradual phaseout by the administration, and the Yatesville Lake project, which was on Carter's original cut list as well, is the only project out of 199 that received no funds in the Reagan budget. The agency, however, was reluctant to give in on even the other 2 projects; as the director of civil works pointed out, these projects were not being terminated or de-authorized; they were only being deferred until some future time when they would be needed.[55] And even Yatesville Lake received some funding for "relocating graves."[56] Ultimately Congress approved an appropriation bill of $2.97 billion, virtually the same level of funding as the previous year.

The Corps appears to have successfully resisted any significant cuts in its budget under the current Reagan administration. It also circumvented many of the cuts that Reagan proposed in personnel. For 1982, the president requested an 8 percent reduction in the agency's full-time permanent positions. These reductions are planned to continue for six years, when they reach a total reduction of 18 percent of the 1982 work force of 32,173.[57] The Corps, however, has sufficient flexibility in its budget to circumvent personnel ceilings through the mechanism of "contracting out" (i.e., hiring outside personnel to compensate for work force reductions). Like several other agencies, the Corps made it clear in the appropriations hearings that it plans to rely heavily on this strategy. In hearings, Congressman Bevill criticized not the Corps but the president, calling this circumvention "phony economics;" he wanted the Corps to do *all* of the work in-house.[58]

The one area in which President Reagan has succeeded in changing the Corps' budget priorities for FY 1982 was in its recreation program. However, at least part of this success can be attributed to the Corps' acquiescence.[59] For many years recreation has been a stepchild in the agency; this perception was recently reaffirmed when an agency spokesman defined low-priority items as recreation and flood control projects.[60] As a result, under the current administration the recreation budget was cut by approximately 30 percent. Most of the personnel cuts sustained by the agency were linked to its recreation functions, and some recreation facilities operated and maintained by the agency will be closed. This comes at a time when there is a move afloat to give back to the federal government those recreational facilities that earlier had been acquired by state and local governments. In times of budgetary retrenchment, neither the federal government nor state-local governments wish to spend scarce resources on outdoor recreation. The FY 1982 Reagan budget also reduced funds for environmental and water quality studies.[61]

In preparing the FY 1983 federal budget, the Reagan administration made an even greater effort than during the previous year to cut substantially the Corps' budget and to alter water policy formulation. The administration's budget proposals called for a 26 percent decrease in funding. The Corps' construction program—the heart of the agency's operations—was to be reduced significantly. However, the Congress once again rallied in support of the agency and passed an appropriations bill that funded the Corps at about the same level as the two previous years.

The Reagan administration, like its Democratic predecessor, also attempted to alter the traditional approach to project funding. First, it tried to augment presidential control over project selection by creating an Office of Water Policy to be chaired by the secretary of the interior, but Congress refused to provide funds for the office's project-review functions.[62] Next, the president responded with an executive order authorizing the Office of Management and Budget to review public works projects, but the Congress continued to consider project authorizations that had not been reviewed by OMB.[63]

The president also challenged the long-standing practice of funding Corps projects with virtually 100 percent federal monies. He proposed that the states pay for a substantial portion of project costs. Initially, it looked like Reagan's cost-sharing proposals might be accepted by the legislative branch, since it too had jumped aboard the economy-in-government bandwagon, but recent opposition from westerners and southerners has reduced the possibility of a standardized cost-sharing provision being enacted. According to one observer, cost-sharing "has become as popular on Capitol Hill and in the ranks of the Reagan administration as an outbreak of mumps."[64]

To date, the Corps has successfully resisted both Carter's and Reagan's attempts to cut project funding, to reduce its autonomy, and to attenuate its traditional sources of support. But the agency has not merely survived—it has thrived. Its 1983 budget was almost $3 billion, and its projects and responsibilities cover an ever-increasing diversity of operations and functions. Another measure of the Corps' health today is the regional diversity of its projects.

A review of Corps projects by geographic region reveals that the agency is constructing water works throughout the United States. As noted above, the Corps is often accused of having a regional bias that favors the South. Recently, for example, Senator Daniel Patrick Moynihan of New York claimed there was "an overwhelming regional imbalance in where Corps projects are built."[65] Northern legislators have complained for years that the Corps favored the South. There are a number of reasons why this is believed to be true. First, many of the Corps' most controversial projects are in the South. The Corps' biggest project, the Tennessee-Tombigbee Waterway, is both very controversial and located in the South. Another reason for this presumed regional bias is the considerable visibility of southern legislators who chair important committees, and who often irritate their colleagues by using their positions, presumably to gain a disproportionate number of projects for their districts or states.

The data presented in table 2-3 indicate that the impact of these southern committee chairpersons has been exaggerated. They have been able to draw projects to specific areas, but not to the South as a whole. In other words, they have not been able to create a regionwide bias in the location of Corps projects. In 1978, only about 16 percent of the Corps' projects were being constructed in the ten states of the old Confederacy (excluding Texas). Twenty years earlier, in 1958, about 14 percent of the Corps' projects were being constructed in the South, so the Corps has long been active across the nation. Actually, a large percentage of the Corps' projects are in the seventeen western states in which the Bureau of Reclamation operates (42 percent in 1978). These percentages indicate that the Corps of Engineers is not and has not been limited to any particular region of the United States. Their nationwide operation is one of the great advantages that the Corps has over the Bureau of Reclamation, the latter agency having been limited to water development in the seventeen western states.

Table 2-3 Corps of Engineers Projects by Region

	South	North	West
1958 Actual Authorized Projects $N = 208$	30 (14%)	87 (42%)	91 (44%)
1978 Carter Budget Request $N = 192$	31 (16%)	81 (42%)	80 (42%)
1982 Carter Budget Request $N = 186$	48 (26%)	67 (36%)	71 (38%)
Proposed Project Deletions, Reagan, 1982-86 $N = 5$	-4	-1	0

Source: Corps of Engineers budget submitted to House Committee on Appropriations, Subcommittee on Public Works.

Notes: South—10 states of the old Confederacy, excluding Texas; West—17 states authorized for Bureau of Reclamation projects; North—remaining states in the Northeast and Midwest. Excluded from sample are cross-regional projects, District of Columbia, Puerto Rico, Alaska, and Hawaii.

We consider the Corps of Engineers to be the epitome of a successful, aggressive, developing organization. But for these very reasons, as well as for several others, the Corps is a controversial agency with no dearth of detractors. Much of what it does brings the agency into direct conflict with, for example, the environmental community. And more recently, these groups have been joined in battle by such politically conservative groups as the National Taxpayers Union, which labeled public works projects "fiscally irresponsible."[66]

Additionally, several articles and books published in recent years attack the Corps of Engineers. With titles such as *The River Killers,* "Dams and Other Disasters," or "Flooding America in Order to Save It," these writers reflect the growing opposition to massive water projects. A Supreme Court justice not too long ago referred to the Corps as public enemy number one. Protest has gone further than just writing, however. Some Corps projects have become the sites of demonstrations in which direct-action tactics are employed.

The opposition has also taken the Corps of Engineers to court. Although fifty-seven court cases have been dismissed recently, forty-one cases are still pending, including a suit against the Tennessee-Tombigbee Waterway project. The plaintiffs in these cases are groups such as Save Our Red River, Save Our Sound Fisheries, and the League of Kentucky Sportsmen. Not all of these suits have been brought by environmentalists. In several instances entire towns have banded together to sue the Corps.[67]

Opponents of the Corps point to a recent audit done by the firm of Price, Waterhouse and Company, which concluded that the Corps had both overbuilt many projects and understated the costs of those projects.

An example is Eufaula Lake in Oklahoma, where only 3 percent of the water is being used, even though the project was completed in 1964.[68] The audit also accuses the Corps of establishing artificially low prices for water, which burdens the national taxpayer while encouraging wasteful water use at or near the site. This complaint has been endorsed by a number of water experts.[69]

The Corps, as a prominent member of the federal establishment, must also face the current conservative, anti-government sentiment that is sweeping through the country. For some people, the agency's activities are just another example of an imperious federal bureaucracy meddling in local affairs. Much of this opposition comes from conservative elements of the population who were traditionally supportive of Corps projects. An example of this public sentiment can be found in the appropriation hearings, where private individuals are asked to address the subcommittee. The following statement was made by a private citizen who was upset by a Corps project next to his home:

> the Corps has been wasteful, unbridled, self-serving, and corrupt. . . . . Recourse to Corps harassment and other actions is difficult because of the size and complexity of the agency, and its taxpayer-funded legal force. . . . The Corps has used its budgetary funds to expand Corps power and influence into the private sector.[70]

Despite this criticism from many quarters, the Corps goes about its business. While opposition may have grown recently, the Corps' traditional sources of support are still sufficiently strong to protect the agency from serious attacks. In the face of criticism of some of its activities, the Corps expands into others. For example, a current proposal before Congress would establish a new "small hydropower" program that would authorize the Corps to do its share of solving the energy crisis by building hydroelectric units at existing project sites.[71] Another bill in Congress would allow the Corps to build, and not just plan, local water treatment plants.[72]

Yet another example of its continuing innovation is the Corps' response to Pub. L. 95-507, a statute that requires public agencies to aggressively seek out minority contractors. The Corps, on its own accord, set up a quota system and thus vigorously complied with the law. More often than not, the agency sees new laws as opportunities for expanding either its mission or its constituency, and sometimes both. This attitude is evident in the following statement from General Heiberg, director of civil works:

> In many cases the water resource business . . . is surrounded by controversy. I think it makes a lot of sense that we try to ensure . . .

that all folks who are the beneficiaries of the project, whether the work itself or the outcome of the work, have an opportunity to participate.

We, quite frankly, are able to see support grow for a project when it includes Blacks and Hispanics.[73]

Finally, the Corps is capitalizing on the current demand for a more secure national defense with National Emergency Preparedness Planning Activities. According to Corps spokesmen, this would allow the Corps to shift some of its work to defense projects: "In a mobilization or wartime scenario, the President and the Congress would want the Corps to turn some of its water resource work . . . to work in our defense."[74]

At this time the future of the Corps looks promising. While the Reagan budget for 1982 called for no new starts, administration officials have stated that as many as 40 to 50 new Corps projects will be funded in 1983 or 1984.[75] There are also pressures from outside the government for massive Corps projects, including a proposal to divert water from the Missouri River to the High Plains at a cost of at least $6 billion; the figure could go as high as $25 billion. The North American Water and Power Alliance wants the government to build a $200 billion canal from Alaska to the western states.[76] On a more realistic note, the Corps is presently conducting 200 studies and investigations, constructing 150 projects, and operating and maintaining 700 existing projects.[77]

In the final analysis, the measurement of the Corps' present and future health is its relationship with Congress. While there are a few dissenters in that body,[78] clearly the Corps' friends in Congress far outnumber its opponents. Congressmen—especially those with projects in their districts—spare no superlatives when talking about the Corps. Mr. Bevill is perhaps the best, if not the most articulate, example: "I think the Corps of Engineers is the most outstanding agency in our government."[79] As a postscript, one should note that the Tennessee Tombigbee Waterway—the Corps' largest project—flows through Congressman Bevill's home district.

The Corps of Engineers has proven itself adept at using its formidable array of resources to dominate other agencies, secure a supportive constituency, and protect its autonomy vis-à-vis its superiors in the executive branch. The agency has scrupulously maintained its traditional sources of political support while at the same time being receptive to new issues that could enlarge its mission. The Corps thus epitomizes a powerful and independent bureaucracy that has the potential for continued expansion. As we turn to a discussion of the U.S. Forest Service, we will see similar patterns of behavior evident in that agency.

THE U.S. FOREST SERVICE

Several agencies came into being around the turn of the century, as the Progressive and conservation movements joined forces to produce significant changes in governmental policy. The movements were combined under the presidential leadership of Theodore Roosevelt, who considered his efforts on behalf of the conservation program to be his most important contribution as president.[80]

Three agencies in this study are the products of what Samuel P. Hays has termed the "progressive conservation movement": the Bureau of Reclamation, the National Park Service, and the U.S. Forest Service. Of the three, the Forest Service stands out as the most complete representation of the several concerns and issues that fueled the early conservation movement in this country. This achievement is due in no small part to the foresight and vision of the Service's first chief forester, Gifford Pinchot, an individual whose crusade on behalf of conservation values was nearly as important as that of Roosevelt's. In fact, the two men in combination were what gave the movement many of its lasting achievements.

> The Eastern hero of the conservation movement, and by far the most influential figure in the field, was Gifford Pinchot. Born in Connecticut of an old Pennsylvania family and educated at Yale, Pinchot chose forestry as a career because of a youthful inclination, and his wealthy father encouraged him to get training in Europe, where the science was most advanced. . . . Pinchot's most important friend was Theodore Roosevelt. . . . They were both Ivy Leaguers who had mastered the out-of-doors, both endowed with boundless energy and interested in translating ideas into action.[81]

Though the Forest Service was not officially created until 1905 with Pinchot at its head, the momentum behind its creation had been building for some twenty-five years. What had been occurring in the United States with respect to one of its most valuable natural resources, the forest, was nothing less than a national scandal. Forest practices, if they could be called that, amounted to cutting down the most valuable trees, abandoning the cut-over land, and then moving on to more lucrative areas. The timber industry moved west with the frontier, and toward the end of the nineteenth century the big timber interests "had been looking forward to cutting a similar path [*of destruction*] across the public domain."[82] In his valuable autobiography, Pinchot described the prevailing mentality in this manner:

> The lumbermen, whose industry was then the third greatest in this country, regarded forest devastation as normal and second growth as a delusion of fools, whom they cursed on the rare occasions when they happened to think of them. And as for sustained yield, no such idea had ever entered their heads.[83]

Beginning around 1870, an increasing number of bills pertaining to the public timberlands were introduced in Congress, but it wasn't until 1891 that "the most important legislation in the history of forestry in America slipped through Congress without question and without debate."[84] The 1891 act, titled *An Act to repeal timber-culture laws, and for other purposes*, dealt principally with the repeal of the 1878 Timber and Stone Act, but a small unnoticed amendment paved the way for the creation in due time of the national forest system. Section 24 of the 1891 Act states:

> That the President of the United States may, from time to time, set apart and reserve, in any State or Territory having public land bearing forests, in any part of the public lands wholly or in part covered with timber or undergrowth, whether of commercial value or not, as public reservations, and the President shall, by public proclamation, declare the establishment of such reservations and the limits thereof.[85]

Presidential initiative in creating forest reserves was quickly forthcoming. By 1897 some 17.5 million acres had been withdrawn from the public domain, and in February of 1897 with just ten days left in office President Cleveland signed an executive order (thereby enraging western representatives and timber interests) to set aside an additional 21 million acres of forest reserves, thus more than doubling the existing forest system.[86]

A good part of the next seven years, from 1898 to 1905, were taken up with the attempt to merge the existing forest reserves—administered by the notoriously corrupt General Land Office in the Interior Department—with the small group of foresters working out of the Agriculture Department. Pinchot was of course tireless in his efforts to provide a secure organizational base for the fledgling national forest system:

> The Government forests—43,000,000 acres of Forest Reserves, and several times more millions of unreserved public timberland—were all in the charge of the Interior Department, which had not a single forester to look after them.
>
> All the Government foresters, the whole two of them, were in the Department of Agriculture, with not a single acre of Government forest in their charge. Forests and foresters were in completely separate water-tight compartments.
>
> It was a fantastic situation.[87]

In 1905 Pinchot succeeded. In January of that year Congress passed an act authorizing the transfer of the forest reserves from the Interior Department to Agriculture, thereby merging the Forestry Division with the forests and placing Pinchot at the head of government forestry.

In recalling the conservation movement of this period, there is a tendency to emphasize only the natural resources aspects of the movement and ignore the political, economic, and social issues of the day. That is why Hays's term, *progressive conservation*, is more appropriate than simply *conservation*, for it connects what time has tended to disconnect. And it is important to an understanding of the organizational history of the Forest Service to remember that Progressivism and conservation were symbiotic concerns. In other words, the development of this agency into a highly professional, dedicated, and powerful organization can be explained only by recalling the philosophy on which it was founded. Perhaps more than any other agency in our sample, the Forest Service owes much of its present strength to its ideological foundation and to its founder. According to Dana and Fairfax, Pinchot's commitment to scientific forestry created the aura of expertise that still surrounds the Forest Service: "Under Pinchot's leadership, the agency began its long history as the epitome of technical competence and scientific management."[88]

Forestry—that is, the scientific management of the timber resource according to the principles of wise use and sustained yield—is the academic discipline upon which Pinchot founded government forestry. This professional base has, as we will point out, served the agency well. But coupled with this base was a reformist impulse that motivated a generation of conservationists to bring about some basic changes in American society. Toward the end of his autobiography, Pinchot wrote directly and eloquently of his conception of conservation:

> The Conservation policy then has three great purposes.
>
> First: to wisely use, protect, preserve, and renew the natural resources of the earth.
>
> Second: to control the use of the natural resources and their products in the common interest, and to secure their distribution to the people at fair and reasonable charges for goods and services.
>
> Third: to see to it that the rights of the people to govern themselves shall not be controlled by great monopolies through their power over natural resources.
>
> Two of the principal ways in which lack of Conservation works out in damage to the general welfare are: (A) by destruction of forests, erosion of soils, injury of waterways, and waste of nonrenewable mineral resources. Here is strong reason for Government control. (B) by monopoly of natural and human resources, their products and application, and of the instruments by which these are made available.
>
> Monopoly means power—power not only over the supply of

natural resources, but also power to fix prices, and to exact unfair profits which lead to higher living costs for the people. It is the very essence of democracy that the greatest advantage of each of us is best reached through common prosperity of all of us. Monopoly is the denial of that great truth.

Monopoly of resources which prevents, limits, or destroys equality of opportunity is one of the most effective of all ways to control and limit human rights, especially the right of self-government.

Monopoly on the loose is a source of many of the economic, political, and social evils which afflict the sons of men. Its abolition or regulation is an inseparable part of the Conservation policy.[89]

The agency's commitment to both progressive, public-spirited values and to scientific forestry ultimately contributed to its growth and widespread acceptability. Dana and Fairfax write that "Forestry was less a movement than a maturing, diversifying profession."[90] This diversification led the Forest Service, in due time, into new areas of activity, and helped create the belief in the public mind of the agency as a highly respected source of expertise and information on natural resources issues.

The evolution of the Forest Service bears many resemblances to the history of the Corps and, as we show in chapter 5, both agencies are today highly regarded and frequently envied by their less influential cohorts. The Forest Service, like the Corps, has sustained itself over a seventy-five-year history by its adherence to utilitarian and pragmatic values. That is, the agency has always stood for the use and development of the public forests of the nation, and it has, by and large, administered the national forest system through applying the general principle of the greatest good for the greatest number, in the long run. How the agency has operationalized this principle is interesting. It began with the recognition that scientific forest management meant that forests were to be managed with a view toward maximizing all possible uses of the forest resource. A constant and assured supply of timber—what Pinchot referred to as tree farming—may have been the primary product of a forest. But foresters were not to lose sight of the forest for the trees: Also of value were, and are, watershed and wildlife management, mineral extraction, grazing of domesticated animals, and outdoor recreation. All potential uses of the forest were to be balanced, somehow, by government foresters who had a sound, practical knowledge of the particular forest in question. This practice of multiple-use management—a concept very similar to the Corps' multi-purpose water development projects—developed over the years, and was eventually given statutory recognition by Congress in its passage of the Multiple Use-Sustained Yield Act of 1960. The Forest Service called this act "a major milestone in the long history of the National Forest."[91]

The history of the Forest Service, like the Corps, reveals a remarkable ability to sense changing public priorities and to adapt its mission to meet those demands. This organizational flexibility is in part a product of the nature of the agency's mission. Both agencies were given broad mandates to manage, conserve, use, and develop the resources in question. Both the Corps and the Forest Service benefited from less scrutiny on the part of Congress and their departmental superiors than has been the case with several of the other agencies in this study. In other words, the agencies were given considerable leeway in how they attained their objectives, and they used this leeway in part to gain further advantages. Congress infrequently challenged the agencies' expertise.

Furthermore, these agencies have benefited from the fact that they are the providers of basic goods and services to a broad-based constituency. The Corps' pork barrel is of course by now notorious; it is perhaps a lesser known fact that there has existed—since even before the actual creation of the Forest Service—a network of interests and alliances supportive of that agency's mission and programs. Gifford Pinchot skillfully utilized interest groups such as the American Forestry Association, the National Board of Trade, and the American Forest Congress in his efforts to found the federal agency. Once created, the Forest Service and the timber industry developed a mutually supportive alliance:

> In practice the Forestry Service allowed timber operators to overcut, even devastate national forests in many places. The line between a cordial relationship and a corrupt relationship was hard to draw when private operators and a public agency became as close as the Forestry Service and the timber industry did. These problems were poorly understood at the time, as the famous Pinchot-Ballinger affair was to demonstrate.[92]

Another strength is that the Forest Service has always conceived of itself as a multi-purpose organization. This was demonstrated early in its history when, in 1918 in an Appropriations Committee hearing, the agency spoke of four principal activities in which it was then engaged. First, management of the national forest system was discussed as a primary function. This function was further broken down into timber production, forest maintenance, recreation, water and power development, and so on. A second principal activity was land classification and surveying. A third area of concern was fire fighting. In the years preceding 1918, droughts had resulted in devastating forest fires throughout the country. In response to these fire losses, the agency emphasized the improvement of its fire-fighting techniques; in the hearings the agency suggested that airplanes be used for this purpose, but the idea was dismissed as too impractical and expensive. The fourth area of activity was research.

The agency has always placed a strong emphasis on forest research, and in 1909 "experiment stations" were first established within the agency to do long-range empirical investigations, from studying the results of various cutting techniques to observing the effects on timber growth of different climatic conditions. Over the years, a period of sustained research on a particular subject has generally preceded the introduction of major new activities in the agency's growing repertoire. Hence the agency's research activity has been an especially fertile source of strength.

Following World War I the Forest Service began developing a major new functional activity. It saw a need to extend scientific forestry practices beyond national forest boundaries, and so cooperative activities with states and with private-forest owners were greatly increased at this time. In 1924 the Clarke-McNary Act was passed which authorized the expenditure of federal funds for federal-state cooperation in tree planting, fire fighting, and forest planning. The Forest Service thus assumed an educator's role with respect to the applied science of forestry. Having had the largest laboratory in the country in which to experiment, it now felt itself ready to, in Pinchot's words, "spread the gospel of practical forestry."[93] In 1980 it continued to be important. The Forest Service's 1981 budget request estimated that "research and cooperative forest activities is . . . to be almost double the 1977 level."[94]

By 1930, the chief forester stated that "a Federal policy of forestry has been developing for almost 60 years. It has been built up by successive legislative enactments and the resulting activities. It is not a specific and limited program, but rather is the gradual unfolding of a national purpose."[95] This statement summarizes the prevailing ideology of successful organizations in our sample. Personnel see their functions as continuous ones, constantly evolving, and intimately linked to the national welfare. This attitude is in marked contrast to the kind of perception informing agency personnel in several of the other agencies in this study. For example, Bureau of Reclamation and Soil Conservation Service officials focus on specific and finite objectives; often in testimony, mention was made of a time when their activities would be completed and they would (God forbid!) go out of business. Not so with the Forest Service, however, nor with the Corps and the National Park Service. On the whole, they see their missions as both permanent and vital to the nation's well-being. An evolutionary perspective is built into these agencies; no fear of extinction is expressed.

Agencies like the Forest Service tend to be innovative in their approach to problems, which is not to say that they cannot also, at times, be conservative in their outlook. Rather, they have an expansive tendency. The history of the Forest Service contains numerous examples of such imaginative thinking. For example, one that we like best occurred in the early 1930s when the agency turned its attention to the problems of soil erosion in the Great Plains states. Following a severe drought in 1934 the agency launched its Great Plains Shelterbelt Project. The project envisioned a huge windbreak of trees to be planted in a strip a hundred miles wide and extending from Texas to the Canadian border. By 1938 the chief of the agency reported that "since 1935, and despite drought, grasshopper plagues, and dust storms, nearly 7,000 miles of new shelterbelts have been established."[96] In 1942, after the Service had planted over 18,000 miles of shelterbelts, the program was turned over to the Soil Conservation Service, another Agriculture Department agency, to administer.

The agency responded in a similar manner during the 1950s, when outdoor recreation demand sharply rose. It initiated Operation Outdoors, a five-year program of repair and expansion of its recreational facilities. In 1961 it instituted its Visitor Information Service to provide visitor centers, nature trails, and interpretive services for the burgeoning number of visitors to the national forests. In all of this, of course, the Forest Service was engaging in healthy competition with its principal rival, the National Park Service, with outdoor recreation being the common, programmatic ground between them.

By 1950 the agency had organized itself into three main functional divisions. This organization has remained the same for the past thirty years. All of the agency's many programs or activities fall under one of the following three headings:

1. Management, protection, and development of the national forest and national rangeland systems—a system encompassing approximately 185 million acres of land

2. Cooperation with state and private-forest landowners in fire protection and in promoting better timber practices

3. Forest and range research

When the current wave of environmental concern swept across the country in the late 1960s, the Forest Service was well equipped to handle the resulting increase in public scrutiny of its programs. To hard-core environmentalists, the Corps was public enemy number one, but the Forest Service also came in for its share of criticism. For example, the Bitterroot National Forest controversy, which concerned the agency's practice of clear-cutting, touched off years of investigation by Congress, and others, of not only the practice itself but of virtually all of the agency's management practices as well as its basic philosophy. The result was the National Forest Management Act of 1976.[97] Despite persistent criticism from environmentalists, the agency's response to the passage of NEPA in 1969 was similar to that of the Corps of Engineers. Neither agency openly criticized the act, nor did either tend to dismiss it or minimize its significance. In 1970, forest officials gave Congress their reaction to NEPA:

Since practically all Forest Service management activities relate directly or indirectly to the environment, this Act supplemented and strengthened historic conservation efforts. However, in keeping with the intent of the Act, the Forest Service now has focused even more attention on environmental situations and is analyzing and studying the ecological consequences of its various activities more thoroughly.[98]

In 1972 the agency estimated that it spent $13 million in implementing NEPA, and by 1974 that figure rose to $28 million. Despite, or perhaps because of, increasing public scrutiny of its programs and practices, the Forest Service committed much time and energy throughout the 1970s to an examination of its own activities.

In response to these various political pressures the Forest Service has stepped up efforts to inventory its lands for either inclusion in or exclusion from the National Wilderness System. Through the RARE I and RARE II programs (Roadless Area Review and Evaluation), the Service has attempted to categorize land as to its suitability for wilderness designation. This inventory included nearly all of the 187 million acres in the national forest systems, and was designed to allow for "massive involvement of the public."[99] Reflecting the Forest Service's continuing commitment to the ideal of multiple use, the RARE II program often was billed as a quest for balance in public land use.[100] Like the Corps, the Forest Service launched an extensive public participation program throughout much of the 1970s in an effort to respond positively to new demands such as this one.

The Forest Service also quickly established itself as a leader in the current movement toward government-wide comprehensive planning. Congress mandated extensive planning programs in the Forest Service through passage of the 1974 Forest and Rangeland Renewable Resources Planning Act (RPA for short), which was amended by the 1976 National Forest Management Act.[101] These acts require the Forest Service to formulate resource management plans for all units of the national forest system by 1985. The RPA required a two-stage process consisting of, first, an assessment, which is an inventory of present and potential future uses of the national forest system, and second, a program stage where various alternative plans are presented and analyzed.[102] While this planning process is certainly not problem-free,[103] the Service has used congressionally mandated planning to expand its budget and justify its many activities. According to Christopher Leman,

Although the RPA has been given too much credit for the Forest Service's subsequent budgetary windfalls, there is no mistaking that the agency has done very well in appropriations since 1974. For example, for the first year after release of the first RPA report, fiscal year 1977 appropriations for the Forest Service increased 47 percent, more than the total increase in the four years from 1977 to 1980 for the Bureau of Land Management, an agency with functions similar to the Forest Service's, but without a total resource assessment and program development effort.[104]

The Forest Service has also actively pursued the requirement for public participation in this process, using to its advantage the requisite public meetings and hearings. The RPA statute has proven to be popular with the Forest Service constituency and with its allies in Congress. Thus the agency has adroitly cultivated its support through a comprehensive planning process that now serves as a model for other natural resource managers. As an indication of its importance, until recently research to meet RPA goals was the fastest-growing component of the Forest Service's budget.[105]

The agency's more recent success—i.e., from 1970 to the present—is reflected in its budget growth. With the exception of a slight slump in the mid-1970s, funding for the Service has risen substantially. For example, the 1980 budget totaled more than $2 billion and included funding for a wide variety of activities, ranging from timber management, citizen participation, and cooperative activities to its public relations programs like Woodsy Owl and Smokey the Bear.[106]

How has the agency fared under the present Republican adminis-tration? In a word, not badly. For example, the FY 1982 Forest Service budget proposed by the Reagan administration maintained a high level of overall funding for the agency, but it substantially altered program priorities. Not surprisingly, funds for recreation and planning were reduced while production-oriented programs are either held at previous levels or increased.

More specifically, the total proposed budget for 1982 was $2.236 billion—a 20 percent reduction from the previous year. However, almost all of this proposed reduction was due to the ultimately unsuccessful attempt to eliminate the Land and Water Conservation Fund, a land acquisition program shared by a number of federal agencies.[107] The Service was also affected by proposed recisions in the Youth Conservation Corps and the Young Adult Conservation Corps, which are budgeted independently but which perform duties for the Forest Service. For instance, the YCC and YACC aided the Forest Service in its reforestation and recreation programs. To compensate for the loss of these youth programs the Service was given a budget supplement for the reforestation work previously done by the YCC and the YACC, but no additional funds for recreation were forthcoming.[108] Thus, in 1982 the total reduction in proposed funding for the Service amounted to $73.8 million, or about a 10 percent budget decrease. This compared favorably to a proposed 14 percent reduction in the Department of Agriculture's budget. The Forest Service thus managed to have its budget cut less than some of its fellow agencies in Agriculture. It should be noted also that nearly all of the Forest Service's budget reduction is in what it considers to be tangential or auxiliary programs.[109] And for FY 1983 Reagan again proposed a budget for the Forest Service that emphasized timber and mineral production while cutting environmental and recreational programs, thereby maintaining an overall funding level of $2 billion.

Under the present administration, the agency has been more affected by a shift in priorities rather than a dramatic increase or decrease in its budgetary base. For example, increased emphasis has been placed on programs that "will improve the supply of products from National Forests" and "make contributions to economic progress."[110] The Reagan budget for FY 1983 shows that receipts from timber sales rose dramatically, from $553 million in 1981, to an estimated $914 million in 1982, to a projected $1.4 billion in 1983. However, the 1983 budget cut funding for tree planting and seeding, timber stand improvement, and soil and water resource improvement.[111] The FY 1984 budget contained similar priorities. The volume of timber harvested from national forests increased from 6.2 billion board feet in 1982 to a proposed 11 billion for 1984. Mineral receipts also increased.[112] Ironically, the increased emphasis on timber production in recent years has resulted in a funding increase for wildlife and fisheries management and support:

> That increase is to be used in support of the timber program. You will recall we are going into roadless areas where we have not previously had detailed information on wildlife and fish. We will be doing land-disturbing activities, so we feel we need to increase support as we move into these previously unroaded areas.[113]

As with the Corps, practically all activities associated with recreation have been cut back. Reagan's FY 1982 budget for recreation represented a decrease of $6.5 million from the Forest Service's proposal (together with a loss of 93 positions); actually, this was an increase of $2 million over the agency's 1981 budget for recreation. However, this modest increase doesn't tell the entire story, according to agency spokesmen: "when you crank in inflation and put in the loss of YCC and YACC, it would be a net reduction."[114]

As a result of this reduction in its recreation program the Forest Service will be forced to curtail a number of activities such as cleanup and maintenance; it may also have to "shorten the season," that is, operate facilities for fewer days out of the year.[115] The revised budget proposed by the Reagan administration recommended a 50 percent reduction in developed-site management as well as the actual closing of some facilities. Their proposal argued that "increased resource degradation in dispersed areas will be minimized through improved management efficiencies,"[116] but a Forest Service spokesman stated in the appropriations hearings that there is a definite potential for "damage to wilderness areas" due to these budget reductions.[117]

Another issue related to recreation, and on which the administration has been particularly vocal, concerns the substandard condition of some visitor facilities in the national forests (and national parks). A 1980 GAO Report found that some of these facilities were a threat to the health and safety of visitors; it recommended that the funds for recreation construction be dramatically increased.[118] But the proposed Reagan budget reduced funds for this purpose by $1 million, which "will reduce or defer our ability to bring substandard water and sanitation facilities to desirable standards."[119] These reductions came at a time when visitation to Forest Service recreation facilities was increasing steadily, from 222 million in 1980 to a projected 233 million in 1981.[120] However, it should be pointed out again that the budget cuts in the agency's recreation programs are quite selective and that the budget total actually represents an increase. We interpret this as testimony to the strength of the Forest Service in that the agency has resisted significant decreases in its budget for such a politically vulnerable item as recreation even during the era of Reagan austerity. While other agencies have been hit hard with budget reductions, the Forest Service has managed to at least maintain funding levels for its "nonproductive" programs. And in the tradition of a self-confident organization, the Forest Service publicizes that it (1) spends less per visitor day than other agencies, and (2) provides 40 percent of all recreation opportunities on federal lands.[121] With this kind of salesmanship, the Forest Service's recreation program has thus far withstood the budgetary ax wielded by departmental officials. John Crowell, a former timber lobbyist who is now assistant secretary for natural resources and the environment in the Agriculture Department, has been described as a "vociferous critic" of the Forest Service.[122] It is Crowell who oversees the agency at the departmental level and who has been most insistent on increasing timber production within the national forest system.

Other aspects of the Forest Service's mission are undergoing scrutiny as well. The Reagan administration wishes to de-emphasize the long-range planning process embodied in the RPA, and it is especially critical of government funds expended for research on planning. The FY 1982 budget proposal not only reduced funds for RPA but also changed program priorities from those recommended by RPA assessment and RPA programs.[123] However, since funding for the RPA has been the fastest-growing program in the Forest Service budget in recent years these reductions appeared fairly trivial relative to the overall budget. As is the case with all other aspects of the Service's budget, Reagan's proposed budget cuts for FY 1982 made a small dent in a massive Forest Service budget. The proposed elimination of the Land and Water Conservation Fund stands out as the only significant reduction in the agency's budget, but Congress has steadfastly refused to abandon the fund, thereby continuing to provide funds for federal land acquisition.

The Forest Service responds to criticism and attacks in a manner similar to the Corps. Rather than resist new policy demands, the agency incorporates them into its growing list of responsibilities and functions. Over time the agency has adroitly absorbed many of the forces that have threatened its domain. An accurate assessment of this unusual ability is provided by Sally Fairfax, who writes that the Forest Service "is an unusually coherent government agency . . . by tradition, most uncommonly apt to comply with, rather than resist or reformulate, commands."[124]

Complementing the Forest Service's capacity to absorb new responsibilities and to formulate new objectives for itself is its professional base.[125] Many observers have noted the high degree of autonomy and independence accorded to this agency within the executive branch structure. Further evidence of its stature is found in biographical reviews of the heads (chief foresters) of the agency: All have been career Forest Service employees with college degrees in forestry. None has been what is commonly referred to as a political appointee. As Culhane notes, "There is no lateral entry into the service; all line officers work their way up from the bottom, giving them a common background and view."[126] The prestige accorded to the discipline of forestry—and the predominance of this profession within the agency—has undoubtedly contributed to the general image of the agency as a valuable repository of scientific expertise. According to recent agency estimates, for instance, 16 percent of its total permanent work force is comprised of foresters. The data compiled by Culhane in his recent work on the Forest Service and Bureau of Land Management underscore this point by noting that 90 percent of the agency's professional staff are trained foresters.[127]

Comparing the Forest Service with the other two principal land-managing agencies—the Park Service and the Bureau of Land Management—one finds that 16 percent is a high figure. The dominant profession in the National Park Service is something called park ranger/park management; it accounts for a little over 12 percent of the work force. In the Bureau of Land Management, 11 percent of the total work force is comprised of what the agency classifies as natural resource specialist. Another telling contrast is found in the fact that both of the latter agencies have at times been directed by political appointees who clearly were not career men rising through the ranks of the agencies. We further discuss these differences in the next two chapters when we examine in detail the BLM and Park Service.

For a variety of reasons, then, there is little doubt that the Forest Service has developed into a well-funded, powerful agency with the ability to use its assets to expand into new areas while at the same time remaining faithful to the agency's original mission and ideology.

SUMMARY: SYNERGISTIC ORGANIZATIONS

Among our seven-agency sample, two federal organizations—the U.S. Forest Service and the Army Corps of Engineers—stand out. They have larger work forces and significantly larger budgets than their five cohorts, factors that we compare in detail in chapter 5. They also have reputations as powerful agencies; though controversy surrounds the tasks they perform for society, even their critics usually accord them grudging respect for their professionalism and for their sense of political acumen. Like powerful politicians who may not always do things we like, respect for them flows from their ability, in this achievement-oriented society, to get things done. And no one has ever accused either agency of not getting the job done.

The histories of the Corps and the Forest Service illuminate an interesting and little-discussed characteristic of organizational behavior— that some agencies are able to put together their various resources in such a way as to produce a powerful combination. In the first chapter we discussed several power sources upon which agencies can draw. If agencies are weak in one area they can try to compensate for that deficiency by being stronger in other areas. But some combinations of factors appear to act within an organization in a synergistic manner: the effect of their combination is not simply a sum of parts, but rather their interaction combines to achieve an effect that each factor individually is incapable of producing. Our finding is that at least certain complex organizations, such as bureaucracies, show evidence of behaving like biological organisms, from which the concept of synergism is drawn.

We thus see bureaucracies as entities, even organisms, that are constantly changing and adapting to their environments, which also are in a certain state of flux. Some agencies are better equipped to make the necessary changes to secure their continued influence, and even survival, than are others. This former group, those that compete better than the others, is blessed with a potent combination of resources. In the case of the Corps and the Forest Service, these include: a pro-development, multiple-use mission; a pragmatic or utilitarian ideology; a clear beginning (through a direct congressional statement of purpose at the time of its creation, or through the work of a strong founder, or both); a scientific and/or military basis of expertise; internal recruitment to leadership positions; a coherent, well-defined public image; and unusually strong support from Congress (or sometimes from the chief executive) as well as from large, well-organized constituencies outside the formal institutions of government. Both the Corps and the Forest Service are, of course, constituent parts of what are commonly referred to now as iron triangles, whose purpose is to protect and promote the interests so arranged.

In our examination of the histories of these two superstars, we did not find the limiting factors, or weaknesses, that seem to handicap the other agencies that we studied. As we go on to discuss in the next two chapters, our five other agencies have not been the beneficiaries of synergism to nearly the same degree as these two have. Thus a more typical pattern of organizational development is our next subject.

CHAPTER THREE

Agencies That Muddle Through:

The National Park Service,
the Soil Conservation Service, and
the U.S. Fish and Wildlife Service

THE NATIONAL PARK SERVICE

When the Pilgrims first landed on the shores of the New World, they considered the American wilderness to be an obstacle in the path of the advancing European civilization. Not until well into the nineteenth century did some individuals begin arguing for the protection of the remaining vestiges of the great American wilderness. These nineteenth-century preservationists and leaders of the romantic movement in America were interested in preserving specific wilderness areas principally for their aesthetic value. This brought preservationists into direct conflict not only with the powerful economic interests of the time but also with the less ideological conservationists, like Gifford Pinchot. Although preservationists and conservationists were allied in their opposition to the unchecked exploitation of the public lands, there was much on which they did not see eye to eye. As a group preservationists were devoted to protecting in perpetuity the pristine character of the remaining public lands, while conservationists supported the utilitarian ideal of "wise use." As a result, these two groups and their conflicting approaches were frequently in direct competition with each other in their efforts to gain control over public lands. The nineteenth-century conservation movement was a movement divided.[1]

The first significant victory for the preservationists occurred in 1872 when Congress created a 2.2 million acre preserve in the Yellowstone Valley, to be "withdrawn from settlement, occupancy or sale . . . and dedicated and set apart as a public park or pleasuring ground for the benefit and enjoyment of the people."[2] Several other national parks were added in the succeeding twenty-five years, and in 1906 Congress passed the Antiquities Act, which empowered the president to establish national monuments by proclamation and without the approval of Congress.[3] By 1916 there were sixteen national parks and twenty-one national monuments in existence. These areas, however, were not the inviolate sanctuaries that the preservationists had envisioned and desired. Due to inadequate funding plus the absence of any federal agency charged with the responsibility of protecting these parks and monuments, they were routinely used for grazing, farming, and lumbering. The parks existed only on paper. Furthermore, the economic exploitation of park lands was often tolerated and even encouraged by local interests who resented federal control—especially if it meant preservation—over the public domain.

The use of park lands for utilitarian purposes reached an apex in 1913 with the bitter struggle over the proposed Hetch Hetchy reservoir project within the boundaries of Yosemite National Park. Developers argued that the reservoir was crucial to the continued growth and economic development of the San Francisco area, and after a protracted conflict they won the right to build a dam within park boundaries.[4] To the preservationists this was indeed a great and painful loss; it also established an important precedent in that it illustrated the political weaknesses inherent in the preservationists' position. As many saw it, their "extremist" position on issues of development would inevitably put them in the minority.

The Hetch Hetchy controversy, however, underscored the need for a new federal agency to manage the recently created park lands. After several years of procrastination and controversy, Congress passed enabling legislation in 1916 establishing a National Park Service with a mandate to do the following:

> regulate the use of . . . national parks and monuments . . . conserve the scenery and the natural and historic objects and the wildlife therein and to provide for the enjoyment of the same in such manner and by such means as will leave them unimpaired for the enjoyment of future generations.[5]

Thus the mission of the new agency was to preserve the parks in a natural state yet also to provide access to these same parks so that they could be enjoyed by the public. An inherent conflict between preservation and public use was written into the original mandate of the new service. In 1918 the secretary of the interior reiterated the need to satisfy both of these goals (without specifying how) in an administrative directive that stated that the parks must be maintained "unimpaired," yet also set aside for the "use and pleasure of the people," including "educational as well as recreational use."[6]

This built-in conflict in the Park Service's mission has repeatedly caused problems for park policymakers. An example of the kind of difficulties created by a dual mission is seen in early Park Service policy in the

Yosemite Valley. Many people felt that Yosemite was the star gem of the entire park system, and so Stephen Mather, first director of the Service, strongly encouraged automobile travel to the valley in hopes that the silent beauty and isolation of the park would encourage people to support the fledgling Park Service. The Service even organized auto caravans that toured valley roads. But within ten years the valley became clogged with cars, and the qualities that had inspired Director Mather to encourage park visitation soon became lost in the effort to use what was also supposed to have been preserved.[7] Some sixty years later, the Park Service continues to grapple with the Yosemite Park Plan in an attempt to solve the conflict between use and preservation. A recently publicized proposal would have visitors tour the park through chartered air service.

By the time of the Park Service's creation in 1916, the split between conservationists and preservationists had grown into an intense rivalry. Gifford Pinchot stated at the time that the creation of a preserve where timber cutting was illegal was nothing more than an indefensible attempt to outlaw scientific forestry.[8] The first director of the Park Service, Stephen Mather, was a millionaire businessman who devoted the last two decades of his life to the establishment of the Park Service. But unlike Pinchot, he never developed a close working relationship with prominent political figures. Although Mather had the support of celebrities like John Muir, the more pragmatic conservationists dominated the centers of power in Washington. As a result, the Park Service was born in the shadow of progressive conservation which was, as we noted in chapter 2, institutionalized in the Forest Service.[9]

Throughout the first thirty years of its existence, the Park Service failed to broaden its mission. Rather it existed on a shoestring budget and continuously grappled with the dilemma created by its conflicting dual mandate. The expendibility of the Service became evident during World War II, when funding was cut from $21 million to $5 million, and central headquarters were moved to Chicago to make room for more "important" operations in Washington.[10]

With the end of the war, however, the parks gained a new and welcomed visibility when postwar prosperity brought record numbers of visitors to the parks. But thirty years of fiscal frugality left the Park Service unprepared to deal with the rush of new visitors. To exacerbate the problem, Congress failed to appreciably increase funding for the Park Service even after the end of the war. The resulting financial bind proved to be not only detrimental to the agency but physically damaging to the parks; there was no way the Service could adequately maintain or patrol them on its annual appropriation. In 1949 Director Newton B. Drury issued a report called "The Dilemma of Our Parks," which described the deterioration and destruction of park land and park property caused by so many visitors and so few staff. A similar report was issued twenty-six years later, and it reached essentially the same conclusions. This one was titled "The Degradation of Our National Parks."

The solution to this problem, as envisioned by the Park Service in 1949, was to initiate a massive development program in the national parks to accommodate increased visitation. At this point in the agency's history the preservation aspect of its mandate became secondary. The Park Service, however, overlooked the possibility that such a development program might in the long run exacerbate the problems it was designed to cure by encouraging even greater visitation than the agency could keep up with. In fact, this spiraling effect, where resources never quite keep up with visitor use, has been a major theme in the history of the Service.

To keep up with public demand, in 1956 the agency launched its Mission '66 program. This was an ambitious ten-year development program that increased visitor capacity enormously but that "has done comparatively little for the plants and animals" and "nothing at all for the ecological maintenance of a park."[11] Another author observed that "some of the Park Service's problems . . . will be traced to its own effort [*Mission '66*] to attract the public."[12] The funding for Mission '66 finally totaled about a billion dollars; it is the only program in the history of the Park Service that has been generously funded. It is also a good example of the Park Service competing successfully with its principal governmental rival, the Forest Service. Culhane notes that "Since the turn of the century, the two services had battled about jurisdiction over especially scenic areas of public lands. The Forest Service generally came out on the short end of the stick, losing a net 4.5 million acres to the Park Service through 1960. Thus, from the Forest Service's point of view, Mission '66 signaled a reintensification of this long-standing jurisdictional duel."[13]

The agency was successful in this instance primarily because it decided to compromise its preservation goal by opting for more publicly attractive utilitarian goals. Although the Park Service may not have consciously abandoned its preservation mission, the agency did not fully appreciate the impact that Mission '66 would have on that primary aspect of park management. In contrasting the operating principles of the Forest Service with those of the Park Service, for example, Darling and Eichhorn state that the "U.S. Forest Service was . . . much more politically aware of the trend of the times, as the National Park Service was naive. Mission '66, instead of being a far-sighted planning operation to conserve these choice areas, seems to have been conceived to allow more complete infiltration and uncritical use."[14] For park enthusiasts the Park Service is unfortunate testimony to the cliché, Damned if you do and damned if you don't.

By the time the Mission '66 program was well underway, park administrators realized that they desperately needed a consistent and coherent management policy that could help solve their historic use-versus-preservation dilemma. Under the leadership of George Hartzog, the Service finally produced a clear administrative policy on this issue; it was officially adopted in a memorandum signed by Secretary of the Interior Stewart Udall in 1964. This new policy appears to have helped resolve the agency's heretofore schizophrenic management of park lands.

The new management framework divided park lands into three categories: natural, historic, and recreational. In his memorandum Secretary Udall spelled out the basic problem that had plagued the Park Service for so long:

> A single broad management concept encompassing these three categories of areas within the System is inadequate either for their proper preservation or for realization of their full potential for public use embodied in the expressions of congressional policy. Each of these categories required a separate set of management principles coordinated to form one organic management plan for the entire system.[15]

The official Park Service explanation of the new plan contained the long-awaited realization that:

> Even though all of the parks come under the mandate of the Act of 1916 . . . it is clear that the purpose and intent of each is not the same as the others. . . . In 1964 we recognized three management categories . . . to encompass this diversity . . . so that resources may be appropriately identified and managed in terms of their inherent values and appropriate uses.[16]

The tripartite management policy had a significant impact on agency operations. Perhaps most importantly, it allowed the agency to adopt a preservationist orientation in *some*—not all—park lands. Thus the criteria for increased use and development, which in the past had simply been to expand everywhere and anywhere within park boundaries to meet public demand, now became linked to physical impact, or as the agency put it, to "ecological health or repose."[17] In practice this simply meant that zoning for use would hereafter guide park management, and that some areas would be zoned for heavy recreational use and others for minimal use. The Service also adopted a new restrictive road policy. These attempts to curtail or diminish development in some areas reflected the newly defined purpose of the "natural area" category: "The single abiding purpose of National Parks is to bring man and his environment into closer harmony. It is thus the quality of the park experience—and not the statistics of travel—which must be the primary concern."[18]

This plan was initiated in 1964, and was the first of several innovations introduced by Director Hartzog in an effort to improve agency operations and to handle the unprecedented influx of visitors. In 1956 visitation was estimated at 55 million, and the Park Service confidently predicted that it would rise to 80 million in ten years. But by 1966 annual visitation had increased to around 133 million, leaving the Park Service unprepared and unequipped. The Service's budget, for instance, had increased threefold during that ten-year period: from $44.8 million (1956) to $136.4 million (1966). With the close of Mission '66, however, the Service suffered a budget cut of over $10 million, which was followed by another budget decrease in 1968. In the meantime, as could by now be expected, visitation increased by another 12 million.[19]

Director Hartzog's new management innovations, including his efforts to establish urban recreation areas, were effective constituency-building devices; they made park lands available to a broader spectrum of people and activities. But they also created management difficulties for Park Service personnel, who were imbued with a traditional concept of parks as natural wonders in a sylvan setting. Urban parks, with their problems of crime and crowding, and recreation areas, which permitted motorized recreation, offended the traditional sensibilities of some Park Service personnel. The historic role of the park ranger, which focused on natural and historic interpretive activity, had to be suddenly expanded to encompass law enforcement, traffic control, and crowd management. This created some morale problems that continue to affect the agency.

In addition to the new management policies, the Park Service was also significantly affected by a number of other developments. Several statutes were enacted, most of them of recent origin, that tended to broaden the agency's horizons. For instance, the Service stated that:

The mandate to preserve historic resources . . . is contained not only in the National Park Service organic act of 1916, but also in five other legislative enactments:

—Antiquities Act, 1906
—Historic Sites Act, 1935
—National Historic Preservation Act, 1966
—National Environmental Policy Act, 1969
—Archeological and Historic Preservation Act, 1974[20]

To this list one should also add:

—Land and Water Conservation Fund Act, 1964
—Wilderness Act, 1964
—"Protection and Enhancement of the Cultural Environment,"
  Executive Order 11593, May 13, 1971[21]

Expansion of the agency's mission during the 1960s is revealed in other ways as well. In just four years, from 1964 to 1968, the number of park areas jumped from 218 to 270.[22] Many of these new areas, moreover, dramatically changed the original conception of a park, which had guided Service activities for over fifty years. For example, the new conception of a park was contained in the authorization that created two urban-oriented park areas (Gateway in New York City and Golden Gate in San Francisco) and two cultural centers (Kennedy Center in Washington, D.C., and Wolf Trap Park in neighboring Virginia). In addition, the Service was given responsibility in the 1970s for orchestrating the American Bicentennial Program.[23]

Yet with these additional responsibilities and enlargements of its original mandate, the Service was unable to secure a commensurate increase in funding. Its budget continued to increase incrementally and thus did not reflect the prodigious changes occurring in and to the national park system. Meanwhile, Director Hartzog continued to force changes in agency operations in an effort to cope with budgetary constraints through increasing the organization's efficiency. He organized the Field Operations Study Team (FOST) to recommend more efficient management and administration strategies.[24] At about the same time Hartzog abolished the use of fifty six administrative manuals and handbooks, accumulated over time, that had become the official Park Service way of "how to do the job."[25]

Another innovation occurring during Hartzog's tenure was the concept of the Golden Eagle Pass, a discounted "season ticket" to all national parks. It is significant because of its quick demise. When instituted in 1965, it was expected that over 30 million passes would be sold that year; but actually only 1 million were bought by the public. The Park Service, together with others who had dreamed up the idea, failed to realize that the American public did not feel it had to pay to get into their own public parks. The Golden Eagle Pass thus raised an outcry of complaints from park visitors who claimed that they should not have to have a ticket to enter a public place.[26] In other words, the public was not very sensitive to the fact that their national parks needed money to operate, and that such money was scarce indeed. For its part, the Park Service appeared remarkably ignorant of the sentiments of its attentive public.

The political and organizational significance of such a public attitude on agency operations has been considerable. Of the Park Service's two primary constituencies, one group—the summer visitors—is broad, diverse, and largely unaware of the political and funding problems facing the Park Service. Most visitors do not know the difference between the Park Service and the Forest Service. The general public tends to demand a great deal from park management, yet it offers very little real constituency support. Environmentalists do, but they are often perceived as extremists who support the agency's preservation mandate but not its public-use one. Moreover, the Park Service has had to compete for funds with other agencies that have well-organized support and that offer pork barrel programs.

Part of the Park Service's problems can thus be traced to public attitudes and to the lack of an organized constituency to support its recreation program. The public considers the parks to be theirs in a rather concrete sense; the Service, therefore, merely regulates the use of this public good. In view of the fact that the parks often have been poorly maintained, understaffed, and overcrowded, it appeared that the Park Service was not an outstanding custodian of this public heritage. To add to the problem, the Service does not appear to have cultivated the active support of its visitor constituency. The director of the Wilderness Society, for example, recently stated that for a long time there has been "a communication gap between the agency and the interested public."[27]

Still others consider the Park Service and its programs to be a low-priority item on the federal agenda. One Bureau of the Budget official explained the agency's financial dilemma in 1969 like this:

> The poor Park Service! First, recreation was considered a "frill." Now its programs are considered a "middle-income subsidy."[28]

Thus, unlike its more powerful competitor, the Forest Service, the Park Service has not been able to claim a constituency organized around economic interests, and hence its mission is not regarded as contributing significantly to the economic productivity of the country. Instead, its natural clientele has been composed primarily of conservation groups whose major objective—preservation—is seen by many as restrictive, narrow, or even reactionary.

The combination of modest-to-low constituency support and a relatively narrow mission have created serious political and organizational problems for the Park Service. The political impotence of the Service was perhaps most obvious during the Nixon presidency. Soon after Richard Nixon entered the White House, he removed the forceful and independent George Hartzog and replaced him with Ron Walker, a political appointee and aide to the president. Walker had been an insurance salesman before joining Nixon's campaign staff, and served as special assistant to the president before appointment to the Park Service. He had no professional experience with parks, or recreation, or preservation.

During Walker's two-year tenure as director, he managed to implicate the agency in an embarrassing boondoggle (shades of Watergate) concerning the development of a campsite reservation system. By 1970, visitation had outstripped facilities to the point where long queues of campers were lining up at the parks, many of whom ultimately had to be turned away. These prospective visitors became disgruntled in the process. Park Service staff felt that a reservation system was the best solution to this critical problem, and so the decision was made to contract out the responsibility of establishing and operating a nationwide park reservation system. (The decision to contract for services was made because the Park Service felt it did not have the personnel or expertise to operate a nationwide system.) The first contract to handle reservations for six of the most heavily used parks was let to American Express. This operation worked well for one season, but American Express refused to renew the contract due to cost overruns caused by the unanticipated volume of reservation requests.

In 1974 the Park Service decided to expand the reservation system to include fourteen more parks, and issued a prospectus for an expanded contract, this time anticipating a huge volume of requests.[29] After a brief review, Ticketron, having assets of $877 million and extensive experience in reservations, was bypassed along with another company, and the contract was instead given to Public Reservation Systems (PRS), a company just recently formed in order to make a bid for the agency's contract. The financial assets of this new company were unknown, but apparently it was clear that it had no experience, expertise, or even adequate equipment to do the job. As could have been expected, their operation was a complete failure; they were unable to handle more than 5 percent of the calls for reservations. A subsequent investigation by the General Accounting Office and an Interior Department inquiry were followed by congressional oversight hearings, which failed to prove any criminal wrongdoing but which did find that PRS had violated its own contract. The investigations also discovered that Park Service Director Ron Walker was a personal friend of the president of PRS and that he maintained "social contacts" with him during the period in which bids were being considered.[30]

For an agency that was already weak politically, scandals of this sort had the potential of undermining what little support there was. For the many park visitors who were the victims of the reservation fiasco, it undoubtedly damaged their faith in the Service's ability to manage the parks in a competent and professional manner. This, coupled with the deteriorating condition of many of the parks, further impaired the Service's image. This attitude was summed up by a statement from the National Parks and Conservation Association in 1975: "There has been an elementary failure to maintain the public property of the American people in the National Park system."[31]

The causes of this failure are due in large part to the long-term funding problems experienced by the Park Service, and its inability to effectively cope with spiraling visitor use. It is less a comment on the commitment of agency employees to their mission. For example, a review of the Service's budget from 1966 to 1969 concluded that "it is generally assumed that the Park Service is operating on a rock-bottom budget."[32] Another author wrote that in 1976 "the funding situation is the worst in 25 years."[33] The Park Service has also been caught in a personnel squeeze. During the 1970s, when visitation continued to soar, the Office of Management and Budget not only set strict limits on funding but set strict personnel ceilings, thereby forcing in some cases a "reduction in force" (RIF). Thus, many congressionally authorized positions were never filled; a number of parks had to reduce their work forces at the same time visitation was rising. From 1972 to 1975, Congress authorized a 7 percent staff increase, but the Park Service received none of this increase.[34] The following year, 1976, the Office of Management and Budget imposed an RIF in the land acquisition program that resulted in 103 congressionally authorized positions going unfilled.[35] What happens to the parks when stringent personnel ceilings are mandated is illustrated by the situation in Rocky Mountain National Park in the 1970s, where visitation increased 77 percent while permanent staff decreased by 20 percent.[36]

The observable deterioration of park lands is only one result of the agency's inadequate budget. There are others that are, in the long run, equally harmful to the viability of the agency. In recent years the Service has become more reluctant to establish new parks. In 1973, for instance, the Service decided to establish a deadline year for "rounding out the National Park System" and since then has established more stringent criteria for the acquisition of new parks.[37] With the exception of Alaskan lands, there has also developed considerable resistance in Congress to proposals for expansion of the park system, given the present, but perennial, funding difficulties.[38] Thus in the face of increased demand for park use, the Service has become hesitant to support plans for its own expansion, and has in fact de-authorized some areas.[39]

Another result of the Service's budgeting and personnel problems is the inability to adequately meet new statutory demands. Chapter 5 will further verify some of the problems the Service has had in meeting the requirements of the National Environmental Policy Act. Another indicator is found in the fact that the Park Service has been unable to complete on time its wilderness reviews as mandated by the 1964 Wilderness Act.[40]

Related to the problems just discussed is the limited ability of the Park Service to research its own operations. The Park Service contrasts sharply with the Forest Service in this regard. In discussing the maze of problems confronting the agency, an assistant director stated that "management has no choice but to concentrate on the effect, whereas the real solution depends upon getting at the cause."[41] In reference to the need for cost-per-visitor research, an investigation found that the

Service cannot do that type of analysis because "they do not have the resources available to them. They are also too occupied with more immediate problems of park operations."[42] Another author even favored giving research funds to the Forest Service rather than the Park Service because "the men who report to the Park Service director have been shockingly weak on research in either natural environments or the sociology of human recreation."[43]

Much of the Park Service's budget and personnel problems can be traced to its rather uneven competition with the Forest Service. While the former has had difficulty meeting its original preservation and use mandate, the latter has successfully expanded its original mandate to include preservation as one of its many activities. Indeed, the Forest Service today manages over 15 million acres of wilderness set aside in the National Wilderness Preservation System as compared with the Park Service's 3.3 million acres.[44] The Park Service has also had to compete with other federal and state agencies as a provider of recreation facilities. Both the Forest Service and the Corps of Engineers, for example, have well-financed recreation programs, though both programs have been attenuated somewhat under President Reagan. The Park Service's rivalry with the Forest Service in this activity is well known. Everhart writes:

> the most celebrated interbureau rivalry in all government involves the Forest Service and the Park Service. . . . The long history of competing and conflicting objectives has developed in each agency a keen but wary respect for the ability of the other to stir up mischief.[45]

Clearly, the Park Service has had its share of problems during its sixty-five-year history—problems in expanding its mission, in the appropriations process, and in competing with more powerful agencies. Despite these weaknesses, however, the Park Service has met with qualified success in a number of areas. The strength of the organization undoubtedly lies in the commitment of its personnel. Perhaps due to its esoteric mission, Park Service employees have demonstrated a deep commitment to the notion of a national park system, and this has bound them together with a strong unity of purpose. Their esprit de corps was quite evident in a survey of Park Service employees completed in 1977.[46] For instance, 15 percent of the respondents "strongly agreed" and 61 percent "agreed" that "there is a strong professional bond among Park Service employees." Also evident in their responses was their commitment to environmental quality. The survey further made clear the fact that Park Service employees did not join the Service for the money. Financial incentives were rated "poor" or "fair" by 29 percent and 42 percent respectively. Indeed, one respondent penciled in: "I'm sure we're the lowest paid agency in the federal government." Despite financial disincentives, 80 percent felt that the Park Service is effective and doing a good job, and 84 percent were optimistic about the Service's future. This zealous attitude is evident in a former director's characterization of Park Service employment as "our high calling as trustees for the greater things of America."[47] In a more subdued tone, another author wrote that the Park Service "is given high marks for its dedication and performance, under increasingly trying conditions."[48] Apparently the public also holds the agency in high esteem, and this despite a reluctance to directly help defray operating expenses through increased users' fees; a recent poll of public perceptions about fifteen federal agencies put the Park Service at the top of the list, with a 77 percent "favorable" rating.[49]

In recent years the number of park areas has increased dramatically despite the agency's reluctance to take on greater responsibilities. The National Parks and Recreation Act of 1978 added fifteen new park areas. Public Law 96-487 authorized the establishment of ten new park areas in Alaska and expanded three previously established areas, also in Alaska. This more than doubled the number of acres under Park Service jurisdiction. At present the system includes 333 separate areas encompassing 73.7 million acres. Park visitation also continues to increase, totaling more than 238 million in 1981 and estimated to be over 267 million for 1984.[50]

These most recent expansions of the national park system have created a political backlash, whose organizational expression is a pressure group called the National Inholders Association. This group organized itself in 1978 to fight against any further federal encroachments on privately held lands lying adjacent to federal lands, and to halt the government's long-standing policy of assuming ownership of lands within national park and forest boundaries (called inholdings). The Association found many powerful allies in the Reagan Interior Department and is a parallel political development to the more widely publicized Sagebrush Rebellion.[51]

In keeping with past tradition, the Park Service is experiencing tremendous difficulties in dealing with this substantial increase in responsibilities and with the political opposition to the park system. The Reagan administration proposed significant new management policies which may have an important impact on future Park Service operations. Former Interior Secretary James Watt of course became embroiled in controversy over his new policies concerning public lands. In short, a number of significant new policies concerning Park Service lands now exist; they deal with the issues of park expansion, park degradation, budgeting difficulties, concessioners, and urban parks.

One of Secretary Watt's first policies regarding the agency was to issue a moratorium on the acquisition of new park lands. In his view, no new acreage should be added to the system until the older, established parks are adequately equipped and maintained:

They [*the parks*] continue to suffer, as they have suffered with the poor stewardship which has been demonstrated in the last years and years and years—when we have been authorizing parks for acquisition, when we can't take care of what we have. . . . I don't think that is good stewardship. It is my strong recommendation that we not ask Congress for authority to add new lands to the National Park System. We haven't taken care of what we have.[52]

The Congress had a different view, however. Throughout his three-year tenure as interior secretary, Watt fought continually with the legislative branch over the issue of park acquisition. First the Reagan administration tried, unsuccessfully, to abolish the Land and Water Conservation Fund, the primary source of funding for land acquisition for the Park Service and other land-managing agencies. When that bold move failed, the administration attempted to drastically reduce the budget for the fund, but the Congress has been persistent in providing monies for land acquisition. For example, the Reagan budget for FY 1983 allocated only $55.5 million for park land acquisition, but Congress increased the final appropriation to $112 million.[53]

Buttressing Watt's views, there have been a number of recent studies, reminiscent of earlier reports, that conclude that the parks are in dire trouble. For example, a report by the Office of Science and Technology, titled "State of the Parks 1980," announced the existence of some 4,345 specific threats to the integrity of the park system, including air and water pollution problems, overuse, overcrowding, and unregulated private development at or near park boundaries.[54] Also, a 1980 GAO investigation examined twelve of the largest and most popular parks, and found that the Park Service had:

not protected the health and safety of visitors and employees using facilities at national parks. . . . Substandard water and sewer systems and hazardous lodges, dormitories, bridges, and tunnels need to be repaired or upgraded or their use should be limited. We estimated that unfunded health and safety projects total $1.6 billion for the National Park Service.[55]

According to the Service's own estimates, there are health and safety problems in 113 separate park areas.[56] The current Park Service director, Russell Dickenson, stated that the figure of $1.6 billion for health and safety cited by GAO is probably low.[57] Yet in 1981, Congress appropriated only $29.5 million to alleviate these operating and maintenance problems. The Park Service requested that this amount be increased to $121.5 million for FY 1982—a fourfold increase—which was not granted. Park acquisition is thus a clear political problem—and dilemma—for the agency. Congress prefers to liberally fund the more glamorous activity of new park acquisition and authorization (What congressperson would not want to get credit for the establishment of a new park in his or her jurisdiction?) while the Reagan administration austerity/efficiency experts pursue the less rewarding, yet necessary, mundane activities of keeping the parks in decent working order. Seemingly the agency is caught in the middle of these competing priorities.

The Reagan administration's budgetary strategy in this regard is to fund these operation and maintenance projects as part of a new line item called "Park Restoration and Improvement." (This category did not exist in the 1981 budget.) The proposed budget for 1982 called for a total expenditure in this area of $105 million, the monies coming from funds previously earmarked for the acquisition-oriented Land and Water Conservation Fund. Health and safety projects comprised only $18 million of this figure, however.[58]

The revised 1982 budget request for the Park Service reflected a small administration-approved increase over the original 1982 request of nearly $500 million. However, this total figure is somewhat misleading because it included funds transferred from the Heritage Conservation and Recreation Service, an Interior Department unit that was phased out of existence by Secretarial Order 3060, dated February 19, 1981. If these transferred funds are excluded, the Park Service's revised budget proposal for 1982 actually represented a decrease of $11.5 million. This decrease represented a reduction in spending for management planning, energy conservation, new area studies, and a 50 percent decrease in the amount allocated to operate the new Alaskan parks. Also, the National Visitor Center in Washington, D.C. was closed.[59]

Secretary Watt's policies led to charges that he was attempting to dismantle the nation's park system. Opponents of the Reagan-Watt administration point to four specific policies that they feel threaten the parks. First, there were charges that the secretary developed a hit list of parks that he wanted to see de-authorized. (As we discussed in chapter 2, a similar hit list existed for water resources projects during the first years of the Carter administration.) A number of departmental memos apparently discussed the desirability of eliminating certain park areas, but in the 1982 appropriations hearings, Watt stated that the Reagan administration

> does not now have, nor has it had, a hit list of National Parks or other areas which the Department would request the Congress to de-authorize. Further, there is no plan at this time to develop a hit list. . . . I have in several forums suggested that that [*de-authorization*] is an option that could be considered.[60]

A second point of controversy concerns urban parks. Secretary Watt, in his confirmation hearings, stated that a greater emphasis should be placed on urban parks but that they should be operated at the state and municipal levels, and not by the federal government: "I will err on the side of public use versus preservation. I don't believe the National Park System should run urban parks."[61] The secretary subsequently made it clear that the Reagan administration would oppose the establishment of any new urban parks. However, the transferral of federal urban property to state or local governments, as with any park de-authorization, would require an act of Congress which we believe is unlikely to be forthcoming.

A third policy of the Reagan-Watt park program generating considerable discussion revolved around liberalized criteria for mining, timber cutting, and other forms of economic development on federal lands. The following exchange between Congressman Sidney Yates of Illinois and Secretary Watt during appropriations hearings helps illuminate the controversy:

> SECRETARY WATT: I want to open up the public lands to faster development in an orderly manner, so that we can protect the environmental qualities of that land.
>
> MR. YATES: May I interrupt for just a moment and ask you to define public lands?
>
> SECRETARY WATT: Those are the lands owned by the Federal Government, excluding the National Park Service areas.
>
> MR. YATES: That would include the Fish and Wildlife Service and the Forest Service.
>
> SECRETARY WATT: It would include all the lands that are open to multiple use. If a refuge or a Park Service area is not open to multiple use, then I am not talking about that. Those lands that are available for use should be used.
>
> MR. YATES: Some of our National Park Service areas are open for multiple use, such as dumping garbage on them. Does that get your attention?[62]

A final policy area that changed under Watt's guidance concerned concessions. In his confirmation hearings Watt described an expanded role for the private concessionaire:

> we need an aggressive program with the private entrepreneurs who are willing to invest and manage resources in the national parks for people. . . . We have tremendous biases. We have a bias for private enterprise. We believe concessioners can do the job.[63]

Clearly, these new Park Service policies were intended to de-emphasize land acquisition and stress physical plant improvements within existing parks. Indeed, recent budgets have given priority to in-park maintenance, rehabilitation, and construction. However, recent construction programs in the Park Service have apparently been troubled by budgeting and planning difficulties that have not helped the agency's "image." A 1981 report by the Surveys and Investigations Staff of the House Appropriations Committee concluded that the Park Service's construction program was plagued by inadequate planning, inaccurate cost estimates, and a lack of credibility due to past errors in Park Service estimates. The report also uncovered a "phantom $131,000 project" to repair facilities at Yosemite Park: "To the amazement of the Investigative Staff, Yosemite personnel were not aware of any repairs." Although this project was funded in the 1980 budget, the Service's Denver Service Center "had no record of the $131,000 project and was not aware of any."[64] In view of these problems, the Congress may be hesitant to approve a large funding increase for Park Service construction activities. Furthermore, there will probably be considerable pressure on Congress and the Park Service to spend at least some funds on acquisition, especially since money has been allocated for that purpose.

To sum up, most of Watt's policy directives were not accepted. Despite administration opposition to park expansion, to the concept of urban parks, and wilderness proposals, these functions continue to be funded at levels considerably higher than Reagan budget proposals call for. In 1982 the Congress increased Reagan's budget for the Service by an impressive $240 million. In FY 1983, Congress provided an additional $151 million over Reagan's proposal even though the administration generously funded park rehabilitation. Nevertheless, Watt's policy initiatives demonstrated the political vulnerability of the National Park Service. That he considered such significant programmatic and budgetary changes within the realm of the possible indicates that the current administration believes the Park Service is politically weak. Watt may well have been more successful had he been less abrasive personally. His successors may gradually bring significant change to the agency.

Whether future Park Service budgets will be adequate to "maintain unimpaired" 73 million acres while at the same time allow for the use of the parks by 261 million visitors remains to be seen. Meanwhile, the list of reports and articles warning of the degradation of the parks goes on: a 1982 report by the Conservation Foundation discussed the "degradation of the park resources" and "serious resource threats originating outside park boundaries."[65] A recent cover of *Life* magazine headlined "National Parks in Peril."[66]

Given the Park Service's almost pathological funding problems, and the severe strain placed on the Service by the new Alaskan lands coupled with the Reagan austerity budget, we can expect to see a continuation of the Service's budgetary problems. Park Service Director Russell Dickenson cogently summarized the condition of the Service and the park system that it operates: "we are in trouble today. The system is in trouble."

The Park Service is not an organizational failure. But it is also clear that it is not an unusually powerful agency. It has never had the budgetary base, the propensity to expand, nor quite the competitive edge that characterizes a rich and powerful agency. While possessing a strong sense of purpose and an impressive esprit de corps, the Park Service has been handicapped by a narrow, "luxury" mission, and has found itself hemmed in to a degree by pro-development interest groups as well as other, more powerful agencies in the federal establishment.

Although the Park Service has occasionally wrested lands from the Forest Service, this success has not been sufficient to transform it into the nation's premier outdoor recreation agency. Both the Forest Service and the Army Corps of Engineers boast of greater annual visitation figures. And recent expansion of park lands has not necessarily led to a concomitant expansion of agency funding, personnel, and political clout (i.e., agency power). The new Alaskan parks and the seventy five new units added in the 1970s (dubbed by critics as the park-of-the-month program) have created seemingly intractable management problems, several new critics, and, in keeping with Park Service tradition, a wholly inadequate budget. The future presents a formidable challenge to the dedicated—but underfunded—personnel of the National Park Service.

THE SOIL CONSERVATION SERVICE

By the end of the nineteenth century conservation had become a salient issue and a viable political movement. The early conservationists were primarily concerned with western natural resources, and for the most part neglected midwestern and Great Plains soil as a resource in need of conservation and attention. It was not until the 1920s that concerned agricultural experts and public officials began the drive for an effective public soil conservation program. Foremost among these men was Hugh Bennett, a government geologist who had done extensive research on erosion in the South. Convinced that soil erosion was destroying American farm productivity, Bennett began what amounted to a one-man crusade against erosion. The first official recognition of his efforts occurred when the Department of Agriculture officially endorsed his paper entitled "Soil Erosion, A Natural Menace."[68]

Bennett's drive for a federal soil conservation program was ultimately realized primarily because of two important events, one physical and one political. First, the Dust Bowl of the 1930s provided a visible confirmation of Bennett's predictions. Up until that time, much of the soil erosion that had taken place was of a more subtle form called sheet erosion, a term originally defined by Bennett. Through this slow yet constant process, farmlands were gradually losing their topsoil. The Dust Bowl phenomenon, however, was anything but gradual. With its monstrous storms quickly stripping away the fertile topsoil of an entire region, it became obvious that immediate action was needed to control all forms of soil erosion. Second, the election of Franklin Roosevelt provided political support for the institutionalization of the soil conservation cause. Secretary of the Interior Harold Ickes became interested in soil conservation in the early days of the New Deal, and promptly settled on Bennett as the "best expert" for the job.[69]

With strong support from President Roosevelt, Ickes set up the Soil Erosion Service within the Department of the Interior and placed Bennett at its head. The new bureau was to function as a part of the National Industrial Recovery Act program; it would provide assistance to farmers for soil erosion control projects and jobs for the unemployed through the Civilian Conservation Corps. At the time of the bureau's creation it was estimated that erosion cost the United States about $400,000,000 annually in soil depreciation and reduced yields.[70]

Bennett's new agency immediately ran into jurisdictional problems with other agencies and hence became stifled in the Department of the Interior. Like Pinchot before him, Bennett soon became convinced that his program would have greater potential for expansion if it were housed in the Department of Agriculture. Although surrounded by powerful and jealous agencies within Interior, Bennett's political expertise nevertheless made possible the continued existence of the fledgling agency. At one point during these critical early years, Bennett arranged for a congressional hearing to be scheduled on the same day a dust storm was forecast to reach Washington. While dark clouds of dust whirled outside the capitol building, the agency director pleaded for congressional authorization to build an enlarged program for soil conservation.[71]

On April 27, 1935, shortly after Bennett's dust storm appearance before Congress, the Soil Conservation Act was signed by the president after being passed unanimously by both houses. The act established the Soil Conservation Service within the Department of Agriculture. According to the act, the new agency had four basic functions:

1. To conduct surveys, investigations, and research relating to the character of soil erosion and the preventative measures needed, to publish the result of any such surveys, investigations, or research, to disseminate information concerning such methods, and to conduct demonstrational projects in areas subject to erosion by wind or water;

2. To carry out preventative measures, including, but not limited to, engineering operations, methods of cultivation, the growing of vegetation, and changes in use of land;

3. To cooperate or enter into agreements with, or to furnish financial

or other aid to, any agency, governmental or otherwise, or any person, subject to such conditions as he may deem necessary, for the purposes of this Act; and

4. To acquire lands, or rights or interests therein, by purchase, gift, condemnation, or otherwise, whenever necessary for the purposes of this Act.[72]

In order to implement the 1935 mandate, the new agency adopted several unique programs and administrative strategies in an effort to overcome political limitations while at the same time dealing effectively with the pervasive problem of erosion.

One of these programs was the establishment of demonstration projects in cooperation with individual farmers. The purpose of these projects was to test different methods of erosion control, to publicly demonstrate these methods, and, of course, to prevent erosion on the land involved. Following a detailed survey of erosion conditions, specific recommendations for preventative practices were made to private landowners. To participate in a project, a farmer was required to sign a five-year contract obligating him to implement the recommended conservation measures. Although the Service strongly emphasized that soil conservation measures had to be designed specifically to fit a given situation, it typically recommended such practices as contour plowing, strip cropping, planting erosion-resistant crops such as alfalfa and clover, periodic retirement of excessively eroded land from cultivation, shifting from soil-depleting crops (e.g., cotton and corn) to soil-conserving noncommercial crops, as well as utilizing small-scale engineering structures such as terraces and dams. By 1936, the Service had established 147 demonstration projects, averaging 25,000 to 30,000 acres each and involving about 50,000 farmers.[73]

Although these demonstration projects were judged to be fairly successful, their impact was limited to a relatively small geographic area; the program was not, therefore, spreading soil conservation principles as quickly as desired. The Service thus began looking for other approaches to soil conservation that would provide a more comprehensive method of administration and utilization and would be developed alongside the demonstration projects. The solution was to encourage the formation of local administrative units called soil conservation districts. The development of these districts not only helped solve the problem of spreading the word, but it also provided the basis for the formation of an active constituency organized into soil conservation district associations. Thus, the desire on the part of the Service to organize farmers into districts was due to administrative, practical, and political reasons, and was explained as such in 1935 by the secretary of agriculture:

The problem of preventing soil erosion is a social as well as an individual problem, and the soil conservation district associations rest on this principle. The organized farmers of an entire land-use area make a united attack on a problem which they could not solve individually.[74]

To pave the way for the formation of soil conservation districts, the Department of Agriculture prepared a standardized state conservation-districts law. This law was then submitted by President Roosevelt in February of 1937 to the governors of all of the states, along with his recommendation for its passage.[75] By 1944 only three states (Massachusetts, Connecticut, and New Hampshire) did not have SCD (soil conservation district) laws, but in 1946 the spokesman for the Service was "happy to report that all three of those states have now enacted legislation in the interest of conservation."[76]

Once a state law had been passed authorizing the formation of soil conservation districts, specific districts were formed by local referenda. Upon petition of at least twenty five farmers, a state soil conservation committee would fix boundaries for a proposed district. After public hearings, a referendum was held; no district could be organized without a favorable majority vote. Once organized, districts received annual appropriations from the state as well as technical assistance from both state and federal agencies. Specific land-use regulations were also submitted to the public for approval. If a majority favored enactment, the regulation was mandatory for all agricultural lands within the district.[77] The number of districts grew at a rapid rate; appropriations hearings for the agency reveal that there were 132 districts in 1939, 989 in 1944, 2,074 in 1949, 2,549 in 1953, and about 3,000, covering 99 percent of the farms and ranches in the nation, in 1977. In a recently published book on the subject, one contributor writes

> By 1980, there were about 2,950 conservation districts covering some 2.2 billion acres, 1.0 billion acres in farms. . . . In other words, virtually all of the land in the United States was within soil conservation districts, though not all farmers in the districts participated in the program. In 1980, about 46 million acres were protected from soil erosion by soil conservation practice.[78]

Although the soil conservation districts have been a noteworthy success, they have not solved the jurisdictional rivalries that have plagued the Soil Conservation Service since its inception. The 1935 enabling act was designed to establish soil conservation as a distinct program and not simply as an adjunct to other existing agricultural programs. But the mandate inherently conflicted and overlapped with the work of several other federal agencies including its closest competitor, the Agricultural Stabilization and Conservation Service (ASCS). These two agencies have existed side by side for over four decades; it is frequently suggested that they be merged.[79] As a result, the Soil Conservation Service has been involved in a series of confrontations with not only ASCS, but with several other federal agencies; these bureaucratic exchanges have been described by investigators as a continuous "state of civil war."[80]

When the Soil Conservation Service was created in 1935, the problem of overlapping jurisdictions could not have been readily apparent. It seemed then as though soil erosion—and the resulting Dust Bowl phenomenon—were problems unaddressed by any existing federal program or agency. To a great extent this was true, but it was the implementation of programs aimed at controlling soil erosion that inexorably led the agency into areas heavily populated by other units of the federal bureaucracy. A reading of the preamble of the 1935 enabling act makes this clear:

> it is hereby declared to be the policy of Congress to provide perma-
> nently for the control and prevention of soil erosion and thereby to
> preserve natural resources, control floods, prevent impairment of
> reservoirs, and maintain the navigability of rivers and harbors, protect
> public health, public lands and relieve unemployment.[81]

This list of responsibilities obviously overlaps with the missions of several powerful agencies, including both the Forest Service and the Corps of Engineers. To fully understand the problems inherent in such a situation, it is necessary to review some of the instances where the Soil Conservation Service was awarded new responsibilities, only to have them later transferred to other agencies. As one author notes, "From 1937 on, SCS was in and out of a number of water supply programs."[82]

In 1938 the secretary of agriculture gave the Soil Conservation Service four new programs to administer. The land utilization program authorized by the Bankhead-Jones Farm Tenant Act was transferred to the Service from the Bureau of Agricultural Economics. This program involved purchase and redevelopment of submarginal lands. All of these lands were acquired by the government because they were extensively damaged or otherwise not suitable for cultivation; so in order to prevent further damage, to bring about proper use of the land, and to improve the agricultural economy of nearby communities, they were transferred to federal control. The purpose of this program was to restore the land to productive use consistent with its capacities. But in 1954, control of the land utilization program was transferred to the Forest Service.

Second, the Soil Conservation Service was assigned drainage and irrigation investigations formerly conducted by the Bureau of Agricultural Engineering. The Service also received control of certain phases of the farm forestry program authorized by the Norris-Doxey Act of 1937.

These responsibilities were expanded in 1942 to include the Prairie States Forestry Project, but in 1945 the Forest Service took control of the farm forestry program.[83]

In 1938, the SCS began work in a water facilities program authorized by the Pope-Jones Act of 1937. Under this program the Service, in cooperation with two other Agriculture Department agencies, developed small irrigation facilities for farmers and ranchers which were beyond the scope of the large irrigation projects that the Bureau of Reclamation was operating. This program also involved water projects other than irrigation, such as the construction of stock ponds. In 1942, however, activities under this program were transferred to the Farm Security Administration.[84]

Another program, transferred to the Service from the Farm Security Administration, was of similarly short duration as an SCS program. In 1945, the Soil Conservation Service began work on water conservation and utilization programs authorized by the Case-Wheeler Act of 1939. The water conservation and utilization program was administered cooperatively with the Bureau of Reclamation, the agency responsible for constructing the water-supply features of the program. The Service was responsible for "developing efficient irrigation farming units for qualified farm families."[85] In practice this involved acquiring the land necessary to establish an operating unit, developing that land for efficient use of water (surveys, leveling, and constructing some water-control structures), selling or leasing developed farm units to qualified farm families, and then providing technical guidance in irrigation farming and soil conservation. By 1949 work had begun on fifteen projects in nine western states, but appropriations hearings held in 1954 reported that only four of these projects were still active; two of these four were scheduled for completion by the end of that year.[86]

Its original mandate to control erosion also brought the Soil Conservation Service into the field of flood control, since water is a primary cause of erosion. As early as 1936 the agency was given responsibilities for water management:

> USDA and SCS responsibilities for water began in 1936 with passage of the Omnibus Flood Control Act. In this legislation Congress recognized for the first time the importance of providing upstream watershed protection to compliment the downstream flood control work by the Army Corps of Engineers.[87]

This new change not only intensified the ongoing rivalry between the departments of the Interior and Agriculture, but also precipitated a clash with the Corps of Engineers. The Flood Control Acts of 1936 and 1944 authorized the Soil Conservation Service to study and carry out watershed protection and flood protection programs. The agency was drawn further into water development with the passage of the Watershed Protection and Flood Prevention Act of 1954. Although effective erosion control would be impossible without water runoff control, the Service was in a poor position to confront the powerful Corps of Engineers. As a result, the Soil Conservation Service limited its water-control programs to small upstream projects, which was essentially all that was left after the Corps had claimed the large, expensive, downstream projects. Underscoring the intra-agency rivalry that was developing, and which became obvious with the 1954 legislation that gave SCS a small watershed program, was the Corps' position on the bill:

> The Army Corps of Engineers, as the principal flood control and dam-building agency of the federal government, opposed the Act. It questioned the need for upstream flood prevention work and the competence of SCS engineers to make flood surveys and design the dams required.[88]

Further indication of the Service's subordinate position vis-à-vis other agencies was the reorganization of the Soil Conservation Service during the Second World War. In 1942 the Service was consolidated with other agencies to form the new Agricultural Conservation and Adjustment Administration. Less than a year later it was transferred to the Food Production Administration where it remained for just four months, then it was transferred to the War Food Administration. At the end of the war the Soil Conservation Service was again placed under the direct control of the secretary of agriculture.[89]

It is clear that the competition between the Service and more powerful agencies has been uneven. Although many new programs have been assigned to the Service over its forty-five-year existence due to the general attractiveness of the soil conservation ideal, actual implementation of these programs has inevitably tread on the toes of the bureaucratic giants. This has not only stifled expansion of the agency's role, but has caused repeated funding difficulties for the programs that have remained within the Service. As early as 1955 budget cuts were causing real problems for recruiting new employees, especially engineers, at levels above GS-11. Salaries were not high enough to be competitive. In addition, personnel reductions were resulting in increased workloads, which inevitably raised questions of whether the quality and availability of assistance to soil conservation districts would suffer.[90]

The Service has been forced to operate within the narrow parameters imposed upon it by a crowded bureaucratic environment. Many of the programs dealing with land use and development that were once administered by the Service have been transferred to other agencies. In the area of water development, the large basinwide projects have been built by either the Corps of Engineers or the Bureau of Reclamation. This has left the small localized water projects to the Soil Conservation Service, and it is in this area that the Service has been able to operate with relative independence. In addition to the flood control acts cited above, a number of statutes and orders from the secretary of agriculture have created new responsibilities in this area for the Service.

In 1953, the secretary of agriculture placed the Soil Conservation Service in charge of administering all departmental flood prevention and river basin investigations. In the same year, the Service was given responsibility for selecting sites for pilot watershed-protection projects and providing assistance to local groups. Work was quickly begun on sixty projects. The purpose of this program was "to test the practicability of complete watershed protection as a means of conserving soil and water; of alleviating damages from floods, silting of reservoirs, and impairment of stream channels; and of solving other upstream land and water problems."[91]

The culmination of previous flood control programs came with the enactment of the Watershed Protection and Flood Prevention Act in 1954. The Service was given primary responsibility within the Agriculture Department for providing technical and financial assistance to local groups in relation to upstream watershed conservation and flood prevention programs. These local groups agreed to carry out and share the costs of these projects. In subsequent years the authority of this act was amended to include municipal and industrial water-supply development (1956), fish and wildlife development (1958), and water-based public recreation (1962) as purposes eligible for federal cost-sharing with local groups. Small watershed projects have been a major focus of Soil Conservation Service activity over the years. From 1954 to 1977, an estimated 1,235 projects were completed.[92]

The Soil Conservation Service has not limited its activities to water projects, however. A number of programs have included a wide array of erosion prevention techniques. One such program is the Great Plains Conservation Project, authorized by Congress in 1956. This program was aimed at the ten Great Plains states most susceptible to serious wind erosion. Under this voluntary program, assistance is provided to ranchers and farmers in developing operational plans and practices that would minimize the adverse effects of the climate (high winds and recurring droughts), conserve water, and protect against erosion. After a master plan had been developed for a farm or ranch, the Service and the producer would then enter into a long-term cost-sharing contract. As long as the producer accomplished the requirements of his operating plan on schedule, he would receive cost-sharing payments that, by law, could not exceed 80 percent of the cost of installing each eligible practice.

Practices eligible for cost-sharing included windbreaks, terrace systems, dams, and irrigation works. By 1959, 1,337 cost-sharing contracts were in force.[93] By the end of 1975, a total of 49,626 such contracts had been signed.[94]

Another addition to the Service's activities is its resource conservation and development program, which was mandated in the Food and Agriculture Act of 1962. The Soil Conservation Service has administrative leadership for this program within the Agriculture Department and works with four other departmental agencies. Like the Fish and Wildlife Service, the agency's mission has recently evolved into one with a heavy emphasis on interagency coordination. The program is designed to expand economic opportunity in an area by helping local organizations devise plans for the development, conservation, and utilization of natural resources and to provide new employment opportunities to local residents. The pattern of providing technical and financial assistance to local project sponsors is, of course, a standard activity for the agency; the resource conservation and development program differs from past programs by its emphasis on improving the overall economy and living conditions in rural areas as well as the wide range of measures undertaken (including recreational developments, rural sewer systems, and municipal water systems, in addition to more typical soil conservation measures). Ten pilot projects were begun in 1964.[95] As of 1973, 123 projects had been authorized.[96]

With the exception of the program just mentioned, virtually all of the programs administered by the Soil Conservation Service emphasize small, local, relatively isolated projects. This has had an important impact on the development of constituency support for the agency. Early on its history it became evident that in order to survive, the Service had to cultivate strong support among small farmers and rural residents. The primary organizational conduit for this support became the soil conservation districts. Over the years the Soil Conservation Service has grown very dependent on this constituency (it is very much like the Fish and Wildlife Service in this regard), and has made assiduous efforts to maintain its support. In a curious way, the relationship has both helped and hindered the agency. It has helped in that the iron triangle—congressional committees, pressure groups (especially the National Association of Conservation Districts), and the SCS—has insured the survival of the agency in the face of attempts to merge it with other federal organizations. On the other hand, the close alliance between the agency and a specialized constituency has not been conducive to agency growth. As one scholar on the subject recently put it,

Many other federal programs are subject to pressures of this type, but the pressures seem to have more severely compromised the objectives of the soil conservation programs because the lobby for soil conservation itself is so weak.[97]

The agency's emphasis on local, geographically dispersed projects is also a result of statutory requirements, such as the 1954 Watershed Protection and Flood Prevention Act described above. Due to the requirement that every project have "local sponsoring organizations,"[98] the Service developed an even closer relationship with a narrow, specialized clientele. As part of its small watersheds program, the Service began to emphasize structural solutions such as stream channelization. This approach was quite popular with agricultural producers since it tended to subsidize production. But by the early 1970s, environmental groups were beginning to protest the long-term impact of stream channelization. A representative of the National Audubon Society explained their view of this practice:

> The channelization emphasis in the Public Law 566 program has to be changed because it leads to the same basic blunders and environmental damages that have resulted from similar projects carried out by the Corps of Engineers and the Bureau of Reclamation.[99]

The Soil Conservation Service could ill afford the wrath of environmentalists since this damaged its image as a conservation organization. At the same time, the Service did not appear to have the organizational capacity to turn to other kinds of projects, especially those referred to as nonstructural alternatives.[100] The agency's inability to diversify in this regard was due to statutory restrictions as well as to the fear of alienating traditional sources of constituency support.

As a result of the Service's cautious attitude toward change and its continued dependence on a small and specialized constituency, the agency encountered considerable difficulty in meeting the requirements of the 1969 National Environmental Policy Act. Rather than view the act as an opportunity to expand its mission, as did the Forest Service and the Corps of Engineers, the Conservation Service approached the environmental impact statement process as merely an opportunity to reiterate past policy decisions. The Service did not request any budgetary or personnel increases in order to meet the new mandate. Richard Andrews observed that:

> SCS policies concerning implementation of N.E.P.A. reflected that agency's traditionally client-centered, negotiative patterns of decision-making. . . . In short, SCS policies and public statements during 1970 and 1971 suggested an official willingness to listen to the comments of other agencies and individuals, but no inclination to change priorities or projects as a result unless its own staff and local sponsors wished to do so.[101]

By the mid-1970s, traditional sources of support, its traditional solutions, and the Service's traditional niche in the federal bureaucracy began to show signs of erosion. The Service was being forced by its outside critics to adapt to change or face extinction. The number of farmers in American society continued to decrease over the years, while the number of environmentally conscious city dwellers increased. Helen Ingram has summarized the agency's dilemma:

> The traditional agricultural support of agencies such as the Bureau of Reclamation and the Soil Conservation Service has ebbed. In place of support, these agencies have faced increasing objections from urban interests who balk at paying the bills for projects not obviously serving their needs.[102]

In response to these pressures, the Service began to search for new priorities. By 1975 land conservation had become an important federal program, primarily in the form of technical assistance. Also changed was the Service's performance relative to NEPA's environmental impact statement requirement. The Council of Environmental Quality had rated the agency's performance as "seriously deficient" in 1970; but by 1974 the Service's impact statements were described as among "the most improved."[103] Perhaps this was because they had such a long way to go.

Efforts to conform to these changing political realities introduced several new problems for the Service, however. Congressional spokesmen for the traditional structural approach to soil conservation began to criticize the newer programs. Due to budgetary constraints, the old programs were perceived by some as being sacrificed to make way for new ones. During the appropriations hearings of 1975, Representative Andrews of North Dakota accused the Soil Conservation Service of leaving its "wife of many years" in order to pursue the "new blonde down the block."[104] Ironically, it would appear that a double standard is at work here. When a large agency, like the Corps, moves into new areas, it is greeted with praise by legislators; when a small agency acts similarly, it receives this kind of criticism.

An important piece of legislation passed Congress in 1977—the Soil and Water Resource Conservation Act of 1977. This statute, like several others passed in the 1970s and aimed at other agencies, instructed the Soil Conservation Service to embark upon a comprehensive evaluation process (called the RCA process) of its missions and objectives; it was intended to force the agency to engage in long-term planning. The results of the four-year effort (1977-81) were, according to researcher Christopher Leman, meager. The agency generated volumes of data but ignored real program evaluation. After a lengthy description of the RCA process within the Service, Leman concludes: "As a whole, RCA did not work very well in my view."[105] Thus it apears that the agency missed another opportunity to broaden its horizons; the Forest Service, for example, greatly capitalized on similar congressional fiats.

By 1980 the largest program in the Soil Conservation Service's budget was in the area of conservation programs, with an emphasis on technical assistance to "individual landowners and operators, community groups, units of government [and] Indian tribes." This program absorbed over half of the Service's budget, while the other functions, in descending funding priority, were watershed flood prevention, resource conservation and development (assistance to state and local governments), the Great Plains Conservation Project, river basin surveys, and watershed planning. A total budget of $523 million for 1980 reflected a small increase over the previous year's budget, but it was significantly less than the agency's 1978 budget.[106] With a high inflation rate, it was hardly an increase at all. However, Leman argues that the agency's budget remained relatively constant between 1969 and 1981, if one adjusts for inflation.[107]

The Service continued to experience incremental budget fluctuations throughout 1981 and 1982. In addition, the Reagan administration placed a number of constraints on the agency's funding. According to a Service spokesperson at the 1982 appropriations hearing:

> Both the fiscal 1981 and 1982 estimates have incorporated into them a series of reductions reflecting the current administration's efforts to reduce federal travel, procurement, use of consulting services and employment levels. Total reductions of $6.3 million in fiscal year 1981 and $2.7 million in fiscal 1982 have been made to reflect these savings.[108]

The total net decrease in the agency's budget proposal for 1982 amounted to nearly $36 million. Typically, the proposed Reagan budget cuts were primarily in the areas of planning, research, and investigations. The Resource Conservation and Development Program, despite strong support from Congress, was scheduled to be phased out entirely by the end of 1982. The Small Watersheds Program was cut. The OMB also eliminated the five new construction starts scheduled for 1982.[109] For the most part, Congress went along with these cuts; it increased the agency's budget request for FY 1982 by less than 2 percent.

The 1983 and 1984 budgets show a continuation of these trends. In 1983, the Service absorbed a 10 percent budget reduction while the administration proposed a further reduction by 8 percent for FY 1984. Funding for the Great Plains Conservation Program has been held relatively constant, despite a recent report by the General Accounting Office which concluded that "soil erosion is becoming more serious . . . and USDA programs are not keeping pace with the problem."[110] The

Reagan administration's controversial approach to soil conservation thus has been summarized as "overall budget cuts accompanied by the targeting of the country's most erosion-prone areas for special technical and financial assistance."[111] For the agency, it means austerity.

The Soil Conservation Service has also had to sustain cutbacks in personnel over the last fifteen years. For example, in 1967 the agency had 15,274 full-time personnel. That figure dropped to 14,522 in 1972, and to 13,869 in 1977. By 1981 agency personnel had dropped to 13,320,[112] which is where it has more or less remained through the 1984 budget cycle.[113] Not only has the number of full-time agency employees declined over the past ten or fifteen years, but perhaps more importantly, the Service did not staff up with economists when other federal agencies were doing so. Leman writes:

> An important difference between the Forest Service and SCS in the 1970s was that the Forest Service began to staff up with economists, while SCS resisted doing so. . . . The Forest Service recognized that if sponsored from within the agency economic analysis could serve in a quite supportive role. Thus, after the demise of PPBS, the agency steadily trained foresters in economics and operations research. . . .
>
> The USDA official who had a permanent role in the late 1970s in overseeing agency policy analysis suggests that "SCS, if it had hired more economists, would have a bigger budget today." Although according to SCS figures the agency in March, 1981 employed a total of 113 economists, this . . . was little more than the agency had in the 1960s.[114]

Although few new responsibilities have been assigned to the Soil Conservation Service in recent years, a lot of work still needs to be done in traditional areas. For example, the Great Plains Conservation Program, despite its lack of budgetary growth, was extended by Congress to 1991.[115] Also the Service, in conjunction with other agencies in the Department of Agriculture, recently completed a study of soil and water conservation problems as mandated in the 1977 Soil and Water Resources Conservation Act. The final report estimates that $205 billion will have to be spent to reverse the decline in the nation's soil and water resources.[116] This study, in conjunction with a related effort called the National Agricultural Lands Study, will undoubtedly point the way to possible future activity by the Soil Conservation Service. Whether the agency has the political strength and budgetary finesse to take advantage of this potential remains to be seen, however.

Although the Service has made some attempts to adapt to a changing political environment, it has met with only limited success. The same problems that have plagued the agency since its inception—a bureaucratic

niche that brings it into conflict with other agencies, a narrow constituency, and some reluctance to abandon the relative security of traditional
programs—still haunt the Service today. During the first few years of
its existence, the Soil Conservation Service was described by a congressperson as "something of an orphan."[117] Forty years later, a legislator on
the Appropriations Committee asked the chief administrator of the Service
if he "had any indication . . . that there is an effort underway to begin
to phase out the Soil Conservation Service."[118] Although we are not
predicting the imminent demise of the Service, it is clear that this agency
has not experienced the growth in funding and personnel, and the addition
of new responsibilities to its repertoire, that characterize more influential
agencies in the bureaucratic establishment.

THE U.S. FISH AND WILDLIFE SERVICE

Of the seven agencies examined in this study, the Fish and Wildlife
Service has the dubious honor of having the most chaotic organizational
history. Tracking the agency's evolution is no small task in itself, for it
has undergone, from its inception in 1871 to its most recent reorganization
in 1970, numerous and frequent permutations. The contemporary agency
is thus descended from what Richard Cooley described as a roving
parentage. This condition of its history is both cause and effect of its
present weak position in the federal bureaucracy, and it serves to
underscore the importance of an organization's history to its ability to
function effectively at any given time.

The genesis of the Fish and Wildlife Service can be traced back to an
1871 act of Congress, wherein concern over the possible deterioration
of the fishery research was voiced. The act resolves

> That the President be . . . authorized and required to appoint, by
> and with the advice and consent of the Senate, from among the civil
> officers or employees of the government, one person of proved
> scientific and practical acquaintance with the fishes of the coast, to
> be commissioner of fish and fisheries, to serve without additional
> salary. And be it further resolved, that it shall be the duty of said
> commissioner to prosecute investigations and inquiries on the sub-
> ject, with the view of ascertaining whether any and what diminution
> in the number of food fishes of the coasts and lakes of the United
> States has taken place; and if so, to what causes the same is due; and
> also whether any and what protective, prohibitory, or precautionary
> measures should be adopted in the premises; and to report upon the
> same to Congress.[119]

By 1892 the fish commissioner together with an assistant inspector were
given the chore of enforcing a congressional prohibition against barri-

cading streams to capture salmon. The government's interest in overseeing the Alaskan salmon industry became evident at this time, and the early history of the U.S. Fish Commission became intertwined with this one particular industry.

A pattern of agency dependence upon the largesse of the fishing industry also began at this time. The fish inspectors were not provided with a governmental means of transportation so they were frequently obliged to rely upon the boats of salmon packers to get from one cannery to another.[120] Related to this was the action taken by Congress in 1903 to create a new agency, the Bureau of Fisheries, and to house it in the then Department of Commerce and Labor. The U.S. Fish Commission in the Treasury Department was assimilated into the Bureau. According to Cooley this transfer was the first step taken to insure that the regulator was controlled by the regulated, since the orientation of the Commerce Department was both positive toward and supportive of the commercial fishing industry.[121] Given a dual mandate from Congress—to conserve and protect while at the same time promoting the fishery resource, the Bureau understandably was beset with difficulties in distinguishing between its two primary, and often conflicting, functions. Like the National Park Service, the Fish and Wildlife Service was originally told to pursue two quite opposed functions, and each agency's history records the numerous problems arising out of an original dichotomous mission. As we will see, the Fish and Wildlife Service was never able to resolve the contradiction to its own advantage.

Not only was the Bureau of Fisheries plagued with problems related to its mission, but in its formative years the agency also became identified with a particular geographic region and a particular industry—Alaska and the salmon business. From its inception in 1903 until passage of the White Act in 1924, the Bureau was utterly unsuccessful at regulating the salmon industry. According to Cooley, it not only lacked the necessary expertise, but also the will. Congress, moreover, was for a long time reluctant to act on the issue of regulating the fishing industry:

> Bills continued to be introduced in each session of Congress "for the protection and conservation of the Alaska fisheries," but for one reason or another they drew sufficient opposition from the interest groups to prevent their passage. As prices of canned salmon soared during the war, the intensity of fishing and canning operators rose to new heights with little interference from the federal government. The factor most responsible for causing a break in the legislative stalemate was the collapse of the markets for canned salmon immediately following World War I.[122]

Passage of the White Act in 1924 temporarily improved the Bureau's situation, for the legislation contained specific and enforceable provisions to regulate the fishing industry in order to guarantee future supplies. As Cooley notes, however, the impetus for the legislation did not arise from a commitment to conservation values but rather from the desire to guarantee continual pecuniary enrichment to the industry.[123] Enacted when the industry was in an economic slump, the Bureau of Fisheries became a convenient scapegoat and was criticized from all sides for not having effectively regulated the industry in the past. Thus while conservation and regulation were temporarily in vogue, with a change in the economic conditions surrounding the fishing industry, the Bureau lapsed back into its ineffectual role. For example, in reviewing the agency's more recent accomplishments, Senator Ernest Gruening of Alaska said:

> It is, in fact, the story of a colossal failure, the failure of a United States government agency entrusted with the high responsibility of conserving this great national heritage to perform its function. The fact is that during the years of their trusteeship the federal regulatory agencies—since 1940 the Fish and Wildlife Service—instead of regulating the industry were regulated and controlled by it. The twenty years of Fish and Wildlife control, from 1940 until statehood in 1959, were the most disastrous of all. These were the years of the decline and near-extinction of the Pacific Salmon in Alaska.[124]

The contemporary agency to which Gruening refers is the result of a 1940 executive reorganization that combined the hapless Bureau of Fisheries with the somewhat more successful Bureau of Biological Survey. This union came a year after a previous reorganization, effected by President Franklin Roosevelt, transferred the Bureau of Fisheries from the Commerce Department to the Department of the Interior, and also brought the Agriculture Department's Biological Survey into Interior. (To this extent Secretary of the Interior Ickes's raid on other departments was successful, although it is worth noting that he was not able to extend his influence over two of the most powerful resource agencies, the Forest Service and the Corps of Engineers. They remained in the Departments of Agriculture and Defense respectively.) As was the case with the 1946 merger that produced the Bureau of Land Management, the U.S. Fish and Wildlife Service was the product of hybrid thinking whose object was the creation of an offspring that combined the strongest elements of its parentage.

An important result of this merger was the transformation of a dominant-use agency into a more diversified organization. The Bureau of Biological Survey brought to the new Fish and Wildlife Service a federal concern for the conservation and protection of wildlife. In 1900 Congress passed the Lacey Act which enjoined the secretary of agriculture to prohibit the interstate commerce of game killed in violation of local laws. With a clear conservationist intent, the act reads in part:

> That the duties and powers of the Department of Agriculture are hereby enlarged so as to include the preservation, distribution, introduction, and restoration of game birds and other wild birds. . . . The object and purpose of this Act is to aid in the restoration of such birds in those parts of the United States adapted thereto where the same have become scarce or extinct, and also to regulate the introduction of American or foreign birds or animals in localities where they have not heretofore existed.[125]

Three more legislative actions enlarged the responsibilities of the Department of Agriculture and its Bureau of Biological Survey before the 1939 reorganization. In 1918 Congress passed the Migratory Bird Treaty Act, signed with Great Britain (for the commonwealth of Canada). This act, as modified by a 1934 statute commonly referred to as the Duck Stamp Act, comprises the statutory authority for the creation of a national wildlife refuge system. The 1934 act provides "funds for the acquisition of areas for use as migratory-bird sanctuaries, refuges, and breeding grounds" and "for developing and administering such areas."[126]

Also in that year the Fish and Wildlife Coordination Act was passed. Transferred to the Fish and Wildlife Service in 1940, this authority may well epitomize the kind of problems subsequently encountered by the Service. The act contains a general statement concerning the importance of preserving the nation's fish and wildlife resources, and implies that any federal project that might affect these resources is to be carefully reviewed and evaluated. It was not clear, however, what projects and which federal agencies were covered by the legislation (or so some reasoned), and thus many agencies simply exempted themselves from the Service's scrutiny. For example, the Atomic Energy Commission, created in 1946, insisted for some time that it was not affected by the legislation and therefore did not have to consider the Fish and Wildlife Service's recommendations. The major limitations of the 1934 act were thus its discretionary nature and the lack of any enforcement provisions. *Coordination* was simply not a sufficiently strong concept to force federal agencies at the time to take an unbiased look at the possible environmental effects of their activities. Thus the effectiveness of the act, as is the case with much of what the Service did and does, depended more on the voluntary compliance of others than it did on the actions of Fish and Wildlife coordinators. In the eyes of many, the Service has been perceived as not much more than an organizational nuisance.

By the time the Fish and Wildlife Service was established in 1940, its environment, functions, and problems were fairly well defined. Since no legislative action was taken on this executive reorganization until 1956, the Fish and Wildlife Service existed for some sixteen years without an organic act. This of course did not help the agency to rapidly develop into an influential protector of the nation's fish and wildlife resources. Moreover, the Service's political development was hampered by problems that it inherited from agencies that it replaced. The Bureau of Biological Survey, previously a unit in the Department of Agriculture, had been for years the locus for an intense battle between wildlife preservationists and sportsmen. The former pushed for the creation of inviolate wildlife refuges that would protect rare and/or endangered forms of animal life; but the latter wanted a refuge system that would insure a continued supply of wildlife for consumptive or recreational use. A third group—ranchers—pressured the Bureau in the direction of predator control. When the Fish and Wildlife Service was formed in 1940 it fell heir to much of this political conflict that previously had plagued the Bureau of Biological Survey. The new agency also inherited the political instability of the Bureau of Fisheries, which had been transferred from Commerce to the Interior Department just two years before it became absorbed in the "new" Fish and Wildlife Service.

The history of the Service from 1940 to 1969 is the description of an agency gradually expanding its services within a clearly circumscribed range. That is, the agency did not actively seek out any new functions, and in fact lost an important commercial function in 1956 due to its inability to reconcile the two missions. Budgetary limitations coupled with a relatively obscure mission go a long way toward accounting for the Service's low profile.

Like the Bureau of Reclamation, the Fish and Wildlife Service's budgetary base for years was derived primarily from earmarked monies. Beginning in 1934, the federal government began collecting a tax on migratory-bird hunting licenses (the Duck Stamp). These revenues were earmarked; 90 percent of it was authorized to go toward the federal acquisition of wetlands and other bird and waterfowl habitats. The remaining 10 percent was to be spent on managing the refuges. Yearly fluctuations in the fund provided an unstable budgetary base for the Service and consequently hindered the agency's activities. Service personnel found it particularly difficult to operate and maintain a wildlife refuge system on an uncertain 10 percent of stamp receipts, and Congress was often reluctant to give the agency an additional appropriation. The appropriations hearings for this period contain frequent references—accusations about and apologies for—the deteriorating condition of the refuges. Finally in 1960 the Duck Stamp Act was amended to give the agency a more favorable financial environment.

Congress's stinginess toward the Service was in part a reflection of the agency's narrow mission as well as the lack of strong, broad-based clientele support. Most of the activities engaged in by the Service have little impact on the general public or on any large segment thereof. While the Service has contributed significantly to the protection and preservation of several species of wildlife, the problem is that these benefits are not experienced or even much appreciated by the public. For example, most waterfowl are not shot on the refuges and the only encounters that the average duck hunter may have with the Fish and Wildlife Service is when he buys a duck stamp at the post office. Similarly, the Service has been of importance in the maintenance of many species of fish in the United States, through both its own research and operation of fish hatcheries as well as through its aid to state fish programs. Unfortunately, none of the fish when caught bear a label attributing them to the Service, and so the agency has suffered from a lack of recognition even on the part of its natural constituency of hunters and sports fishermen.

Consequently, of the two primary conservation activities engaged in by the agency, neither has experienced an impressive growth rate. When the Service was established in 1940, there existed 90 federal fish hatcheries. Twenty-five years later, in 1965, there were 89. Ten years later the Service had increased its hatcheries to a total of 90. Most recently, the Reagan administration reduced the number of hatcheries to 69, and in 1984 proposed they be cut to 45 units. The number and size of national wildlife refuges did undergo some growth during this time, but not, according to agency personnel, fast enough to keep up with the public demand that burgeoned in the 1950s. In 1941, the Service managed 267 refuges, totaling 13.77 million acres. By 1967, the number was up to 307, covering some 28.8 million acres. However, with the recent additions of new Alaskan lands as authorized in 1980 legislation, the acreage contained in the refuge and wildlife system skyrocketed to 88 million; the number of separate refuges climbed to 413. But despite this rather dramatic increase in both units and acres, a concomitant rise in recognition or political "credit" has not occurred. The Service seems to be perennially overshadowed by better known agencies. For example, by 1970, the Fish and Wildlife Service managed more land than did the National Park Service,[127] yet the latter agency enjoyed considerably more public recognition than did its lesser-known counterpart. In addition to its obscure mission the Fish and Wildlife Service has been a distinctly regional agency: as of 1984, 86 percent of its total land holdings were contained in three Alaskan refuges, and nearly all other refuges were located in a few western states where population has been sparse until very recently. Undoubtedly this regionalism accounts in large part for the agency's lack of national visibility.

By 1956, considerable interest had developed on the part of Washington policymakers in restructuring the Fish and Wildlife Service—in particular, in depriving it of a primary part of its duties. With the 1940 reorganization the Service began to view itself principally as a research and refuge-managing agency with a pronounced conservation-oriented mission. Consequently, the commercial fisheries section of the agency had received short shrift. Pressure from the fishing industry thus induced the government to reorganize the Service, and after lengthy debates between the two houses of Congress and the executive, a compromise measure was reached. The legislative result was enactment of the Fish and Wildlife Act of 1956. This statute gave the agency its long-awaited organic act, but it also laid out a rather elaborate reorganization that effectively bifurcated the Service. The legislation created the position of assistant secretary, within the Interior Department, for fish and wildlife, plus the position of commissioner of fish and wildlife. Beneath these positions there was created a U.S. Fish and Wildlife Service, but "consisting of two separate agencies,"[128] each of which would have the status of a federal bureau. Thus came into existence the Bureau of Commercial Fisheries and the Bureau of Sports Fisheries and Wildlife, plus a kind of phantom agency called the U.S. Fish and Wildlife Service which existed at the assistant-secretariat level.

While on an organizational chart the reorganization may have looked like the Service was at long last getting the recognition it deserved, this was clearly not the case. The assistant secretary for fish and wildlife soon became the assistant secretary for fish, wildlife, and parks, and by 1976 the Bureau of Outdoor Recreation also came under that official's direction. During the reorganization hearings a departmental official had characterized the Service as "merely a little branch buried in the Department of the Interior."[129] The 1956 reorganization did little if anything to change that condition, and indeed the division of the Service into two distinct bureaus presaged future trouble. In 1970, in what has been the last (so far) in a long series of reorganizations, the Bureau of Commercial Fisheries was returned to its original home in the Commerce Department to be merged with the newly created National Oceanographic and Atmospheric Administration. The Bureau of Sports Fisheries and Wildlife, which was what remained of the original agency after it succumbed to the powerful centrifugal forces that operate in many natural resources agencies,[130] became—again—the U.S. Fish and Wildlife Service. That is where things stand in 1984.

The recent history of the agency, from its 1956 reorganization to the present, shows a familiar pattern of behavior. The major problem of the Service has to do with its organizational character—that is, its outlook and orientation to public policy. The agency is perhaps best characterized as a secondary service organization. It has not been able to break out of this conservative orientation. The attitude of agency personnel is basically that of being enthusiastic, behind-the-scenes helpers. Rather than becoming a leader in the environmental movement that developed during the 1960s, the Service maintained its traditional low profile and was frequently criticized for its timidity. A Department of the Interior spokesperson commented on this in 1972:

> When I came to Washington to assume jurisdiction over the Bureau of Sports Fisheries and Wildlife just 9 months ago, I expected to find a small, hard-hitting, nationally influential protector of fish and wildlife. . . . One element of my image of the Bureau proved accurate—it was small. Other than that, it was not exaggerating to characterize the organization as a paper tiger. . . . Here we had, then, a group of highly motivated, well trained professionals who were frustrated and somewhat demoralized in achieving their mission.[131]

And in 1973, the secretary of the interior admonished the agency for still not having become the biological arm of the department. The apparent reluctance of the agency to take on new responsibilities may be a result of the Service's past failures to hold on to existing programs.

After the 1956 reorganization, for example, the Service sustained yet another blow to its mission. As described earlier, the agency had supervision over the game and fish laws for the territory of Alaska, and it shared with other Interior Department agencies the general responsibility for the federal administration of Alaska throughout the first half of the twentieth century. However, when Alaska became a state in 1959 much of this authority was turned over to the state. The Service retained control only over those same duties that it had in the other states—the administration of its federal refuges and fish hatcheries, which admittedly are large, and a limited supervision of wildlife programs on the other federal lands in the state.

Throughout the 1960s the agency followed behind the growing environmental movement in this country. An irony of the Fish and Wildlife Service's position with respect to the environmental issue is found in its commitment to a rodent and pest control program at this time. In a study commissioned by the secretary of the interior, the Service was criticized for its zealousness in pursuing this particular activity, and was in effect told that it had gone far beyond the bounds of necessity in implementing a minor program. At the same time, the Service, which had long had the authority to review the use of pesticides for their effect on fish and wildlife, did little to further the movement to regulate pesticide use. It supported such actions, but again it did so in its traditional role. Taking the lead in any activity or issue was an alien role for the agency.

The environmental movement and the ensuing legislation passed by Congress dealing with environmental quality issues had a major impact on the Fish and Wildlife Service in the decade of the 1970s. Organizationally, the agency was unprepared to deal with the overwhelming increase in its workload resulting from the new legislation and new programs. The 1969 National Environmental Policy Act, the planning and construction of the trans-Alaska pipeline, the stringent Endangered Species Act of 1973, plus the several air and water quality acts virtually overwhelmed the small agency. The Service was well aware of the potential for its own aggrandizement contained in these acts, but since it had never developed a strong organizational infrastructure it was ill equipped to take advantage of the moment.

Consequently, the word *overcommitment* runs like a red thread through congressional oversight and appropriations hearings in the early 1970s. It may provide the most accurate assessment of the Service in this period. Within established programs, the Service tried to put the greatest emphasis on its refuge program, yet the consistent conclusion of agency officials and others was that the refuges were understaffed and in a process of disintegration. Agency figures for fiscal year 1973, for example, show an average of three administrative personnel per refuge. One member of the appropriations subcommittee complained about the poor condition of the refuges, stating "I don't think there is a single member of this Congress who is not beseiged by mail to upgrade refuge facilities."[132]

The workload and resulting paper work that soon became the most obvious result of a national concern with environmental quality proved to be an enormous burden on the small agency. In 1971 the Service anticipated having to do the following "coordination" work: reconnaissance and feasibility studies for 50 Bureau of Reclamation projects, 140 Corps of Engineers projects, and 410 other federal water projects; the review of 6,000 Department of the Army permit applications for work on navigable waterways, leading to the preparation of 400 reports; 130 nonfederal applications for the Federal Power Commission, 50 for the Atomic Energy Commission, and 16 for the Forest Service and the Bureau of Land Management.

In addition, the Service expected to review at least 1,200 environmental impact statements during the last half of fiscal year 1971. Understandably, the Service felt itself inundated. An agency official complained in 1972 to the appropriations committee: ". . . our management resources include 30 million acres of habitat, 629 field stations, personnel of 3,958 . . . there is a situation of imbalance, this is imbalance of programs to our capability which does result in an overcommitment."[133] There was simply no way that the agency could effectively deal with the staggering increase in its duties that resulted from a concern for the environment.

The Service's problems in meeting the mandate of the National Environmental Policy Act were exacerbated by what has been called a "brain drain" from the agency. With the passage of NEPA, federal agencies were suddenly in need of biologists and related professionals who could prepare impact statements for agency activities. The Fish and Wildlife Service, which employed such people, began losing its personnel to higher-paying agencies. Thus NEPA, which was highly congruent with the agency's environmental mission, could have been expected to contribute substantially to the Service's growth and visibility. Instead, it caused innumerable problems for an agency quite unprepared for new mandates and for the predatory activity of other federal agencies.

Funding for the Fish and Wildlife Service in recent years has likewise taken a cautious, incremental path. From 1975 to 1980 the Service received a moderate increase in funding, culminating in a 1980 budget of $433 million.[134] This somewhat helped the agency keep up with its duties, but under the Reagan administration it faces the executive budgetary ax. Secretary of the Interior James Watt voiced considerable criticism of the Service in the 1982 appropriations hearings, and promised to revamp the agency's priorities:

> there will be major—and I want to underline the word "major"—there will be major changes in the management of the Fish and Wildlife Service. . . . It [the Service] need not stop economic activity, economic growth and job opportunities. In too many instances I believe that it has. . . . With the changes in budgetary requirements that I am requesting, we will get the attention of the management of the Fish and Wildlife System and new ways and new techniques will be installed throughout that service. I mean throughout, not just in Washington.[135]

The 1982 proposed budget for the Fish and Wildlife Service underwent a curious series of revisions, primarily because of the conflicting demands generated by Secretary Watt on the one hand and an enormous increase in responsibilities on the other. As we mentioned earlier, the 1980 Alaska National Interest Lands Conservation Act (ANILCA) established nine new units of the National Wildlife Refuge System, and enlarged and consolidated several existing units. As a result, the total acreage of National Wildlife Refuge lands administered by the Fish and Wildlife Service in Alaska jumped from 22 million to 76 million.[136] In spite of these increases, the Reagan administration cut the agency's budget. The Department of the Interior originally intended to increase the agency's budget, with OMB's agreement, and so $5 million was added for resource management. In a subsequent round of budget decisions, however, the agency's funds for this particular item were reduced by $42.6 million. In fact, during a recess in the appropriations hearings, several last-minute cuts were made by the administration; this action necessitated a repeat discussion of items already reviewed by the subcommittee because, in the space of a few days, the totals had changed significantly.[137] The acting director of the Service described his agency's budget *before* these reductions were made as "a bare-bones budget" that did not provide sufficient funds "to carry out all the responsibilities which Congress has given us."[138]

Indeed, a wide array of agency programs have been targeted for either elimination or significant reduction. Congress has resisted some, but not all, of these proposed cuts. In 1982 the Reagan administration succeeded in eliminating the cooperative funding portion of the Endangered Species Program. These monies assisted states in establishing their own programs for protecting endangered flora and fauna. Several states quickly announced that they would be forced to discontinue their programs if they did not receive federal aid.[139] In response to the imminent curtailment of these state programs, Congress chose to fund the cooperative program in 1983 and 1984, over administration objections.

The entire Endangered Species Program has been the object of considerable budgetary conflict. President Reagan has repeatedly asked for major cuts but much of the money deleted by the executive has been restored by Congress. Nevertheless, under Watt's tenure as interior secretary, budgetary brakes were put on the program: only 17 new species were put on the endangered species list during the last three years, compared with 103 during the Carter-Andrus years.

Recently, a few other changes affecting the management and administration of the Service's facilities have been made. In 1982, in an effort to reduce administrative costs, eighteen area offices were closed and the personnel transferred to regional or other field offices. Also, nineteen fish hatcheries were removed from the Service's budget; they were transferred to either state control or to the Bureau of Indian Affairs. This left the agency with only 69 fish hatcheries—a number the administration wishes to see lowered even further.[140]

In a few program areas, however, the Service has managed to maintain the status quo, or even to slightly increase funding. Like the National Park Service, more money is being spent on maintenance and rehabilitation activities these days, and despite administration efforts to zero-fund land acquisition, Congress in 1984 allocated $4.3 million for that purpose.

In recognition of current political realities, the Fish and Wildlife Service has made an attempt to expand its operations to include more activities designed to support natural resource development. For example, the Service considers its habitat preservation program a "prime example of this broadened mission."[141] The Service also plans to "increase participation in the [Interior] Department's coal-leasing and Outer Continental Shelf programs, and expand scope of assistance to the Bureau of Land Management in oil shale and tar sands leasing activities."[142] Yet even these activities were subjected to Reagan budget cuts in 1982. While stronger agencies received increased funding (or at least avoided decreases) for programs related to resource development, the Fish and Wildlife Service has been unable to expand into this new area. Obviously, the Reagan administration views the

Service as an impediment to, rather than a promoter of, increased resource exploitation.[143]

This view of the Fish and Wildlife Service as a hindrance to economic growth can be seen most clearly in recent funding levels for the agency's technical assistance program, which provides information to other federal agencies concerning the impact of their projects on wildlife. The Fish and Wildlife Service has repeatedly asked for increased funding for this program, claiming that the additional funds would allow them to do more comprehensive planning and research, and thus expedite development and project construction. But the program has always been underfunded; only about 50 percent to 60 percent of the requests for assistance can be met. As a result, "many projects with substantial adverse impacts to fish and wildlife habitat are planned and constructed without benefit of fish and wildlife information and recommendations."[144] The Reagan administration's FY 1982 budget called for further decreases in funding for this program.[145] By 1983 it disappeared entirely from the budget.

In looking towards the future, it appears likely that the Fish and Wildlife Service will continue to struggle to meet new responsibilities with a small budget and work force. For example, the new tasks given the Service by the Alaska National Interest Lands Conservation Act not only substantially increased the total acreage of the National Wildlife Refuge System, but presented some unique management problems. The Service must learn to deal with the "sensitive issue of subsistence use" of wildlife resources, and with the "frontier lifestyle" of many Alaskans. This will call for "management expertise not normally utilized on Service lands."[146] Also, much of the new acreage is extremely remote, rugged, and subject to unusually harsh climatic conditions. And there is a history of "questionable mining activity and other forms of trespass."[147] Yet staffing for these new areas is virtually nonexistent; some of the new refuges are massive, encompassing over 3 million acres, and not staffed by a single employee.[148] Clearly, ANILCA will severely test the organizational capabilities of the Fish and Wildlife Service.

The Alaska-based refuges are not the only ones causing management problems for the agency, however. A 1983 survey of refuges disclosed numerous threats to the integrity of the system, including increased poaching activity on some 260 refuges.[149] Nonetheless, the administration's FY 1983 budget proposal cut funding for "surveillance activities involved in the protection of endangered species."[150]

Under the present administration, with its implementation of decremental budgeting, the Service will find few opportunities to grow beyond its traditional role as an auxiliary agency with a narrowly defined and not particularly popular mission. In its relatively new coordinating role the Service performs some useful functions on behalf of the nation's fish and wildlife resources, so perhaps the agency has at last found a relatively secure, though limited, niche in the federal bureaucratic structure. While it is not nearly so influential as some of the other resource agencies analyzed in this study, the Service is not yet ready to be put on the endangered species list of federal agencies. But it is close. Through most of its history it has been subjected to some very harsh criticism for its failures to meet its objectives. There are some good reasons for this poor track record, of course, but cataloging those rationalizations may not help the agency for much longer if the present era of public sector frugality continues indefinitely, as some believe it will.

SUMMARY: AN INCREMENTAL MODEL OF DEVELOPMENT

Both the circumstances and the behavior of the three agencies discussed here contrast sharply with the two largest resource managers, the Corps and the Forest Service. These smaller organizations are by no means failures, if one is judging failure by evaluating their respective records of accomplishment; yet one gets the strong impression that they have not developed to their fullest potential. Certain limiting factors have produced a history and a pattern of behavior that we think is aptly described as incremental. And, just as Lindblom by no means meant to disparage the bureaucratic behavior that he characterized as "muddling through," we intend no invidious comparison when we point out, for example, that the National Park Service is not the U.S. Forest Service, despite a long history of competition between them.

The conditions that circumscribe the behavior of these agencies include the following: the nature of the mission, the professional base of the organization, and the nature of their constituencies. In the histories of the Park Service, Soil Conservation Service, and Fish and Wildlife Service, one can see the circumstances that produce a "typical" federal agency. Two agencies, the Park Service and the Fish and Wildlife Service, had to wrestle with an original, dichotomous mission. Both were given at the time of their creation two independent and essentially conflicting goals—to preserve on the one hand and to use on the other. As we pointed out, this led to some schizophrenic behavior on the part of the agencies in trying to reconcile that which is difficult to reconcile. It also led to considerable criticism. In one case, Congress eventually took away entirely the development function from the agency; in the other case, zoning for dominant use (or nonuse) seems to have settled the issue. But in both cases the agency's early development was hurt by the existence of contradictory ambiguous goals. These divided the organization and its constituency in a way that seemed to produce, to the outside observer, excessively vacillating behavior.

The Soil Conservation Service did not have a contradictory mission with which to wrestle, but it did have a relatively narrow one. In a recent book on the subject, two scholars suggest that the agency has not grown significantly because public attitudes about soil conservation have remained relatively static. In looking at data on federal funding for soil conservation from 1950 to 1980, Easter and Cotner find:

> Over the 30-year period, the expenditure in deflated dollars per year has remained in the $700 million to $750 million range. Therefore, public expenditures to support conservation programs have not increased. This implies that society, through its governmental processes, has assigned about the same level of priority to conservation investment now as it did 40 years ago. In fact, the implication may be a lower priority because total public expenditures have increased rapidly during this period.[151]

This is another way in which organizations get boxed in: either their functions or their constituencies (or both) are originally limited, and so the agency finds itself competing with other, more flexible organizations. The Park Service's attentive public—the environmentalists—are perceived by many as "far out." The Fish and Wildlife Service had for a time both the Alaskan salmon industry and the sportsmen as its attentive publics; it was accused of becoming a captured agency until Congress, in the 1950s, reorganized it into two separate bureaus. Now the Service has only the sportsmen and conservationists as its major clientele, and both of these groups operate somewhat on the edge of the mainstream of American politics. They provide the agency with no more than average group support. Finally, the Soil Conservation Service came on the scene in the mid-1930s, only to find several other federal agencies already in existence and performing some of the activities the Conservation Service was mandated to do. Competition with agencies like the Corps, the Forest Service, and the Bureau of Reclamation ultimately left the agency with little room to grow, so the SCS found a secure, though limited, niche in providing small-scale services for farmers living primarily in the heartland of America. As we noted, the Service became relegated to providing the little projects after the bigger agencies got the cream of the crop.

Professional forestry is at the foundation of the Forest Service; civil engineering is the area of expertise for the Corps. The three agencies discussed here are more or less amalgams of several professions and so do not exhibit the predominance of a single profession. They are, in other words, more interdisciplinary. This characteristic appears not to appreciably help a federal agency develop political influence. The control of information is of course a major source of power for a bureaucracy, and if it can convince those outside the organization that it is one of the few possessors of a certain body of information, then it has an advantage vis-à-vis those that do not have it. Both the Corps and the Forest Service have convinced many people, over many years, that they are the experts at doing certain things; but this is less true for interdisciplinary organizations like the three described in this chapter. Time and again, for

To state with certainty that the incremental model is the most typical development pattern in the executive establishment would take a much larger sample than the one we have. We suspect, however, that relatively few superstars can be found in this population (we have not heard of many if they do exist), nor are there a great many of what we call shooting stars. Furthermore, observing ordinary human behavior prompts us to conclude that most organizations, like most humans, have certain extenuating circumstances that cause them to move along at a more or less steady pace rather than to soar. Based on our research, this may be an appropriate redefinition of the term *pathos of bureaucracy*.

Organizational Shooting Stars: The Bureau of Reclamation and the Bureau of Land Management

THE BUREAU OF RECLAMATION

The Bureau of Reclamation, created by the Reclamation Act of 1902, was an organizational expression of America's westward movement. The act was an imaginative attempt to resolve certain dilemmas posed by our expansion into regions and territories very unlike the lush eastern half of the United States. The historian Bernard DeVoto gives what still is the most succinct and accurate definition of the American West: It is where average annual rainfall measures less than twenty inches.[1] This simple climatic reality is the key to understanding much of the history and development of the western half of the United States.

The reality of the arid West was for most of the nineteenth ·century ignored, despite mounting evidence to the contrary. Of the westward march, one author writes:

> From the Mississippi River westward, events unfolded like a bad joke. Early reports of a "great American desert" were simply ignored as inconceivable, impossible. But eventually the accumulation of evidence, including rainfall records, established beyond a doubt that west of the vicinity of the hundredth meridian — a line approximately bisecting the Dakotas and extending south to Laredo, Texas—nearly all the land below 8,000 feet ... was too dry for unirrigated agriculture. And west of the Rockies it deteriorated to a lot of inhospitable desert.
>
> When ignoring the situation didn't make it go away, we tried to drive it away with myth and fantasy. Rain would follow the plow (because of the increased evaporation from washed soil); rain would follow the train (because of smoke particles for drops to form around); rain would follow the telegraph (because of electricity in the air). . . . There were even those who came right out and said what everyone else was more or less hinting at: rain will follow settlement for no reason other than the presence of good people with a destiny to fulfill.[2]

The government of course greatly assisted and encouraged attempts at settling the West. Throughout the nineteenth century vast pieces of the public domain were given to various commercial interests, in particular to the railroads, for the purpose of developing the western half of the continent. During the Civil War an important bill passed Congress which for the first time made public land available to all prospective settlers regardless of race. This legislation, the Homestead Act of 1862, allowed heads of families to acquire up to 160 acres of surveyed public domain (i.e., western land) for a small fee.[3] The Timber Culture Act of 1873 and the Desert Land Act of 1877 had similar intentions.

Despite these governmental actions to assist not only the corporations but ordinary settlers as well, one overriding reality remained: land in the West was virtually useless without water. A settler had nothing if he did not also have some water, "and before the West was going to be settled it was going to have to be irrigated."[4] Major John Wesley Powell, a government scientist and explorer, was the first to propose a solution to this troubling dilemma. In an 1877 governmental report, Powell outlined a settlement proposal of the West by irrigation districts. Though specific features of Powell's report were not implemented, his realization of the paramount importance of water to western development was acted upon. The idea was codified in the 1902 Reclamation Act.

The Reclamation Service was organized within the U.S. Geological Survey to administer the act; five years later, in 1907, the Service was removed from the Geological Survey and established under a director. In 1923 another organizational change was effected; the secretary of the interior created the position of commissioner of reclamation and renamed the Service the Bureau of Reclamation. It remained the Bureau of Reclamation until 1979, when the interior secretary announced another name change, together with a change in direction and some change in functions. The Bureau was called briefly the Water and Power Resources Service; the name change reflected an attempt to come to terms with the fact that the Bureau had outlived its original mission and was actively seeking out new ones. Under the present Republican administration, however, its name has been returned to the Bureau of Reclamation. That is the title we will use in this study.

The 1902 Reclamation Act provided that monies from the sale and disposal of public lands in the sixteen western states (Texas was added to the list in 1906) would go into a special fund in the U.S. Treasury known as the reclamation fund. This fund would then be used

> in the examination and survey for and the construction and maintenance of irrigation works for the storage, diversion, and development of waters for the reclamation of arid and semiarid lands in the said States and Territories.[5]

Thus the original mission of the Bureau was a lofty and even romantic one: It envisioned nothing less than the transformation of the West "from a land of sprawling cow towns and crude mining settlements in the midst of barren desert waste into prosperous modern communities supported by lush farmland."[6] That such transformations did in fact occur—metropolises such as Los Angeles, San Diego, and Phoenix were made possible by engineering the movement of water from its natural courses—is testimony to the fact that the Bureau, for a time, accomplished extraordinary feats that combined sophisticated technology with imaginative goals.

The Bureau of Reclamation, however, was beset with problems almost from the start. The financial arrangements contained in the 1902 act for financing these reclamation projects were novel, at least when they were compared with the financing of projects by the government's other water resource developer, the Corps. First, the Bureau's surveys and investigations of potential projects—and these were limited to the seventeen western states named in the act unless Congress specifically authorized action in other areas (a rare occurrence since the Corps was already ably servicing the rest of the country)—were to be financed by earmarked monies, e.g., the reclamation fund. At least in theory, then, this limited the agency's funds to what came in to the U.S. Treasury from sales of public land. The financing of the Corps' initial surveys was never circumscribed in this manner. Second, once a congressionally authorized project was underway, the estimated costs of construction provided the basis for calculating the charges, per acre, that water users would be required to pay back to the government:

> The said charges shall be determined with a view of returning to the reclamation fund the estimated cost of construction of the project, and shall be apportioned equitably: Provided, that in all construction work eight hours shall constitute a day's work, and no Mongolian labor shall be employed thereon.[7]

Further, repayment by water beneficiaries of the construction costs was not to exceed ten annual payments.

The reclamation fund was thus envisioned as a revolving, "pay-as-you-go" plan, which would refinance itself approximately every ten years in order to underwrite a continuing program of reclamation in the West. The original intent was that of a low-cost, partially federally financed, loan program wherein the actual users of the reclaimed water would repay the federal government in ten installments.

This financial arrangement contained a quite different philosophy from that pertaining to the Bureau's major competitor, the Corps, and it caused serious problems for the agency. While "cost-sharing" became a major feature of some Corps' projects (with the ratio varying according to the nature of the project, but with the federal government totally financing some projects), this cost-sharing was of a different kind from actual monetary repayments. Beneficiaries of Corps projects—principally local and state governments, but sometimes private water development associations—were to contribute to Corps projects by defraying certain planning and construction costs. For example, local interests were to provide rights-of-way, easements, the condemnation of land necessary to the project, and the like. Costs to the local beneficiaries were thus payments in kind and in services rather than outright cash transactions. This cost-sharing mechanism had the added bonus of virtually assuring Congress and the Corps that substantial local and regional support existed for the federal projects. In other words, a Corps project would rarely get underway unless local assurances of the nature mentioned above were forthcoming. This scheme helped defray costs to the federal government, but of equal importance it assured the agency of minimal local opposition to its projects. Thus the Corps had not only a hundred-year headstart on the Bureau of Reclamation in the water resources field, but it also operated in a more liberal financial environment.

The early history of the Bureau highlights some of its problems. For the first three years of its existence most of the work of the Reclamation Service focused on general surveys and the preparation of construction plans. By 1906, plans were approved for some twenty irrigation projects, which exhausted nearly all of the reclamation-fund money. Hearings before the House Committee on Irrigation of Arid Lands in 1906 revealed that the agency had no problem in finding takers for its irrigated land; many of these initial water users were homesteaders because the bulk of the land irrigated by early projects was public domain.

By 1914 the Bureau's problems became more apparent. In subcommittee hearings in that year, spokesmen for the Service were asked about charges that their agency had begun to stagnate. Agency officials responded by discussing certain technical and financial problems they had encountered in their first twelve years of existence: The construction of a reservoir that leaked; large cost overruns that were due to admittedly inadequate planning; and some unexpected effects caused by irrigation in arid environments. In some areas, it turned out, irrigation caused the water table to rise to such an extent that farms were turned into virtual swamps—a situation as unproductive as the original desert. This problem could of course be alleviated by drainage of the land, but the solution would increase project costs. Drainage, however, turned out to be essential in many areas due to the natural salinity of the desert land.

In addition to these technical, trial-and-error problems, the reclamation fund was running into difficulty. Income from the sale of public lands was insufficient to cover the costs of projects. Increasingly, water beneficiaries were unable to pay back the government in ten years; so the time period of repayment was extended to twenty years. Also, the revolving fund was not turning over as rapidly as anticipated, and this put severe restrictions on new project planning. All in all, the reclamation fund, envisioned as a sort of perpetual motion machine, was seen to need considerable human intervention after all.

An example of the Bureau's problems with regard to its financing formula is seen in the plans, and end result, of the Uncompahgre project in Colorado. It was initially estimated to cost $1 million and put approximately 140,000 acres under cultivation. The project actually cost three times as much and benefited only half as much land. In effect, the Bureau had made a major miscalculation that would raise the necessary charges per acre sixfold. In this case, as in others, Congress unilaterally reduced the amount to be repaid by water users. By 1939 some $17 million had been written off in this way. Congress also acted frequently to defer payments on specific projects for a number of years. The agency's accounting procedures to keep track of deferrals and cancellations were clearly bewildering to many congressional members, not to mention the general public. Even few experts in the Bureau could keep up with the increasingly byzantine budgetary process.

Matters did not substantially improve overnight. In the 1923 appropriations hearings the Service discussed some twenty-six projects, but money was still a big problem. A large backlog of uncompleted projects led the director of the Service to admit: "In the present state of the fund it is not advisable to take up new work for some years to come."[8]

By 1939, however, the Bureau was recharged with energy. FDR's New Deal, and some spectacular engineering feats such as the Boulder Dam (renamed the Hoover Dam in 1947, after Roosevelt's death),[9] gave the agency a new lease on life. In discussing its past, the Bureau noted: "These mistakes were not engineering mistakes, but rather were the result of pioneering in a new field."[10] Moreover, the reclamation fund, always short of money, had been essentially refinanced. Repayment periods were extended to forty years, and this allowed the Bureau to claim that repayments were coming in on schedule. More importantly, however, the fund had been augmented in several ways: Since 1921 part of the oil, potash, and potassium royalties derived from the public lands were to go into the reclamation fund, along with royalties and revenues from some other federal undertakings.

Also by 1939 the Bureau was able to effectively capitalize on the power-generating aspects of its irrigation projects. Power was not mentioned as an objective in the 1902 statute, but by 1939 hydroelectric power had become an important ingredient in water resources development. The Bureau could proudly point to some engineering masterpieces in that regard. The revenue derived from power sales also helped to defray construction costs and to lower rates to water users to an economically manageable level.

According to one case study of the Bureau of Reclamation, the agency began to show signs of an organizational decline from a 1950 high point.[11] By this time the Bureau had skimmed off the cream of the most economically attractive reclamation projects. Good dam sites and potentially rich farm lands became increasingly scarce, and the Bureau was able to pursue its mission only by granting longer repayment periods at low interest rates.

Stratton and Sirotkin state, and our more recent data support, the contention that in the period from 1950 to 1955 the appropriations to the Bureau of Reclamation fell from approximately $364 million to about $156 million. While in 1950 Bureau employees comprised about 61 percent of the entire Interior Department work force, five years later they accounted for only 38 percent.

Beyond budget and personnel declines the impoverishment of the Bureau of Reclamation can be monitored by the number of political defeats it suffered. First, it lost an important claim to hegemony over water development west of the hundredth meridian. As multi-purpose rather than single-purpose water projects came into fashion during the 1940s, a fierce competition developed between the Bureau and the powerful Army Corps of Engineers. In a study of the Kings Rivers project in California, Arthur Maass describes how even the support of such a powerful president as Franklin Roosevelt was not sufficient to wrench control away from the Army Corps.[12] In the Corps' eventual victory on this project, however, the attitude of local residents must also be ranked high. Testimony in March of 1945 by Representative A. J. Elliott of California before a subcommittee of the House Appropriations Committee states flatly that

> local interests are so strongly in opposition to a project built under reclamation law that they have stated that rather than have the project built by the Bureau of Reclamation they prefer no Federal project at all.[13]

The Bureau also began to suffer some embarrassing setbacks to its developmental mission at the hands of conservationists and the National Park Service—organizations that never have been a potent political force. As good dam sites became increasingly scarce the agency began to scan the environs of national parks, national monuments, and wilderness areas for possible project sites. In the Echo Park controversy of the 1950s, conservation forces defeated an attempt by the Bureau to invade Dinosaur National Monument with a man-made reservoir.[14] The most definitive defeat, however, came in the Colorado River Basin Bill of 1968 when conservation groups turned back a Bureau proposal to authorize the construction of two dams in the Grand Canyon region of the Colorado River.

In its heyday the Bureau of Reclamation enjoyed a great deal of professional esprit de corps. During the 1930s when jobs were scarce, the best engineering students from western universities were recruited into the Bureau. Reclamation engineers took great pride in the construction of their monumental arched gravity structures such as the Glen Canyon Dam. Traditionally, Bureau of Reclamation engineers proudly compared their skills with those of the Corps, which preferred "easier," earth-filled dams. Nevertheless, from about 1950 on the agency was finding its role increasingly threatened by the existence of a more powerful competitor in the water resources field and also by its own reclamation laws.

In the face of a threat to its continued existence, the Bureau tried to diversify and broaden its mission, but too often these attempts were thwarted. For instance, by 1950 the agency had begun doing hydroelectric power investigations in Alaska, but this once again brought it into direct competition with the Corps. In the 1954 House Appropriations Committee hearings, questions were raised about a potential duplication of effort. It soon became clear that the Bureau would come out on the short end of the stick, for the Corps claimed that it was operating in Alaska under legislative authority contained in the 1948 Flood Control Act, whereas Bureau of Reclamation operations were based on the generality that they had requested appropriations for investigations of this type in the past and had received them. Once Congress remembered that the Bureau's mission was limited to the seventeen western states, excluding Alaska, the agency was told to get new legislative authority for its investigations. Legislative authority for an expanded Bureau role, although frequently mentioned, never materialized.

During the 1950s the Bureau latched on to the then-popular recreation boom, and in its 1961 appropriations hearing recreation was frequently mentioned as a benefit deriving from reclamation projects. But while important, recreation benefits could hardly sustain a public works agency for very long. Once public and governmental attention waned, so did the Bureau's recreation program.

By the mid-1960s, competition with the Corps had become increasingly bitter; the Bureau could make few inroads to the Corps' growing monopoly. Secretary of the Interior Stewart Udall, testifying in 1965 before Congress, summed up the Bureau's dilemmas by noting that agency activities were hampered by closer congressional scrutiny of individual projects as well as by its historic repayment requirement. Simply put, he commented that "we have to run through a higher hoop."[15] By this time the Corps was doing more planning and construction than the Bureau, even in the Bureau's "own" original territory (the Pacific

Northwest turned out to be the Corps' most fertile area for water resources development).

The 1970s were clearly the decade of decision for the Bureau of Reclamation. Problems arose in a number of areas. For example, nearly all of the prime sites for reclamation projects had been developed. It appeared that the Bureau's principal mission was close to completion. In the 1974 appropriations hearings, the agency admitted that "the original objective [of the Bureau] has been met. . . . The West is now developed."[16]

The Bureau was also a conspicuous target for environmentalists, whose political strength had grown remarkably by the middle of the decade. The Ralph Nader-inspired book, *Damning the West*,[17] was typical of the environmentalists' literature condemning the agency. Environmental impact statements, as mandated by 1969 legislation, also caused problems for the Bureau throughout the 1970s. It experienced considerable difficulty in meeting the extensive requirements for environmental review and for the planning of nonstructural alternatives.

In the midst of a trying decade, the Bureau felt itself victimized by Mother Nature when, on June 5, 1976, its Teton Dam failed. This earth-filled dam disintegrated through a combination of seismic activity and erosion, with the result to society of extensive loss of life and property. Damage claims were expected to exceed $400 million.[18] The disaster shook public confidence in the Bureau.

At the same time that the Bureau was attempting to recover from the Teton Dam disaster, Jimmy Carter was campaigning for the presidency on a platform that emphasized environmental protection, government reorganization, and the elimination of waste in federal government expenditures. After his election he ordered his transition team to investigate possible cuts in public works projects. As we also discuss in chapter 2, only a month after assuming office he initiated a review of nineteen marginal projects, eight of which were under construction by the Bureau of Reclamation. In April of 1977, the results of the presidential review were announced, with these recommendations for Bureau projects:

—Fruitland Mesa, Colorado; delete funding and deauthorize project

—Savory Pot Hook, Colorado; delete funding and deauthorize project

—Narrows Unit, Colorado; delete funding pending project reevaluation

—Auburn Dam, California; delete funding until seismic safety studies are done

—Oahe Unit, South Dakota; delete funding and modify in accordance with local demands

—Garrison Diversion Project; eliminate certain aspects of the project

—Bonneville Unit, Central Utah Project; eliminate certain aspects of the project

—Central Arizona Project; eliminate certain aspects of the project

Due to these suggested reductions, the budget proposed by Carter for the Bureau's FY 1978 appropriation was $609.6 million, significantly less than the $840.4 million budget proposed by President Ford the month before.[19] The Senate responded by passing a bill that required the president to spend the funds necessary to continue the projects.[20]

Although western politicians predictably resisted the cuts in water projects, some of them were quite candid about the future prospects for massive western water projects. Governor Richard Lamm of Colorado, who fiercely resisted the project cuts—three of which were in his state— nevertheless admitted that

> The days of large-scale Western water projects are coming to an end. Grandiose schemes about making deserts bloom? Some of us have more modest goals and expectations now. I very strongly believe there is a limit to the carrying capacity of the West.[21]

But Lamm also echoed the sentiments of his colleagues in stating that projects should not be deleted once they had been started. Westerners were particularly disturbed that four of the five largest western water projects were on the Carter list. Interest groups such as the Western States Water Council and the National Water Resources Association— the traditional clientele of the Bureau—joined forces with congressional allies in an effort to preserve continued funding for these ongoing projects. The six western senators on the Senate Appropriations Committee and the fifteen western congresspersons on the House Appropriations Committee led the fight to fund all of the projects. Ultimately, the Congress agreed to a compromise bill that stopped work on Auburn Dam until safety studies could be completed, and deleted funds for the Bureau's Fruitland Mesa, Narrows Unit, Oahe, and Savory Pot Hook projects. The Congress also reduced funds for the Central Arizona Project.[22] The House, which was a reluctant partner in the compromises made in the final appropriations bill, noted in the conference report that "the Congress retains the right to select water resource projects for funding," and promised to renew the fight for the projects the following year.[23]

The final budget compromise was due in part to the efforts of several northern legislators who were opposed to big western water projects. Another reason the Congress agreed to delete funds for at least two Bureau projects was due to local opposition from the alleged recipients of the project. Senator James Abourezk of South Dakota proposed an amendment to the appropriations bill that deleted funds for the Oahe Diversion Project in his state because area farmers and ranchers—those who were listed as project beneficiaries—opposed the Bureau's project.[24] The Narrows Unit in Colorado was also deleted because of local opposition. Even the Central Arizona Project, which is popular among most of the state's residents, faced opposition from a local group called Citizens Concerned About the Project.

The FY 1978 budget described above went into effect on October 1, 1977, the same day that the new Department of Energy came into existence. In another effort to reduce the operations of the Bureau of Reclamation, Carter transferred the agency's responsibilities for marketing power to the new department. With the continuing diminution of prime project sites and the rising political momentum of budget-cutters and environmentalists, the loss of this function was a notable setback for the Bureau at a time when it could ill afford it.

As promised, the debate over the water projects continued throughout 1978. The administration once again attempted to stop the Garrison Diversion Project, which was bogged down in a lawsuit brought by the Audubon Society. This project was also the subject of a controversy with Canada over the potential impact of the project on international waters. The Bonneville Unit of the Central Utah Project was also targeted for deletion. In June, Carter submitted a list of twenty six projects—nine of which were being constructed by the Bureau—that he wanted to have deleted or modified. Included on this list was the $55 million Oroville-Tonasket Unit of the Chief Joseph Dam in the state of Washington.[25] The proposed Carter budget for the Bureau was $618 million, a reduction of $63 million from its appropriations for FY 1978. Carter again imposed a no-new-starts policy for FY 1979.[26]

At the same time that the battle over the budget was taking place, the Bureau lost an important case before the U.S. Supreme Court. In *California et al. v. United States,*[27] the California State Water Resources Control Board argued that the Reclamation Act required the Bureau of Reclamation to satisfy state-mandated water quality controls. The Bureau in turn argued that federal water projects were exempt from state controls. Amici curiae briefs were filed against the Bureau by every western state except Utah. In a reversal of past opinion, the Court narrowly construed the federal government's powers and ruled against the Bureau:

> From the legislative history of the Reclamation Act of 1902, it is clear that state law was expected to control in two important respects. First, and of controlling importance in this case, the Secretary would have to appropriate, purchase, or condemn necessary water rights in strict conformity with state law. . . . Second, once the waters were released from the dam, their distribution to individual landowners would again be controlled by state law.[28]

This case is another example of a limiting provision of the law which affects the Bureau of Reclamation but not the Corps of Engineers; the

Court's decision is based on section 8 of the Reclamation Act. The Corps is not limited by such legislation.

New challenges faced the Bureau in 1979. In January, Carter issued an executive order that required federal water projects to meet new criteria. Specifically, Carter ordered the Water Resources Council to establish a new set of standards and principles for project planning and to complete an "impartial technical review" on all preauthorization studies. The council was also charged with developing a new planning manual for calculating costs and benefits and for applying them in a consistent manner.[29]

Carter also proposed a reorganization plan that would formally transfer all of the planning and analysis functions from both the Corps and the Bureau of Reclamation to the Water Resources Council. The plan further called for the transfer of all of the Reclamation Bureau's design and construction functions to the Corps. Obviously, this would leave the Bureau of Reclamation with little to do. Although the plan was never approved by Congress, it illustrates the former president's attitude toward this agency. Even the Corps was preferred over the Bureau by Carter.[30]

Another indicator of its precarious situation is the fact that the Bureau underwent a name change at this time. Although the agency wanted to keep the word *Bureau* in its new title, Secretary Andrus forced the agency to adopt the term *Service*, thereby erasing any reference to the former title. The name change of course had symbolic significance, illustrating that in politics a rose is not a rose by any other name. It signified for many that the end of the Bureau's traditional role as a builder of massive reclamation projects in the West was about to expire. Commissioner Higginson euphemistically explained that the "initial purpose of reclaiming arid western lands had expanded to a much broader responsibility for water and power resource management."[31] A more realistic explanation was provided by Secretary Andrus, which stressed the administration's desire to stringently limit future construction activity by the agency: "National needs now call for greater efficiency in the operation of *existing* structures and their integration in new programs for renewable resources and alternative energy."[32]*

The Bureau's "broader responsibility" included some new programs such as wind energy research and investigations into cloud seeding. But these new responsibilities did not rescue the Bureau from a steadily shrinking budget. The agency's total appropriation for FY 1980 was $356 million less than its 1977 appropriation,[33] with the administration

---

*Not only was the new name a complete change from the old one, it was difficult to remember and awkward to use. In hearings Congressperson Smith remarked that her people referred to the agency as "Wipers," based on the new acronym, WPRS, which stands for Water and Power Resources Services.

requesting that no funds be appropriated for the Garrison Diversion Project or the Oahe Pumping Plant. The former was still in trouble with environmentalists and the Canadian government, and the latter was voted down by the board of directors of the local conservancy subdistrict. Also, the Auburn Dam was again delayed pending a safety study.[34]

In late 1979, in a speech entitled "The Bureau of Reclamation Faces the 1980s," Commissioner Higginson assured the National Water Resources Association that

> The Water and Power Project construction program is still strong. But it is changing. It is responding to new political criteria, economic pressures, present and future water and energy shortages and environmental concerns, but it is a going program.[35]

Commissioner Higginson cited several examples of new programs recently initiated by the Bureau, including the Public Involvement and Environmental Education programs. These are notable because they appeared long after other natural resource agencies developed such programs.

Commissioner Higginson also cited "Indian water resource development" as a Bureau activity, but this would more appropriately be described as a major problem area for the Bureau rather than a new program. The Bureau has long been at odds with Indian reservations due to conflicting water rights. The western United States developed a doctrine of water rights that is quite distinct from the riparian doctrine used in the East. Due to the scarcity of water in the American West, the riparian doctrine was unsuited to that environment, so the western states adopted an entirely new approach known as the prior appropriation doctrine. The 1902 Reclamation Act requires the Bureau to allocate water according to state law, or, in other words, to abide by the prior appropriation doctrine, since it is used by nearly all of the states within the Bureau's jurisdiction. But Indian tribes are not subject to state law — they have an exclusive relationship with the federal government — so the federal courts have developed a separate water law doctrine for Indian reservations and other federal lands. This reserved rights doctrine (or Winters doctrine as it is sometimes called) directly conflicts with state water law; hence there has been considerable conflict between the Bureau and western Indian reservations. The Corps of Engineers, which builds only about a third of its projects where a conflict exists between state and federal water doctrines, is less affected by this problem than is the Bureau of Reclamation.

The Bureau's conflict with Indian tribes has a long history. It began with the agency's first project in Nevada. Recently Indian tribes have become more politically sophisticated and therefore present a significant challenge to the Bureau's modus operandi. A case in point concerns

Orme Dam, which was proposed as a component of the Central Arizona Project. The CAP, as it has come to be known, is currently the Bureau's largest project. According to the agency's original plan, the dam would have inundated 70 percent of the Fort McDowell Indian Reservation, home of the Yavapai Indians. The Indians battled the dam for thirteen years, claiming that the Bureau was insensitive to cultural values and minority interests. The protest against the dam culminated in a thirty-mile march called the "Trail of Tears." Finally, under intense pressure from Indians from all over the West, and their environmental allies, Congress voted to abandon the Orme Dam in November of 1981.[36]

Notwithstanding these major setbacks, many hoped that the Bureau's lot would improve after the 1980 presidential election because of the simple fact that Jimmy Carter would no longer be in the White House. During his tenure as president, he reduced the Bureau's budget by 37 percent (while the Corps of Engineers' budget increased by 24 percent). He attempted to transfer the agency's planning functions to the Water Resources Council and its construction and design functions to the Corps of Engineers. Carter also imposed a new set of criteria on the agency which stressed environmental values and nonstructural alternatives, two policies the Bureau had fiercely resisted. There were "no new starts" during the Carter administration, either.

The Reagan administration promised a new beginning in western water development, and Secretary of the Interior James Watt assured western governors that the "War on the West" waged by Carter was over.[37] But the new administration was also committed to substantially cutting the federal budget, much of which is generally considered uncontrollable. However, Interior's budget was vulnerable. As Leman notes, "the proportion of controllable funds in the 1979 budget for the U.S. Department of Health and Human Services was less than 3 percent, while in the U.S. Department of Interior, it was 63 percent."[38] Secretary Watt therefore was forced to explain that, at least initially, he would concentrate on reducing the budget of the Department of the Interior rather than embark on an ambitious water development program. Although the Reagan administration allowed a $171.6 million increase in the Bureau's budget in 1981, its 1982 budget was a big disappointment to the. agency. In hearings before the Subcommittee on Energy and Water Development, Secretary Watt explained his attitude toward the Bureau of Reclamation:

> I had hoped, Congressmen, that we would have a new start in the Reagan 1982 budget for the Bureau of Reclamation. The planning has been so depleted — and the intentions of the past management — not to have such things, means that there wasn't one that I could pull out and put in the Reagan budget.
>
> I am sorry about that. We wanted to . . . send a signal to the west

that the war on the west is over. The best way we knew how to do that was to say we will have a new reclamation start in 1982 for Reagan's budget, but the depletion, the denigration of the planning process over the past years is such that there was not one I could identify to put in our 1982 budget.[39]

As a result, the Bureau's budget was cut once again, with a proposed $62 million reduction in the total budget. This included a 5 percent cut in the construction program, thus delaying construction on eight projects.[40]

In the same subcommittee hearings, Representative Virginia Smith from Nebraska offered the observation that the Bureau is facing the end of an era—the era of big reclamation projects: "A professional in the WPRS says in his opinion two major projects in my district are probably the last irrigation projects that will be built in the United States."[41] One of these projects, the North Loup Division, was among the eight chosen by the Reagan administration for reduced funding. The other one, the O'Neill Unit, was halted by a court order that barred further construction until the Bureau of Reclamation prepared an adequate environmental impact statement.[42] It would appear that Representative Smith's suspicions regarding the agency's future are well founded.

Another event of significance occurred in 1982. The Reagan administration changed the name of the Bureau (i.e., the Water and Power Resources Service) back to the Bureau of Reclamation. However, given the terminal state of the reclamation mission, this may not be the harbinger of a bright future.

Typical of the agency's cyclical pattern of development, however, the Bureau has received increasing support from the Reagan administration. Beginning with FY 1983, the Bureau's immediate budgetary outlook began to improve. The traditional clientele of the Bureau— western agriculture, ranchers, and associated businesses—strongly supported Ronald Reagan in the 1980 presidential election. Sensitive to this source of political support, the president has begun to heed their demands for continued water development in the West: "there are signs that water projects soon may begin to move again under President Reagan, who is more sympathetic than Carter—at least rhetorically—to the dependence of western states on federal water projects."[43]

The Reagan administration's commitment to reclamation projects has turned out to be more than just rhetoric; for FY 1983 the administration requested a 21 percent increase in the Bureau's budget. The request for FY 1984 called for another substantial budget increase.

The present administration also provided critical support for the Bureau and its constituency in the long struggle with Congress to review the 1902 Reclamation Act. In 1982 Secretary of the Interior Watt testified in favor of raising the acreage limitation from 160 to 960 acres, a reform that has long been sought by the large corporate recipients of project water. Ultimately the 960 acre proposal became law.

But the recent good fortune of the agency has been tempered with criticism from a variety of sources. Increasing pressure is being placed on the Bureau to change the way it finances projects. Originally, reclamation projects were to be funded through a strict repayment plan, but this requirement has been liberalized to the point where projects are now viewed by some as excessively generous subsidies to the West. A recent study by the General Accounting Office, for example, concluded that the Bureau's repayment plan only covers 10 percent of actual project cost.[44] The Bureau's statistics contradict this estimate, and place the figure at an 84 percent rate of return.[45] Nevertheless, there is a widespread perception that reclamation water is considerably underpriced. The Reagan administration and environmental groups have been pushing for increased user charges, which would reduce the cost of the program to the federal government and which might encourage water conservation efforts.

The Bureau has also been criticized in recent years for managerial problems. Two years after the 1979 reorganization of the Bureau a GAO investigation found that the agency experienced a decrease in efficiency and an increase in costs as a result of the reorganization.[46] An internal audit of the agency by the Department of the Interior in 1982 revealed numerous management problems.[47] Such problems—in addition to the many other factors we have discussed—may explain why the Corps of Engineers but not the Bureau of Reclamation received new construction starts in the 1983 Reagan budget proposal (although in a subsequent budget amendment the Bureau received two new starts).

In the long run, however, the greatest limitation to the Bureau's future lies in its narrow mission. Senator Malcolm Wallop, a long-time supporter of reclamation projects, succinctly described the terminal nature of the Bureau's mission: "The reclamation system, as it was envisioned, is nearly complete. There may be one or two big projects left."[48]

From its high point in the 1930s and 1940s, the Bureau fell victim to a slow process of organizational decline. Its attempts to diversify were only partly successful, for it was never able to find new functions as uniquely its own as irrigation once was, and as popular among its western constituency. For a time, the Bureau succeeded in capturing the imagination and aspirations of the American West, but once that mission was accomplished the agency found itself too hemmed in by competing organizations and its own restrictive laws to make a major breakthrough. It appears that the agency is doing reasonably well with a westerner in the White House, but it seems unlikely to us that it will achieve the kind of eminence it once had when its engineering expertise was combined with the lofty ambition of "making the deserts bloom." If the Bureau does make a resurgence, it will probably be due to long-term demographic

changes that show a national shift in population to the West and Sunbelt
states. But the Bureau will have a long time to wait before reaping any
organizational benefits from a more populated West.

THE BUREAU OF LAND MANAGEMENT

In terms of sheer acreage, the Bureau of Land Management is the federal
government's largest land manager. It is responsible for the administration
of over 310 million acres of public lands, a figure that accounts for
almost 60 percent of all of the federal lands. Nearly half of this land is
in Alaska; the remainder is almost entirely to be found in the eleven
most western states of the nation. If an agency's power were to be
measured solely in terms of real estate, then surely the Bureau would be
a powerful organization. But this is not the case. The Bureau of Land
Management has been, until very recently, a politically weak organization
that survived primarily because nobody knew what to do with the land
that it managed.[49]

The Bureau is an old-new organization. It came into existence in its
present organizational form through a 1946 executive reorganization
that combined two failing agencies in the Department of the Interior,
hoping that they might lend strength to one another. The Bureau is thus
the direct descendant of the Grazing Service, established under the 1934
Taylor Grazing Act, and the rather infamous General Land Office, which
had been in existence since 1812 and whose history was intimately bound
up with the history of the public domain. What in essence the Bureau
fell heir to was a set of problems and issues, never adequately resolved,
having to do with grazing on the old public domain lands. Throughout
much of the nineteenth century the General Land Office was given the
next-to-impossible charge of administering the public domain. Adding
insult to injury, however, it discharged its duties so as to benefit the
vested interests of the time at the expense of the individual homesteader:

> In 1874, an Oregon correspondent for the *New York Sun* questioned
> the justice of a system which permitted "the local offices to receive
> applications for homestead and preemption rights and to encourage
> settlements and improvements on the public domain, only to" receive
> "instructions from the General Land Office in Washington to drive
> the settlers away and turn their improved property over to some
> railroad corporation." The main trouble, insisted the correspondent,
> was that the Interior Department was conducted almost entirely in
> the interests of land grabbers and monopolists, that it paid little or
> no attention to local laws or customs.[50]

The conservation movement of the late nineteenth century was, as we
saw, directed at reforming this scandalous misuse of the public lands;

thus from about 1870 on large tracts of the best land were withdrawn from the public domain to be set aside for particular uses. Even so, a lot of unappropriated acreage remained under the Land Office's management, land that was best suited for cattle and sheep grazing but upon which homesteading was also attempted. The closing decades of the nineteenth century saw the public range rapidly deteriorating through a large-scale application of the individualistic principles that give rise to "the tragedy of the commons." The historian Samuel Hays describes in a vivid manner the conditions then prevailing on the open range:

> Much of the Western livestock industry depended for its forage upon the "open" range, owned by the federal government, but free for anyone to use. Moving their livestock from the higher alpine ranges during the summer to the lower grazing lands in the winter, cattle and sheepmen could operate profitably with little capital and no privately owned land. Chaos and anarchy, however, predominated on the open range. Congress had never provided legislation regulating grazing or permitting stockmen to acquire range lands. Cattle and sheepmen roamed the public domain, grabbing choice grazing areas for their exclusive use, but competitors cut the wire. Resorting to force and violence, sheepherders and cowboys "solved" their disputes over grazing lands by slaughtering rival livestock and murdering rival stockmen. Armed bands raided competing herds and flocks and patrolled choice areas to oust interlopers. Absence of the most elementary institutions of property law created confusion, bitterness, and destruction.[51]

These real and often bitter conflicts over public land use remained unresolved for a long time. In trying to find a solution, President Theodore Roosevelt found himself caught between the livestock industry on the one side and western farmers and homesteaders on the other. Despite attempts by his administration to force the issue and to obtain a leasing measure from Congress, none was forthcoming. A leasing proposition for the public domain was not approved until 1934.[52]

The deterioration of the public domain, evident in the latter part of the nineteenth century, continued unabated. According to the historian Roy Robbins the end of the First World War witnessed the beginning of a severe agricultural depression in the United States. This again raised the question of what to do with 160 million acres of unreserved federal lands:

> The submarginal wheat frontier came to an end. In the 'twenties, the High Plains of America presented a gloomy spectacle: abandoned homesteads everywhere; grazing lands in very poor condition, some

beyond rehabilitation; and more significant still, the big stockmen gradually extending their influence as well as their fences over the public domain.[53]

President Herbert Hoover, who favored ceding the remaining public lands to the states in which they lay, in 1929 appointed a commission to study the transfer plan and to come up with recommendations as to its implementation. A year later the Garfield Commission published its report and, not surprisingly, unanimously supported the president's proposal of turning the public domain over to the states.[54] However, there was much public criticism of the report. One commentator said that "the plan, in essence, is one of monopoly and eviction, antisocial, undemocratic." Another concluded his analysis of the report by urging congressional action: "When Congress comes to consider the commission's proposals, its duty is clear. It should shelve the report."[55]

That is what Congress did. In the 1930 congressional elections the Democrats gained control of the House, and when the bill containing the commission's proposals was introduced it was severely lacking in support. Not only did eastern congressmen oppose it, as was expected, but rather surprisingly, so did much of the West, including the powerful livestock association interests. Robbins concludes: "Thus ended the dramatic attempt to turn over to the states the remaining public domain."[56]

Nevertheless, reform on the range was essential, not to mention long overdue. Franklin Roosevelt, together with the tough-minded and staunch conservationist Harold Ickes, formulated a new deal with regard to the conservation movement in the United States. Secretary of the Interior Ickes combined the immediate and pressing needs for depression relief with conservation objectives to come up with a comprehensive natural resources program. This program included action on the public domain issue:

> Lastly, the Secretary dealt with the great unsolved problem of the remaining public domain—some 173,000,000 acres, mostly grazing lands. Scorning the Republican proposal of ceding these lands to the western states, the Secretary boldly declared that these lands should become, like the national forests, a part of the permanent national domain, with grazing use and rehabilitation governed by means of leasing. This plan would insure not only law and order, but also intelligent use and preservation of these grazing resources for years to come.[57]

The legislative result of these actions was the passage of the Taylor Grazing Act in 1934, "perhaps the greatest contribution of the New Deal administration to the history of the old public domain."[58] According to Culhane, securing the passage of this controversial legislation from a reluctant Congress was no mean feat:

> Supported by the Department of Agriculture and the president, Ickes waged one of his famous campaigns, testifying aggressively for the bill, threatening to withhold Civilian Conservation Corps . . . camps from the public domain without the bill, and finally (having dredged up a few obscure legal authorities) threatening to withdraw the whole public domain on his own authority. The Taylor Grazing Act was passed June 28, 1934, as a result of Ickes' pressure, Taylor's legislative skill, and the considerable influence of the dust storms of that year.[59]

Though the act had its shortcomings, and these became increasingly evident in the ensuing decade, nevertheless the statute firmly established the federal interest in controlling the public domain. Of this significant action, Robbins writes:

> For over forty years historians had been heralding the passing of the frontier; without a doubt the old frontier had now passed. . . . Thus ends an era. The land of opportunity—opportunity measured in terms of free land—had officially closed its doors. America had come of age.[60]

The resolution of the public domain question proved to be an intractable one, however. Political controversies during and after World War II engulfed the Grazing Service, leading ultimately to a 1946 executive reorganization. The ostensible issue during these years was one of money—i.e., grazing fees—but the underlying issue, according to Culhane, was one of control of the Grazing Service. Nevada senator Pat McCarran, chairperson of the Committee on Public Lands and champion of the Nevada grazing interests, led the attack against a federal increase in grazing fees in the 1940s. A good description of the conflict again is provided by Culhane:

> The fiscal year 1947 compromise appropriation—which slashed the Grazing Service budget to 53 percent of its 1945 level, thus reducing personnel by 66 percent, barely enough to maintain a skeleton staff— was the principle victory in McCarran's crusade to reduce the Grazing Service to dependence on range users. Local stockmen's advisory boards contributed $200,000 . . . to the 1947 appropriations of $550,000 to help pay the salaries of local graziers. Grazing Service officials were thus literally paid by the users they were supposed to regulate. Thoroughly cowed, the Grazing Service was led behind the

barn and put out of its misery; President Truman's Reorganization Plan Number 2 of 1946 consolidated the Grazing Service and the old GLO to form the Bureau of Land Management.[61]

However, the president's action occurred without specific authorizing legislation by Congress, so the new agency, the Bureau of Land Management, survived some three decades without a statutory base. From 1946 to 1976, the Bureau was essentially an organization without a mission. As was often the case with the public domain lands, the administering agency—this time the Bureau—acted as sort of a holding company awaiting clear statutory direction.

The primary reason for this is found in the residual nature of the public domain lands. The Bureau manages land that no one wanted when it was quite literally free for the taking. Even in 1930 when President Hoover and his commission proposed transferring this land to state ownership, many in the West were uninterested in acreage "on which a jack rabbit could hardly live."[62] Federal land disposal policy through the nineteenth and early twentieth centuries resulted in the existence of scattered and hard-to-manage plots; essential pieces, like watering holes, had been carved out for private control. And until very recently few interests, much less the general public, knew or cared about the public range lands. (A 1970 study commission report estimated that the public lands account for just 3 percent of all the forage consumed by livestock in the United States.)[63] Moreover, those interests that have cared about the Bureau's lands had a direct, economic stake in forestalling the creation of a strong federal range-managing agency. Philip Foss, in *Politics and Grass*, argues that western ranchers wanted the Taylor Grazing Act administered so there would be both peace on the range and a halt to overutilization of the range resource—in their interests, in other words. They would have foregone these benefits if it meant any drastic changes in grazing rights, closer regulation of use, or higher fees.[64] The Bureau thus found itself in the unenviable position of being closely identified with a single interest; it is not saying too much to state that the agency for a long time epitomized the captured agency phenomenon.[65] It found it difficult to build support for a broadly conceived range management program which might have partially neutralized the political power of the livestock industry. For instance, eastern congressmen exhibited sustained interest only in the budgetary aspects of the Bureau's program; they more or less ignored rangeland conservation. Because of this situation, for most of its thirty-year history the Bureau was not able to efficiently manage its large land holdings; rather, it negotiated. Few changes were put through over strong ranching opposition.[66]

The Bureau's "capture" by ranching interests can be more fully appreciated by comparing it to the Forest Service, an agency that most observers admit has been more successful at neutralizing constituency pressures. A number of differences exist between these two land managers. One, the Bureau has been chronically underfunded when compared with the Forest Service. Culhane documents this, as do Dana and Fairfax in their recent book on forest and range policy. The organizational result has been to make the Bureau more vulnerable to the demands of its local attentive public:

> BLM has never and will never control the land it administers the way the Forest Service does. . . . BLM has roughly one-seventh the personnel, one-third the money, and four times the land of the Forest Service. . . .Thus, BLM managers are on thin ground. They must, therefore, rely extensively on the cooperation of land-users to implement management programs.[67]

Whether budget and personnel resources are the cause or the effect of an organization's relative deprivation is difficult to determine; it is a chicken-and-egg kind of question. But in either event the practical result for the BLM has been to place it in a catch-up position vis-à-vis the Forest Service, the latter agency serving as a role model for the former. As Culhane notes, the early directors of the Grazing Service frequently were recruited from the ranks of the professional foresters of the Forest Service.[68]

A second factor making the BLM more susceptible to local grazing interests concerns management techniques. As Kaufman noted in his classic study, *The Forest Ranger*, the long-standing Forest Service policy of personnel rotation did much to guard against agency professionals "going native." Regular and routine rotation from one locale to another has had the effect of reinforcing the national perspective, as opposed to local and regional perspectives, among Forest Service employees. The BLM, however, has not followed a strict rotation policy and so agency personnel have been subjected to more pronounced local pressures than have their cohorts in the Forest Service.

A third and final reason for the Bureau's dependence on its local constituency has to do with the professional orientation of the agency and with its personnel recruitment practices. Range management, which constitutes the agency's predominant profession, is a comparatively new discipline, and it is offered in only a few colleges in the country—primarily western agricultural schools. In fact, appointment to its immediate predecessor, the Grazing Service, was for a time officially biased toward the West. From 1936 to 1946, only bona fide residents of western states for at least one year were eligible for top management positions in the Service. The Taylor Grazing Act also recommended that the Civil Service Commission consider practical range experience in hiring agency personnel. The result was that many Bureau employees were former ranchers, and many more were the sons of ranchers. Bradley and Ingram note that "Even now, the line officers of BLM are still predominantly Western natural resource professionals—26 percent of the BLM's managers are Utah State University graduates, 55 percent graduated from other Western universities."[69] In addition, the social pressures on agency employees were, as Wesley Calef suggests, in the direction of increasing Bureau dependence on the livestock interests:

> Local BLM officials are quite probably strongly affected by adverse social pressures on themselves and their families. Most BLM offices are located in small western towns whose culture and livelihood are largely oriented to the range livestock industry. Public opinion is entirely that of the ranching interests. Consequently, a district manager who strongly antagonizes the local livestock interest will soon find himself and his family largely isolated from the social life of the community. Few managers or staff members experience this social disapproval, because they rarely antagonize the rancher community.[70]

In comparing the Bureau of Land Management with the more powerful and independent Forest Service, Calef too finds that "the Bureau of Land Management administration is much looser, more flexible and more permissive."[71]

The ranchers' dominance over the BLM prevented the agency, for most of its existence, from developing new activities and new constituencies. This resulted in what Dana and Fairfax refer to as "the enduring obscurity of the Bureau of Land Management."[72] A good example of this situation was the increasing political importance of wilderness and recreation issues, which scholars claim bypassed the agency in the 1960s:

> In spite of all the public outcry and congresional attention to parks and wilderness, the management of public domain lands continued to be underfunded and essentially unattended to. Although the BLM made some progress, to be discussed below, the best index of the stature of the BLM during this period is probably to be found in the Wilderness act. The act omitted public domain lands and did not mention the Bureau. This was not the result of special pleadings or policy but simply an oversight. Four hundred and sixty-five million acres of public domain lands were simply forgotten.[73]

Given this set of political and organizational conditions one may well have predicted a dreary future for the Bureau. In recent years, however, there have been indications that the agency was making an effort at breaking away from its impoverished and subservient situation relative to range interests. In a recent article on the Bureau the authors note that during the 1950s the agency started to become increasingly "professionalized": i.e., it began to move from being a dominant-use agency, as mandated by the 1934 Taylor Grazing Act, to incorporating a multiple-use philosophy like that of the Forest Service. They state:

> . . . professional land management is dominated by a multiple-use philosophy. Thus, BLM officers desired a multiple-use mandate similar to that of the Forest Service. Such a mandate would have the same advantages for the Bureau as it had for the Forest Service, allowing the agency to moderate conflicting demands of single-use consumption-oriented clients.[74]

By the 1970s, Culhane reports that the BLM professionals had become "indistinguishable" from their Forest Service counterparts in at least one crucial respect—their strong commitment to multiple-use management and progressive conservation values.[75]

The Bureau in fact got such a mandate from Congress in 1964 when it passed the Classification and Multiple Use Act. The act, however, was only of a temporary nature and was due to expire in 1970 because Congress also passed legislation in 1964 creating the Public Land Law Review Commission. It was the task of this commission "to conduct a review of existing public land laws and regulations and recommend revisions necessary therein."[76] A large part of the commission's task, therefore, was to attempt to resolve what had been attempted several times in the past—to find a permanent political and organizational solution for the public domain.

In 1970 the commission completed its study and issued its final report, *One Third of the Nation's Land*. Many of its recommendations concerned the plight of the Bureau of Land Management and its 465 million acres. In particular it recommended against any large-scale disposal of these lands and emphasized the necessity of an organic act—a firm, statutory base—for the Bureau. In 1976 Congress acted upon these and other recommendations by passing a fifty-page statute, the Federal Land Policy and Management Act, for the Bureau. Thus, after a long, insecure and conflict-ridden existence, the agency finally became legitimized.

Over the past decade the Bureau has benefited from the change in public attitudes toward the environment as well as from changes in the national agenda. A different set of public values have come to be applied to these residual lands. Barren canyon country that offers poor grazing conditions is now praised for its scenic and wilderness qualities. Coal and oil deposits once thought uneconomic to develop are today identified as the key to our energy independence. As a result, wilderness preservation and outdoor recreation have become important components of the Bureau's multiple-use mission. In recent years the jurisdiction inherited from the General Land Office has taken on new importance, and consequently much of the agency's attention is currently given to mineral leasing and development, both on the Outer Continental Shelf and on the Bureau's own land holdings. At the same time, ranchers have lost a portion of the influence they once exercised in western politics. For the first time in its history, the Bureau has a diversified constituency that pays attention to what the agency is doing.

Since the passage of the 1976 Federal Land Policy and Management Act (FLPMA), the Bureau has successfully shifted to a multiple-use management system. This has resulted in a diversity of programs and activities which has allowed the Bureau to shift priorities in response to prevailing political winds. Throughout the late seventies, the agency placed increasing emphasis on wilderness and recreation, culminating in its Wilderness Inventory. Mandated by FLPMA, and modeled after the Forest Service's RARE programs, this study will eventually inventory 174 million acres of Bureau lands for possible inclusion in the National Wilderness System.

Under the Reagan administration, however, a dramatic shift away from wilderness and recreational use and toward increased development and production of natural resources has occurred. For instance, the largest appropriation in the agency's proposed 1982 budget, an item called "Management of Lands and Resources," called for an increase of $16.6 million for accelerated leasing of oil, gas, oil shale, and tar sands, and leases for the Outer Continental Shelf. The total budget for these activities was estimated at $117 million.[77]

The Reagan administration—and former Secretary of the Interior Watt— did more than shift priorities within the Bureau of Land Management, however. The agency has come under attack in recent years by western-based conservative interests that form an important segment of the president's constituency. The new administration has responded to these demands in a number of ways, each of which illustrates the relative lack of power, and political vulnerability, that still plague the Bureau.

The most obvious manifestation of this contemporary conservative mood is the so-called Sagebrush Rebellion. Of course it is well known that former Secretary Watt is closely associated with this movement whose principal demand is that federal lands in the West be turned over to the states in which they lay. Meeting this demand would have put, for all practical purposes, the Bureau of Land Management out of business. The following exchange during appropriations hearings between Congressman Sidney Yates and Secretary Watt made it clear that the Bureau was the principal target of the Sagebrush Rebels. Watt adds insult to injury by comparing the Bureau unfavorably to the Forest Service:

MR. YATES: Okay, tell us. What organized them [the Sagebrush Rebels]?

SECRETARY WATT: The attitudes of the Bureau of Land Management.

MR. YATES: None of the other Bureaus?

SECRETARY WATT: They are not on the cutting edge.

MR. YATES: Not the Forest Service?

SECRETARY WATT: One of our objectives will be to make the Bureau of Land Management successful in building community relationships by adopting the management techniques they use in the Forest Service.[78]

Acting Bureau Director Edward Hastey agreed that the Bureau of Land Management had become the lightning rod for the Sagebrush Rebellion: "It ended up centering pretty much on the BLM and the land we manage."[79] During the appropriations hearings, Watt offered an explanation as to why the Bureau was the primary target of the Sagebrush rebels: "there has been an attitude of distance, arrogance, and disregard for local interests."[80] Of course, the local interests to which Secretary Watt is referring are the ranchers who dominated the Bureau's activities until the passage of FLPMA in 1976. The rebellion got most of its strength from grazing interests who object to the Bureau's new policies concerning grazing fees, wildlife, native plants, and predator control. A 1981 article in *American Forests* describes this viewpoint: "Ranchers become angry and are quick to blame the 'new' BLM, which suddenly, because of the recent 'organic act' [FLPMA] legislation, has become an active management agency rather than a custodian."[81] The article also quotes a prominent Utah rancher who complains bitterly about the Bureau's scientific grazing management policies: "The BLM hires young kids straight out of college who suddenly become experts and tell seasoned ranchers how to manage the rangeland. . . . Federal employees sit around a big table and come up with a plan to manage the land you've grazed for a half-century or more."[82]

The agency's problems with ranchers were exacerbated by a 1972 ruling in a legal case, brought by the National Resources Defense Council, that accused the agency of inadequately preparing its environmental impact statements. The court handed down a decision that ordered the Bureau to prepare 144 separate impact statements on grazing. Although the Bureau fought the decision, these court-mandated impact statements have been cited by ranchers as a typical example of "useless paper work" produced by the Bureau of Land Management.[83] To some, it looked as though the Bureau was caught for a time between two extremist movements.

Although the main thrust of the Sagebrush Rebellion was to force the transfer of federal lands to state or private ownership, Watt said that he opposed massive transfers of land unless the transfer met the criterion of being in the public interest. The following exchange is from an appropriations hearing, with Representative Yates again leading the attack:

> MR YATES: Does the Sagebrush Rebellion carry with it returning any of the federal lands to the states?
>
> SECRETARY WATT: Some of the proponents of the Sagebrush Rebellion advocate that. I do not.
>
> MR. YATES: So to the extent that you have the power to do so you will not turn back any of the federal lands to the states except for the kinds of transfers of small holdings such as you described this morning?
>
> SECRETARY WATT: That is basically correct. We do not anticipate any massive land transfers. It will just be that which is done in the public and national interest.[84]

The Sagebrush Rebellion remained a potent political force through 1980, but since then it has lost much of its momentum. There are two reasons for this. The first concerns the election of Ronald Reagan. Recent studies of the rebellion indicate that federal control per se was not the critical issue. Rather, it was the new management policies of the BLM; these were the natural result of the FLPMA mandate, which broadened the mission of the BLM and transformed it into a multiple-use agency. Thus environmental factors—and environmental constituencies—became more important to the agency while ranchers experienced a proportional decrease in their traditional influence over the agency. The Carter administration encouraged this shift in mission. Hence, the problem as perceived by Sagebrush rebels was that the federal government no longer supported their concept of land use. A recent study concluded that: "The Sagebrush Rebellion is better understood as a conflict in values rather than a sectional conflict . . . the issue is not federal ownership per se but how and for what purposes the lands are to be managed."[85] With the election of Ronald Reagan the federal government shifted back to a pro-development approach, thereby satisfying the rebellion's principal demand.

The president's interest in placating the rebels became apparent with the appointment of James Watt as secretary of the interior. Watt was a long-standing proponent of the rebellion, and as an attorney for the Mountain States Legal Foundation he had fought the federal government—especially the BLM—in an effort to increase development on federal lands. As he said: "I took them to court and whipped the BLM in the 10th Circuit."[86] Although Watt was forced out of office in October of 1983, William Clark is expected to continue many of Watt's pro-development policies, albeit in a low-profile manner.

Secretary Watt was not the only ally whom ranchers have had in the

Interior Department, however. The present director of the Bureau of Land Management, Robert Burford, is a prominent Colorado rancher and an acknowledged leader of the Sagebrush Rebellion. He has for several years vociferously opposed the policies of the agency he is now directing. This is another example of the agency's vulnerability. Burford is both a political appointee and, until his appointment, held a grazing permit from the bureau.[87]

The second reason why the Sagebrush Rebellion has lost much of its steam concerns the impact that privatization would have on grazing fees. Many of the Sagebrush rebels promoted state control only as an intermediate step; their ultimate goal was to transfer land ownership to private ranchers, thus giving the rancher direct, legal control over the lands he grazed. But as talk of privatization became more common, fears developed that grazing lands would be bought for speculative purposes, or to generate profits from grazing fees which would be priced at market value. Ranchers soon realized they might be better off with a benign BLM, which has always charged less than market value for grazing fees, and even less than does the Forest Service. Ultimately the possibility that grazing lands would be bought by private entrepreneurs and managed for maximum profit contributed to the demise of the Sagebrush movement. So by 1981 the Sagebrush rebels were no longer a force confronting Washington—they were *in* Washington.

The Reagan administration's priorities can be clearly seen in the component parts of the agency's proposed FY 1982 budget. Under the "Management of Lands and Resources" item, the Reagan budget called for a $2 million increase (and thirty new positions) to accelerate OCS oil and gas leasing, coupled with a $10 million reduction in OCS environmental studies. Thus, more offshore leases would be granted but much less research would be done on the environmental impacts of these leases.[88]

Similar objectives are being pursued in regard to onshore oil and gas leasing, with an increase of $1.5 million to cover the costs of intensified leasing and exploration efforts, and a concomitant reduction in the intensity of data collection related to resource considerations in the preparation of the environmental statement. This accelerated leasing activity represented a marked increase over the previous year when a moratorium was placed on oil and gas leasing because of alleged widespread fraud and abuses in the program.[89] At that time the responsibility for managing the leasing program was shared by the Bureau of Land Management and the Geological Survey. According to the latter agency, the Bureau has been unable to maintain accurate records and, as a result, revenue from the program has been lost. The Bureau of Land Management denied these charges.[90]

In Reagan's proposed FY 1982 budget the funding for the coal leasing program was reduced but the projected number of leases was expected to rise sharply.[91] The rangeland management program was also cut, although its workload was held constant. Part of this reduction was due to a $1.6 million decrease in funds for preparing the court-ordered environmental impact statements for the Bureau's grazing programs. This of course poses a difficult problem for the agency, since the court order contains a specific deadline for completion.[92] Monies for the agency's dam safety program were also cut, despite the fact that "Serious problems are known to exist in several major structures."[93]

The planning program was substantially reduced by nearly $1.5 million. According to the agency, planning is necessary in order to "insure that we don't have a serious impact on vegetation, soils, and cultural resources. We need to find out what is there so when we do cause an impact we know what we are impacting; or if we do find something we decide should not be impacted, at least we know what we are doing."[94] Such inventories are primarily a response to increased concern for environmental factors; hence, it comes as no surprise that the Reagan administration cut expenditures for inventories in all resource programs. During appropriations hearings for FY 1982 Congressperson Yates succinctly described the Reagan philosophy with regard to inventories:

> Under this proposal you are reducing the intensity of resource inventory into oil shale, you are reducing the level of inventories in grazing, you are reducing the level of intensity for inventory in natural cultural resources, you are reducing or actually you are deferring all inventories for recreation resources . . . and you are also reducing the level of intensity for inventories under wildlife.[95]

The de-emphasis on planning, data collection, inventories, and EIS preparation was part of a push to reduce what Secretary Watt called "paralysis by analysis." Conversely, increases in funding for leasing programs were designed to accelerate those approvals with a minimum of interference from studies and regulations. He said: "We have studied too many things too long. We need to make American move."[96] The catchword used throughout the 1982 Reagan budget was *streamlining*, which was frequently given as the explanation for such reductions. Some of these proposed deductions were quite large: The recreation and wilderness management program was cut by 29 percent. This constituted a reduction of $7.12 million, of which $7.10 million was justified as streamlining.[97]

The Bureau of Land Management's Wilderness Inventory was still another target of the Reagan budget-cutters in 1982. They called not only for funding reductions but for a decrease of four hundred permanent positions, almost all of which were related to the Bureau's recreation or wilderness programs.[98] This cut resulted in a reduction in wilderness studies, reduced staffing of the Bureau's 357 million acres used for recreation, and, in some cases, in an absence of law enforcement protection on these federal lands. An agency spokesperson said bluntly: "As far as visitor protection is concerned, that is something that most visitors are going to have to take on at their own risk."[99]

The 1982 budget was an important precedent, not only because it was Reagan's first budget, but because Congress acquiesced to most of the president's proposals. The final 1982 budget for the BLM was about the same as the previous year's appropriation because the increases for resource extraction offset the reductions in environmental protection and related functions.

The Reagan budget proposals for FY 1983 and 1984 continued to stress the priorities outlined in 1982. Increases were requested for leasing activities but these programs became mired in a number of political controversies. First, the plan to lease the entire Outer Continental Shelf (OCS) lands for oil drilling was opposed by legislation that banned drilling in sensitive areas off the coasts of New England, Florida, and California. Congress, in spite of heavy administration opposition, has voted during the last three years to exempt these areas from the lease sale.

A second area where the Reagan administraion's leasing program has met political resistance concerns the coal leasing program. Secretary Watt planned to dramatically increase coal leases, but Congress placed a ban on the lease sales until after an ad hoc coal commission investigated the lease; a report by the General Accounting Office had concluded that the Watt leasing schedule lost $100 million in revenues.[100]

A third area of controversy over BLM leasing involved the agency's Wilderness Study Areas (WSAs). The Bureau intended to study 24 million acres of land selected for possible inclusion in the National Wilderness Preservation System. Secretary Watt had planned to open that land to mineral and oil development, but after an intense battle with Congress Watt announced a temporary ban on leasing in the potential wilderness areas.[101]

Another heated controversy that involved BLM lands was the Reagan proposal to sell 35 million acres of "excess" public lands. The proposal was short-lived, but it created a noisy political furor that caused at least a few BLM people to wonder what the future held for the agency.

By 1984 the BLM could best be described as in a state of flux. Not only had the agency been the object of three years of intense combat over public land issues, but a 1984 reorganization actually halved the agency's budget and removed some important functions. By secretarial order the BLM's offshore oil leasing responsibilities as well as some onshore receipt-collection duties were transferred to the Minerals Management Service, which just recently became independent of its parent agency, the Geological Survey.[102] The BLM leasing program has been the subject of extensive criticism in recent years, with the U.S. Geological Survey being one of its more vocal critics. The loss of these important functions has reduced the agency's role in energy development—the first priority of the Reagan administration. It also reduced the agency's budget from $1.2 billion to $539 million. However, most of this reduction was due to the loss of lease receipts and so did not result in an appreciable loss of personnel.

At present the Bureau of Land Management is experiencing a host of cross pressures and continued conflict. A brief listing of potential problem areas affecting the agency would include:

Coal. The Commission on Fair Market Value Policy for Federal Coal Leasing recently issued a report highly critical of James Watt's coal leasing policies. In response to the report, and continued public criticism, Secretary Clark may back away from Watt's program.[103]

Tarsands and Oil Shale. The BLM has a prototype program involving leases in Colorado and Utah, but activity in these areas may be stalled by the recent drop in oil prices and reduced demand.

Grazing. The 1972 lawsuit by the Natural Resources Defense Council forced the BLM to write extensive EISs for each of its grazing activities and the council has gone back to court, claiming some of the EISs are inadequate. A BLM spokesman stated that "we are not doing the voluminous EISs we once did," but that the statements were "receiving highest priority" and were on schedule.[104]

Management Problems. A recent probe by the Interior Department discovered problems with the onshore oil and gas leasing program; at least 196 tracts were offered illegally. This report follows other accusations that the BLM mismanaged offshore leases.[105]

The Watt Controversy. James Watt's policies created considerable controversy and exposed the BLM to intense political cross pressures. Although Mr. Watt resigned, his policies will continue to be pursued by remaining political appointees, such as BLM's Robert Burford. Hence, the controversy over BLM policy will undoubtedly continue.[106]

Wilderness. Congress banned oil and gas exploration in wilderness study areas with a rider to the FY 1984 appropriations bill. The Reagan administration has actually increased funding for wilderness review in an attempt to speed up the selection process, which would open to development all WSA lands not chosen as wilderness. This promises to be a contentious issue.[107]

Clearly the BLM faces an uncertain future. Perhaps more than any other agency the BLM has undergone rapid changes to its mission and its priorities; it has been the agency most affected by the Reagan-Watt

policies. The agency was unable to solidify support from its new constituencies resulting from FLPMA before the policy shifts of the 1980s
altered the agency's direction. Also, recent accusations of mismanagement
have damaged public perceptions of agency expertise. And last, the
creation of the Minerals Management Service and the loss of important
functions have again narrowed the agency's mission and created yet
another bureaucratic competitor.

To summarize, a lot has happened to the Bureau of Land Management in the space of eight years. On the one hand, the Bureau's broadened
mission, as defined by its 1976 organic act, has created a more diversified
constituency and a greater range of activities for the agency; at last, it
seemed, the Bureau escaped from the ranchers' capture. But has it? The
agency still has a long way to go before one could consider it to be a
powerful and autonomous agency. Recent challenges, such as those just
discussed, make it quite evident that the Bureau remains vulnerable to
those who oppose its broadened mission, and it is as yet unable to react
as forcefully or as quickly to changes in its environment as, say, the
Forest Service has been able to. The budget and personnel data analyzed in
chapter 5 will show that neither the environmental movement nor the
initial concern about energy shortages produced significant increases in
these indicators of agency strength. The Bureau was favored under Jimmy
Carter, but this has not been the case, so far, under Ronald Reagan.
Indeed, it appears as though the Bureau were targeted for elimination. If
it is to emerge as a countervailing power to the various interests now
descending on the public domain, the agency will need a considerable
boost in the basic agency resources of manpower, money, and expertise.
To date, the agency's potential remains woefully underutilized and its
future is in doubt.

SUMMARY: MISSIONS ACCOMPLISHED AND INTERRUPTED

To a greater extent than the five other agencies discussed in this study,
the Bureau of Reclamation and the Bureau of Land Management have
had what might be termed a variegated history. That is, their development
is characterized by more ups and downs than is typically the case. They
neither display the steady, impressive growth that sets the Corps and
the Forest Service apart, nor do they move along at the slower but
steady pace of the other three agencies. Unpredictability and uncertainty
are almost built into the character of these organizations.

In the case of the Bureau of Reclamation the agency got off to an
impressive start, but just a decade later it ran into financial difficulties.
These problems were eventually ameliorated, and so the Bureau made a
comeback during the FDR era; many of its most impressive accomplishments date from the 1930s and 1940s. But this zenith was again followed
by a sustained period of organizational decline that began about 1950

and continued until recently. The agency is currently enjoying considerable support from the Reagan administration—unlike the other agency discussed in this chapter—but that support could change should a change occur in the White House. One also might have thought that the energy crisis of the 1970s would have breathed new life into the agency, but the data indicate that the Bureau did not appreciably benefit from this crisis; it remains an agency with an uncertain future.

The conditions that appear to have most constrained the agency's growth are these: From the outset, the Bureau was geographically limited to working in only the seventeen westernmost states of the nation. In other words, it has been a decidedly regional agency. This constraint was exacerbated by the existence of another federal agency, the Corps, which was not so delimited. Thus the Corps could literally build support for its activities throughout the country; it could challenge, often successfully, the Bureau even on its own turf.

Furthermore, as a former Interior secretary pointed out, the Bureau had to act under a set of legislative directives far more stringent than those under which the Corps operated. Monetary payments by beneficiaries of Bureau projects were unable to keep the agency solvent over the long term; and even after Congress liberalized the sources of money going into the reclamation fund, it never entirely let go of the idea that the Bureau should work with earmarked monies. In contrast, Corps projects were never so conceived. As time went on, the competition between the two ater developers became increasingly uneven: as the Corps's fortunes snowballed, the Bureau's diminished.

Unlike the Bureau of Reclamation, the Bureau of Land Management did not get off to a fast start. It came into existence through a 1946 executive order, but its creation was not quickly followed by congressional action. Thus for some thirty years the agency was forced to act as a sort of holding company until the federal government could decide what it wanted to do with the enormous public landholdings under the Bureau's jurisdiction.

Once Congress passed an organic act for the Bureau, however, it embarked on what appeared to be an impressive take-off stage of development; by 1976 the future looked bright indeed. Moreover, the agency fared very well under Carter. The president appointed an intelligent individual with a strong pro-conservation record to head the agency during these critical, agency-building years. Both the president and Bureau's director, Frank Gregg, were committed to transforming the agency from being a single-use, rancher-dominated organization into a multiple-use, professionalized one. The bureaucratic model used to effect these changes was that of the U.S. Forest Service, and the Carter-Gregg alliance even bore some resemblance to that of Teddy Roosevelt and Gifford Pinchot—the happy alliance that gave the Forest Service its strong start some seventy years earlier. As the data presented in chapter 5 show, the Bureau's budget increased substantially between 1976 and 1980, an indication that the agency was on the move.

During the 1970s, the Bureau not only benefited from this presidential interest in its mission but from changing public values and concerns. As we discussed previously, what were once thought of as utterly useless, unproductive lands now promised to contain both material and spiritual wealth for a nation concerned about resource depletion. For example, one of the Carter administration's primary solutions to solving the energy crisis was switching from expensive imported oil to abundant, domestically produced coal. Bureau lands were a virtual treasure trove for that particular resource. They contained not only valuable energy resources, however; the rugged, "god-forsaken" character of much of this land began to be valued for precisely those features that earlier were viewed as its drawbacks. The result was that the hundreds of millions of acres under Bureau management became the focal point of competition for control over them.

But the agency's takeoff was barely begun when a new president, with a quite different ideology, entered the picture. Ronald Reagan, together with Secretary Watt, and a new Bureau director, Robert Burford, halted the agency's takeoff in midair. These policymakers were sympathetic to the so-called Sagebrush Rebellion and therefore considerably less interested than their predecessors were in creating a strong and autonomous Bureau of Land Management. Expectations that the Bureau would develop into another Forest Service, therefore, have been disappointed by recent changes in the political environment, and the agency's future, as so often the case in the past, is once again up for grabs.

A Cross Validation of
Agency Power: Budget,
Personnel, and Status Rankings

Our research into the histories of seven resource agencies should go a long way toward accounting for the observable differences among federal bureaucracies in the ways each uses its power and influence in the political process. In this chapter we are interested in broadening the historical analysis of agency power by examining other indicators of organizational strength. We do so because the statistical and attitudinal data presented here are not only intrinsically interesting but also because these measures provide an important check on the interpretations drawn from the historical records of each agency. In this endeavor we follow the methodological advice of the authors of *Unobtrusive Measures*, who argue for cross validation of this type:

> No research method is without bias. Interviews and questionnaires must be supplemented by methods testing the same social science variables but having *different* methodological weaknesses. . . . The issue is not choosing among individual methods. Rather, it is the necessity for a multiple operationism, a collection of methods combined to avoid sharing the same weaknesses.[1]

Two of the most frequently compared categories across organizations are budgets and personnel. From the relative size of an agency's budget and work force inferences can be drawn about the organization's power. The Corps of Engineers, for example, with its annual budget of over $3 billion and a work force approaching 30,000 engaged in civil works planning and construction is far ahead of the other six agencies in this study. Moreover, budgets and personnel are not just indicators of strength but are themselves among the most valuable resources upon which an agency can draw to further enhance its position. Thus they are both cause and effect of an agency's power.

A third indicator has to do with an organization's reputation. To answer the question, How does one know who is powerful and who is not?, one uses the simple method of asking people. This is what we have done. Agencies, like people, have reputations for power and influence. So in order to complement the historical research and the budget and personnel statistics, we personally interviewed policymaking staff in each of the seven agencies in our sample. They were asked to rank six agencies (excluding their own) according to four variables.[2] These findings, as will be shown, strongly reinforced the conclusions obtained from the other data. These four essentially independent sources of information thus allow us to draw some rigorously tested generalizations concerning agency power differentials. Before reviewing those generalizations, however, the three variables of budget, personnel, and perceptions will be briefly analyzed and discussed.

AGENCY BUDGETS

Budgets are an extremely useful source of information, as Wildavsky and others have shown. The data are relatively accessible and they provide a standard unit of comparison. Budget data do have their limitations, however, so they should be used in conjunction with other methods of measurement and/or other kinds of information.

The principal limitation of budget data is that they do not, by themselves, explain anything. Their interpretation depends on a familiarity with the political, social, and economic contexts in which budgets are made. For example, figure 5-1 displays the total annual budget appropriations of our seven agencies for the years 1950-80. One might make much of the fact that each agency's budget is absolutely larger in 1980 than it was in 1950. But this observation is less impressive when one considers the rate of inflation over this period. Taking into account inflation means that agencies, like the rest of us, have to have more money just to stay even. A statement by an official of the Fish and Wildlife Service in 1973 illustrates the point:

> Using 1967 as a base, the fund level of available monies to the Bureau has actually decreased. You will also notice the committee has been most generous in the last several years in increasing the appropriations but with the degree of inflation . . .[3]

In interpreting budgets one must also be sensitive to the impoundment issue. Our budget data are for annual budget authority (BA), which is what Congress authorizes the agency to spend in a given fiscal year. However, certain presidential administrations have had their own opinions about agency expenditures, so a frequent practice by the Office of Management and Budget has been to restrict or impound an agency's appropriation. This practice reached its extreme during the Nixon years, and in 1974 a statement by a Corps of Engineers official shows the potential for misinterpretation of raw budget figures.

The total amount we are requesting for fiscal year 1974 for civil works is $1,479,000,000. This compares with an appropriation last year including supplementals of slightly over $1.85 million. However, linked with the budget request for new funds is a decision by the administration that $116 million of our fiscal year 1973 appropriation wil be carried over unobligated for use in fiscal year 1974. The effect of this is to balance off the two fiscal years at close to the same level.[4]

With considerations such as these in mind, our budget data for the seven natural resources agencies in this study yield some interesting comparisons. Figures 5-1 and 5-2 show funding levels for each agency over a thirty-year time span. One almost obvious interpretation is that the Corps of Engineers and the Forest Service are in a class by themselves. Budgets for both agencies have grown faster than any of the other five agencies in this study; these five all cluster more or less at the bottom of the graph. In 1980, the Corps in fact goes off the top end of the graph with a budget authority of over $3 billion.

The Corps and the Forest Service thus possess the budgetary characteristics of powerful agencies: From relatively modest bases in 1950, both agencies have shown remarkable growth, leading to absolute annual appropriations significantly higher than any of the other agencies. Their budgetary growth suggests the ability, previously discussed, to expand into new areas of activity without sacrificing their traditional functions. Both have been able to maintain congressional and/or executive approval for their programs and have been monetarily rewarded for providing such services.

In contrast, the Bureau of Reclamation, Soil Conservation Service, National Park Service, Bureau of Land Management, and Fish and Wildlife Service all demonstrate lower levels of funding and usually incremental annual increases. There is displayed a gradual widening of the gap between rich and not-so-rich agencies. Figure 5-2, which shows only the years 1950 and 1980, illustrates this more forcefully. For example, the budgetary woes of the National Park Service during this period are amply documented.[5] Although national park visitation rose dramatically during the 1950s and 1960s, and while the number of national parks was also augmented, the Service failed to achieve a commensurate increase in funding for operations and park management.[6] This forced it into deficit spending in 1969.[7] The director of the agency went to the extreme of threatening Congress that he would close down the parks if it didn't respond more generously to the Service's impoverishment, which in 1970 Congress did.[8] But this generosity did not last long.

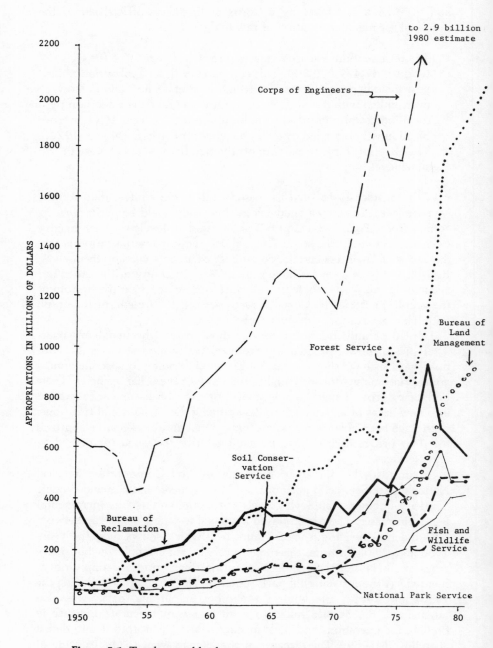

Figure 5-1. Total annual budget appropriations of seven agencies for the years 1950-1980. *Source:* Office of Management and Budget.

Also evident in these figures is the Bureau of Reclamation's decline from a position of relative strength. The Bureau's competition with the Corps, which is discussed in the histories of the two agencies, is seen in figures 5-1 and 5-2, where a "mere" $250 million separate them in 1950, but where a whopping $2.3 billion is testimony to the Corps' increasing monopoly on water resources development and related activities. The Bureau in this critical time period failed to broaden its activities while the Corps successfully assumed responsibility for an increasing diversity of operations.

To a somewhat lesser extent, the Park Service and the Fish and Wildlife Service have also suffered from competing with the formidable strength of the Forest Service in a number of overlapping program areas. The Bureau of Land Management has been successful in recent years to the extent that it has imitated the Forest Service. But that behavior, as we show in chapter 4, had its costs as well. Fenno's research, as does ours, corroborates the finding that powerful agencies marshal their resources in a cumulative manner and often at the expense of their less powerful rivals.[9] Defining agency power as the ability to get Congress to appropriate what the agency requested, Fenno found the Forest Service to have strong committee support, while the Park Service, Fish and Wildlife Service, Bureau of Land Management, and the Bureau of Reclamation were characterized by weak committee support.[10] Fenno's study was for a time period of fifteen years—from 1947 to 1962. One can infer from the budget data displayed in figures 5-1 and 5-2 that this situation has not changed a great deal since 1962.

Figures 5-1 and 5-2 thus provide an illustration of the total expenditures for the seven agencies and how they have increased or decreased over time. We can extend our understanding of these budgets by taking a closer look at how they change over time. A number of methods have been developed in the public policy literature which examine budgetary change in terms of percentage increase or decrease.[11] These measures are appropriate for examining the rate of change occurring in a particular agency's budget, but they are less useful for a comparative study, such as this one, because percentages do not take into account absolute differences. For example, both the Corps of Engineers and the Soil Conservation Service have experienced a mean annual budget increase over the last thirty years of about 7.5 percent. This is an interesting comparison, but it must be kept in mind that the Corps' budget is so much larger than the Soil Conservation Service's budget that a 7.5 percent rate of increase for one is not the same as a 7.5 percent increase for the other. Thus we argue that for comparative purposes relative changes in agency budgets are best explained in terms of absolute amounts, since these provide a clearer picture of what each agency has to work with.

Table 5-1 provides the mean annual change in appropriations for

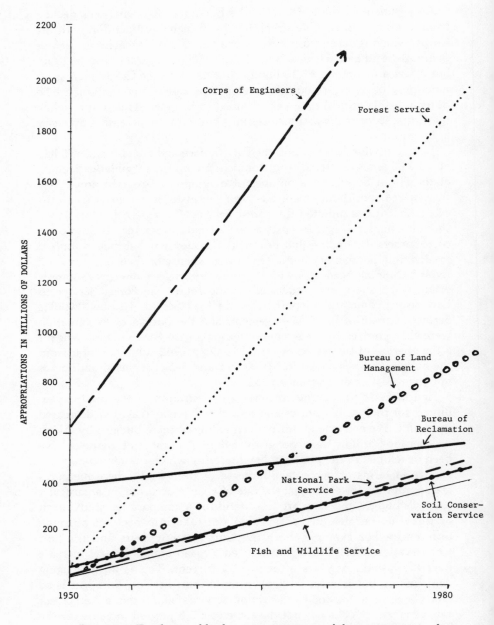

Figure 5-2. Total annual budget appropriations of the seven agencies for 1950 and 1980. *Source:* Office of Management and Budget.

each of the seven agencies. The data are divided into three columns. The first column gives the mean annual increases only and indicates the number of years (out of a total of 33) that the agency experienced an increase in funding. The second column is concerned only with decreases, while the third column totals all 33 years to arrive at the mean annual change in appropriations from 1951 to 1983 (appropriations for 1983 are estimates).

Table 5-1   Mean Annual Change in Approppriations, 1951-83
in THOUSANDS OF DOLLARS

Agency	Increase	Decrease	Total
Corps of Engineers	159,603 (N=20)	64,573 (N=13)	71,291
Forest Service	102,260 (N=24)	68,957 (N=9)	55,564
Bureau of Land Management	42,532 (N=29)	21,106 (N=4)	34,818
National Park Service	74,332 (N=18)	59,998 (N=15)	13,272
Bureau of Reclamation	60,976 (N=21)	39,216 (N=12)	24,543
Soil Conservation Service	27,338 (N=25)	27,476 (N=8)	14,050
Fish & Wildlife Service	20,422 (N=25)	9,132 (N=8)	13,257

Source: U.S. Budget, 1952-84.

A number of observations can be made regarding the data displayed in Table 5-1. The Bureau of Reclamation has sustained budget reductions in 15 of the last 33 years. These reductions average about $60 million. The two agencies with the largest budgets, the Corps and the Forest Service, also have received substantial average cuts, but they, unlike the Bureau of Reclamation, have compensated for these reductions by substantial increases in other years. Still, the Bureau has not been totally deprived of significant increases, for it ranks a distant third—behind the Corps and Forest Service—in terms of increases. The data indicate that the Bureau of Reclamation has experienced a rather capricious budgetary history that parallels its organizational history as discussed in chapter 4.

Some of the Bureau's funding fluctuations can be traced to the organizational difficulties that the Bureau of Reclamation has had to endure. However, since both the Bureau and the Corps of Engineers have been subjected to a larger number of decreases than the other agencies in this study, one could also conclude that water resources development as a program area has been the object of a greater deal of capriciousness on the part of the purse holders than is the case with other program areas. The Corps has survived these vagaries quite well, however, while the

Bureau has not; and as a result, the latter agency has experienced a very low mean annual budget growth. Only the budget of the Fish and Wildlife Service has averaged a lower annual growth.

The budget of the Bureau of Land Management also presents an interesting case. Prior to 1976, the year in which the Bureau's organic act was passed, the agency had a mean annual budget growth of only $15.4 milion. But after Congress passed the Federal Land Policy and Management Act the Bureau's budget increased dramatically. Also the agency has managed to escape a large number of annual budget decreases, sustaining in fact only four negative growth years since 1951.

In sum, a principal message of table 5-1 is that the Corps of Engineers and the Forest Service have experienced high levels of budgetary growth *despite* significant losses during negative growth years. The overall growth of their budgetary bases is impressive. The bureaus of Reclamation and Land Management present a different picture. These two agencies have experienced greater fluctuation and hence greater inconsistency in their fiscal development. It becomes difficult, therefore, to predict their future funding situations. Both agencies have experienced success but it has been generally short-lived. Finally, a third pattern emerges with the National Park Service, the Soil Conservation Service, and the Fish and Wildlife Service, three agencies that demonstrated relatively unremarkable annual budgetary growth. The budget for the Park Service shows a cyclical funding pattern, but overall it has grown at a rate only half that of its major competitor, the Forest Service. The Soil Conservation Service and the Fish and Wildlife Service, the tortoises of the pack, creep slowly but steadily along.

Finally, we wish to look at and analyze the budgetary fortunes of these seven agencies during the decade of the 1970s and through the first two years of the Reagan administration. During the last decade, and continuing to the present, several issues came to the forefront of public attention which related directly to natural resources policy and which presumably then had an impact on these seven resource managers. First, the country witnessed the environmental crisis. Shortly thereafter, i.e., about 1973 or 1974, the nation was confronted with the energy crisis, which continued through the Carter administration and was a major preoccupation of the president's. By 1980 these issues had culminated and coalesced into a generalized public concern over shortages of all kinds, with the 1980 presidential election largely being fought over who, Carter or Reagan, could better deliver on bringing economy and frugality to the nation's capitol and to its governmental structure.

What impact did this substantial public concern over environmental crises and energy shortages, and the concomitant 1980 changing of the guard, have on the agencies herein analyzed? First of all, the data support the thesis that the rich get richer and, by comparison, the poor stay poor. For example, neither the Corps nor the Forest Service was much affected by the changes in public attitudes toward environmental issues. One might have suspected that pro-development agencies such as the Corps and the Forest Service would have been materially hurt by the environmental quality issue, and conversely that those agencies with a clearer preservationist orientation, like the Park Service and the Fish and Wildlife Service, would have been rewarded. This seems not to be the case. Long-term trends in agency budgets predominated over what Anthony Downs has described as relatively short-term "issue-attention cycles."[12] To some extent, all seven resource agencies benefited from increased public attention to these issues, but those benefiting the most turn out to be the two agencies in the best position to capitalize on both the environmental and energy crises. Those agencies, the Corps and the Forest Service, happened to be the two organizations whose histories show a marked ability to incorporate new missions and new programs into their repertoire. The agencies faring less well were those that saw "nothing new" in the National Environmental Policy Act of 1969, or that resisted it, or that were in a precarious position to begin with. A point that we will return to in the conclusion of this study is the observation that the fortunes of agencies, as measured by the size of their budgets, has more to do with what Matthew Holden described as an organization's "disposition" than it has to do with the nature of the agency's mission.[13] Preservation-oriented agencies do not, in other words, automatically or necessarily benefit from an era of environmental awareness; this is especially true when the era is immediately followed by an energy crisis that would logically have an opposite effect on the agencies.

The decade of environmentalism was followed by the age of Reaganomics, and with it came unprecedented presidential attempts at budget cutting. Budget data for this period are presented in table 5-2. The table compares presidential requests and congressional appropriations for the fiscal years 1981 to 1984. It should be noted that the presidential requests for both 1981 and 1982 are the former Carter administration's figures; the 1983 and 1984 requests come from the Reagan administration. It was not possible to derive a Reagan request for 1982 because, upon his election, the Carter requests went through a complicated series of revisions at the hands of the new administration. No exact figures were readily available. However, since the Congress largely accepted the Reagan proposed changes in the Carter budget requests during the transition year, it is the "congressional appropriation" for fiscal year 1982 that fairly accurately reflects Reaganomics during the transition year.

A comparison of the 1981 and 1982 appropriations shows that Reagan succeeded in reducing the budgets of the seven agencies by an average of 2.26 percent. This is not an impressive amount. But what must be

Table 5-2 Presidential Requests and Congressional Appropriations, 1981-84
in THOUSANDS OF DOLLARS

Agency	1981		1982			1983	1984
	Req	App	Req	App	Req	App*	Req
Corps of Engineers	2,991,764	3,073,597	3,340,500	2,970,052	2,197,000	2,958,188	2,315,108
Forest Service	2,028,279	2,141,866	2,206,201	1,887,066	1,985,607	1,904,715	1,684,972
Bureau of Land Management	996,795	1,034,346	1,099,074	1,239,476	1,255,630	1,162,421	584,177
National Park Service	809,452	788,180	906,713	773,205	936,520	810,922	974,910
Bureau of Reclamation	518,900	868,959	562,395	801,192	734,578	885,576	737,525
Soil Conservation Service	535,247	588,233	566,354	577,044	515,816	518,330	474,406
Fish & Wildlife Service	445,684	424,225	459,904	438,253	412,353	465,194	472,382

*Estimate.

kept in mind is that the administration's cuts were made according to functional categories and not along agency lines. This is to say, as we discussed in chapters 2, 3, and 4, that pro-development programs were increased and nondevelopmental functions (or what were seen as anti-development programs) were decreased, regardless of agency. The point is that in order to appreciate the current administration's impact on agency budgets one must disaggregate the data; using *agency* as the standard unit of comparison is no longer sufficient by itself.

The 1983 appropriation figures are only preliminary estimates, but they nevertheless reveal a significant change in congressional support for the president from the previous year. In 1982 President Reagan's budget proposals were accepted over Carter's without major revision. In 1983, however, the president's honeymoon was over and so his influence over Congress had likewise eroded; as a result appropriations differ substantially in some cases from the presidential request. This is most evident in the budget for the Corps of Engineers, which Reagan proposed to cut by a phenomenal 26.8 percent. However, Congress refused to accept such a cut and increased the president's proposal by 36.2 percent, thereby allowing the Corps to maintain a "status quo" budget. Working in the opposite direction, congressional budget-makers decreased the president's proposal for the Bureau of Reclamation by 13.4 percent.

Overall, the Reagan administration has implemented only marginal reductions in the budgets of the seven agencies. However, we emphasize again that much of the budgetary action under the Reagan administration has taken place *within* the agency budgets; significant decreases in some program areas were offset by increases in economic development functions. As the Conservation Foundation recently observed, budget figures for the Reagan administration "reflect the administration's emphasis on development of natural resources and deemphasis on resource planning and environmental protection."[14]

The 1984 budget will undoubtedly reflect the changes in Congress produced by the 1982 midterm elections in which a number of pro-environment legislators were sent to Washington. As a result, there may develop an even more pronounced difference between requests and appropriations in 1984 than was the case in 1983.

AGENCY WORK FORCES

An indicator similar to agency budgets is total number of personnel. Figure 5-3 displays statistics on the approximate size of the work force for each of the seven agencies. Figure 5-3 shows the total number of permanent positions allotted to each agency from 1950 to 1980 in five-year intervals. Once again, as shown in figure 5-3, the Corps and the Forest Service exhibit substantial growth in their work forces. The Corps moves from second to first place, and the Forest Service moves from third to second. The National Park Service, Bureau of Land Management, Soil Conservation Service, and the Fish and Wildlife Service increase more slowly. The Bureau of Reclamation's decline starting around 1950 when it had the largest work force of the seven agencies is also evident in these statistics.

With the average salary for federal employees increasing about 118 percent from 1950 to 1976,[15] even a modest increase in personnel requires a prodigious growth in an agency's budget. In this light the rapid growth of the Forest Service and the Corps is even more impressive than it appears in the figures. It indicates an unusual ability to acquire new positions necessary for expanding and diversifying agency operations even during a period when inflation and salary increases were neutralizing much of the organization's real, or noninflationary, growth.

In terms of personnel, by 1980 the Corps and the Forest Service are two and three times larger than their cohorts. This suggests that these agencies are far better off than the smaller agencies in terms of slack resources; with work forces of 25,000 to 30,000, organizational flexibility is certainly more assured than when an agency's work force is stretched to the limit. The plight of the Fish and Wildlife Service during the late 1960s and early 1970s comes to mind in this regard. Numerous new responsibilities of coordination, enforcement, and research were thrust upon an agency unequipped to handle the great increase in workload. Consequently, traditional programs suffered and the agency was criticized, as it had been in the past, for not doing its job. The Park Service and the Bureau of Land Management have also been in a similar budgetary

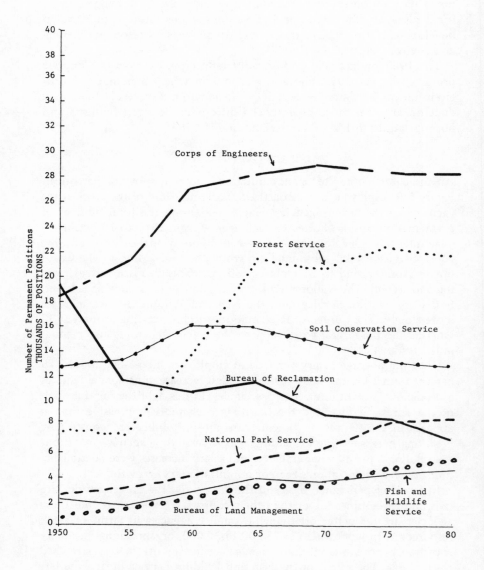

Figure 5-3. Total number of permanent positions in seven agencies for the years 1950-1980, in five-year intervals. *Source:* Office of Management and Budget.

and personnel bind, with some Park Service employees feeling that they must be the lowest-paid employees of the federal government. The Bureau of Land Management, with its now-valuable energy resources, is also stretched very thin given only modest increases in its work force and budget.

Some retrenchment in personnel occurred during the Carter years, but hiring freezes and RIFs (reductions in force) gained momentum under the current Republican regime. It has been estimated that in just one year in office Reagan reduced the size of the federal work force by more than 30,000 positions, and that the president's 1983 fiscal year budget envisioned eliminating tens of thousands of additional jobs.[16]

This policy has of course put additional constraints on agency activity, but it hits hardest those already stretched very thin. The more influential agencies, however, like the Corps of Engineers, have found means to lessen the impact of personnel reductions, primarily through a stepped-up practice of "contracting out." According to recent Appropriations Committee hearings, rather than have the work done in-house, by agency employees, the Corps has increased its use of outside consultants to keep abreast of its sizeable workload. The Soil Conservation Service has also liberally used this practice to get around hiring freezes. The practice has encountered considerable criticism both within Congress and from groups hostile to an agency's programs; nevertheless it is another indication of the degree to which congressionally backed bureaus manage to obviate even clearly articulated presidential directives.

PERCEPTIONS ABOUT AGENCY POWER

Finally, how do bureaucrats view each other? Are the perceptions of agency personnel in these seven organizations consistent with the findings presented above? Despite—or perhaps because of—some intense interagency rivalry, do they see a hierarchical pattern of agency power?

The answer to the above questions is yes. In order to cross-check our historical research and the budgetary and personnel data, we interviewed agency personnel in each of the seven agencies. The sample ($N=20$) consisted of mid- to upper-level officials working in the agencies' Washington offices, and whose positions were associated with policy analysis and/or environmental programs. Each respondent was asked, among other things, to rank six agencies (excluding his or her own) on four variables. The variables were: (1) the agency's relative power within the executive branch; (2) the agency's close relationship with Congress; (3) the range of its interest group support; and (4) the quality of its response to the 1969 National Environmental Policy Act.

Table 5-3 gives the mean rankings for all seven agencies on all four variables. These means are also presented in graph form in figure 5-4. A score of one (1.0) represents the highest possible ranking; each successive

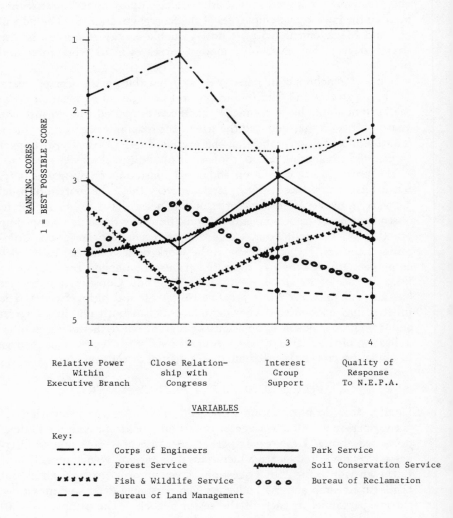

Figure 5-4.
Mean Rankings (1 = best possible score).

score indicates a lower ranking. This scoring system allowed each respondent to choose only one agency for each position, thus emphasizing the more extreme scores: only one agency could receive a score of one, and one had to be ranked sixth.

Table 5-3   Mean Rankings

	Overall Mean	Variable 1 Relative Power within Executive Branch	Variable 2 Close Relationship with Congress	Variable 3 Interest Group Support	Variable 4 Quality of Response to NEPA
Bureau of Reclamation	4.1	4.2	3.4	4.2	4.5
Bureau of Land Management	4.5	4.4	4.4	4.5	4.7
Corps of Engineers	2.1	1.8	1.4	3.0	2.3
Fish & Wildlife Service	3.9	3.6	4.6	3.9	3.6
Forest Service	2.7	2.6	2.8	2.7	2.5
National Park Service	3.5	3.2	4.0	3.0	3.7
Soil Conservation Service	3.7	4.1	3.8	3.3	3.7

For variable one (relative power within the executive branch) a clear hierarchy of scores emerges. With a mean score of 1.8, the Corps of Engineers is ranked well above the other agencies. The Forest Service is ranked second, while the other four agencies scored moderate to low rankings. For variable two (close relationship with Congress), the Corps of Engineers again scored well above all other agencies with a mean of 1.4. The Forest Service was again ranked second.

The findings for variable three (interest group support) are less conclusive. Although the Corps of Engineers and the Forest Service still scored quite high, so too did the Park Service. The results therefore are less definitive, with all of the scores clustering at the moderate and low ranks. What might account for this result is some confusion over our term *interest groups*. Since much of the discussion in the interviews centered around natural resources policy and the environmental movement, respondents may have assumed that this variable was concerned only with *environmental* interest group support and not with pro-development lobbies. This is only one possible explanation for the results on this variable, however; it may be that the results accurately reflect the perceptions of the respondents, that is, a clear consensus does not exist concerning which agencies have the strongest network of alliances.

On variable four (quality of response to NEPA) the Corps of Engineers and the Forest Service once again received the highest scores by a considerable margin. We were interested in the agencies' response to

NEPA because in the policy literature it is often used as a measure of an agency's ability to change and innovate. This in turn is related to agency survival. To provide a general ranking for the four variables combined, we calculated an overall mean that includes all the scores across all four variables contained in table 5-3. These scores average the results from each of the four variables, and emphasize the first-place ranking of the Corps of Engineers and the second-place ranking of the Forest Service. One of the advantages of using this type of ranked scoring system is the exclusivity of the highest rank. Since only one agency can be ranked first, the respondent must carefully select the one agency that would receive the highest rank. Table 5-4 gives the total number of respondents that ranked each agency first on each variable. The stark contrast between agencies is apparent. The Corps of Engineers dominated the highest ranking. For variables one, two, and four, the Corps received 55.6 percent, 83.3 percent, and 68.8 percent, respectively, of all first-place rankings for those variables. The exception again is variable three (interest group support), where no agency received a clear lead. It should be noted that the Corps of Engineers and the Forest Service were the only agencies in the sample to score first-place rankings on all four variables, however. All other agencies received no first-place ranking on at least one of the four variables.

Table 5-4   First-Place Ranking for Each Agency on Each Variable

	Mean	Variable 1 Relative Power within Exec-utive Branch	Variable 2 Close Relation-ship with Congress	Variable 3 Interest Group Support	Variable 4 Quality of Response to NEPA
Bureau of Reclamation	3 (1.7)	0	0	1 (6.7)	0
Bureau of Land Management	0	0	0	0	0
Corps of Engineers	10 (57.8)	10 (55.6)	15 (83.3)	4 (23.5)	11 (68.8)
Fish & Wild-life Service	1.8 (11.2)	0	2 (12.5)	4 (25.0)	1 (7.1)
Forest Service	4.4 (27.5)	6 (37.5)	3 (18.8)	4 (25.0)	4 (28.6)
National Park Service	1.3 (8.3)	3 (20.0)	0	2 (13.3)	0
Soil Conser-vation Service	1.3 (7.7)	0	2 (11.8)	3 (18.8)	0

Note: Total number is given first. Number in parentheses is adjusted percentage.

The other extreme in ranking is the lowest ranking, number six. Again, the ranked scoring system requires all respondents to rank one agency last on each variable. Table 5-5 gives the total number of respondents that ranked each agency last on each variable. The Corps of Engineers and the Forest Service scored impressively with the lowest number of last-place rankings. At the other extreme, the Bureau of Land Management received, by a substantial margin, the greatest number of last-place scores.

Table 5-5   Last-Place Ranking for Each Agency on Each Variable

	Mean	Variable 1 Relative Power within Executive Branch	Variable 2 Close Relation- ship with Congress	Variable 3 Interest Group Support	Variable 4 Quality of Response to NEPA
Bureau of Reclamation	2.5 (16.6)	3 (18.8)	1 (06.3)	3 (20.0)	3 (21.4)
Bureau of Land Management	5.8 (37.1)	6 (37.5)	4 (25.0)	8 (50.0)	5 (35.7)
Corps of Engineers	.75 (04.7)	0	0	0	3 (18.8)
Fish & Wild- life Service	1.6 (11.2)	2 (12.5)	2 (12.5)	2 (12.5)	1 (07.1)
Forest Service	.5 (03.4)	0	0	1 (06.3)	1 (07.1)
National Park Service	2.5 (16.7)	3 (20.0)	5 (33.3)	2 (13.3)	0
Soil Conser- vation Service	2.6 (16.7)	3 (17.6)	5 (29.4)	1 (06.3)	2 (13.3)

These findings lend support to the hypothesis concerning power differentials among federal agencies. Among currently existing natural resources agencies, the Corps of Engineers and the Forest Service have clearly established a reputation as powerful, innovative agencies. Furthermore, support for this perception is not limited to one or two rival agencies, but rather is broad-based. For example, at least one respondent from every agency in our sample ranked the Corps first on variables one, two, and four. There was also across-the-board support for ranking the Forest Service either first or second on all variables. For variable four (quality of response to NEPA), at least one respondent from each agency in the sample ranked the Forest Service either first or second.

For the other agencies, however, there was little consistency or agreement among respondents. For example, scores for the Soil Conservation Service and for the Fish and Wildlife Service varied dramatically, often covering the entire range of possible rankings. This may indicate that these agencies have yet to establish a clear reputation as either strong or weak agencies within the executive establishment.

In contrast to the scores described thus far, the Bureau of Reclamation and the Bureau of Land Management consistently scored well below the other five agencies. There was widespread agreement among the agency personnel in the sample to rank these two agencies at the lowest rankings.

Our data also show evidence of possible competitive attitudes between agencies, resulting in a form of mutual, if grudging, respect. This was most obvious between the Forest Service and the National Park Service, where respondents from each agency consistently ranked the other higher than average. All of the Park Service respondents ranked the Forest Service first on variable one (relative power within the executive branch). Conversely, all of the Forest Service respondents ranked the Park Service either one or two on the same variable. The competition over management practices and policy, which gave rise to the creation of these two agencies in the early part of the century, obviously continues unabated to the present day.

CONCLUSION

The combination of archival research, budget and personnel data, and subjective perceptions about agency power reinforce one another. Without unduly belaboring the point, two federal agencies have pulled out from the pack of seven to distinguish themselves (for better or for worse) within the bureaucratic establishment. The others either move along at a slower but steady pace or experience alternating periods of growth and stagnation. We consider this to be a highly interesting, empirically verified finding; we shall speculate on its consequences for public policy— particularly for resources policy—in the next and final chapter.

CHAPTER SIX

Resource Management
in the 1980s:
Who Guards the Guardians?

Over one hundred years of federal involvement in natural resources management has been described and analyzed in this study. Were they alive today, men such as Theodore Roosevelt, Gifford Pinchot, Stephen Mather, and John Wesley Powell—who set in motion most of the governmental organizations herein described—could of course take pride in their creations, and in the fact that the organizations have endured well beyond the span of their own lifetimes. But one wonders if they would not also entertain misgivings as to whether their deeply held conservation values—so appropriate to the nineteenth and early twentieth centuries—were being adequately protected and promoted by the bureaucratic order presently in existence. The literature of the nineteenth century is full of concerns about the developing new social order, with these writers' worst fears being expressed in such fantasies as Frankenstein and Jekyll and Hyde. More recently, of course, these same concerns have been a preoccupation of writers like Kafka, Orwell, and Huxley, who saw in the development of a technological, bureaucratized society great threats to individual liberties and freedoms.

One does not have to go so far afield, however, to find examples of concern, then and now, over an excessive concentration of power by the few. In chapter 2 we quoted at length from Pinchot's autobiography, *Breaking New Ground*, where he defines conservation policy. Aimed not only at protecting, preserving, and wisely using the earth's natural resources, his policy had two other, equally important dimensions as well—controlling our resources for the common good, *and* insuring that that control would not fall into the hands of the great monopolies. He is worth quoting again:

> Monopoly on the loose is a source of many of the economic, political, and social evils which afflict the souls of men. Its abolition or regulation is an inseparable part of the conservation policy.[1]

Though Pinchot was referring to the power concentrated in the hands of the nineteenth-century capitalists, whom the historian Frederick Lewis Allen refers to as "the lords of creation,"[2] Pinchot and his fellow Progressives challenged monopoly in whatever form, public or private. Whether it was the power of a big city boss or that of a chairman of the board, Progressivism as a policital movement was aimed at diffusing power and thereby maintaining self-government.

Such concerns are at least as appropriate in 1985 as they were at the turn of the century, although the context in which they are addressed has undergone a great transformation. In the United States of 1900 there was no "bureaucratic state" to speak of; government at all levels was still relatively small—often ineffectual and corrupt, as reformers of the time noted with dismay. Hugh Heclo has argued that big government is a twentieth-century phenomenon, a product of war and economic collapse:

> Each of the two World Wars had a noticeable ratchet effect (a sharp increase and then a decline to a higher than original level) on the trend of government spending and employment. But whereas after World War I Republican administrations did much to dismantle the instruments of national government power accumulated during the war, the ratchet effect was much larger after 1945. Post-World War I federal employment was up 20 percent over the average of prewar years, but after 1945 it remained 120 percent larger than in the immediate pre-World War II years; federal spending tells a similar story.[3]

By midcentury, then, the administrative state was firmly in place; consequently people began to wonder whether it had not, itself, become the primary threat to self-government. As a historian of the 1950s has argued, the Eisenhower administration's domestic agenda was aimed primarily at "holding the line" against governmental growth.[4] We shall return to this point presently.

In tracing the evolution of these seven resource-managing agencies over roughly a one-hundred-year time span, this study lends credence to several theses developed by other scholars of organizational theory. First, this study presents a rigorous validation of Holden's thesis concerning "imperialism" in bureaucracy.[5] As Holden and others have pointed out, the executive branch of government has developed in the twentieth century into virtually a fourth branch of government. Competition among these hundreds of agencies and bureaus that comprise the federal bureaucracy is keen. What this study of agency power differentials shows is that over time the competition increasingly becomes unequal; a single agency comes to dominate a particular program area. In the water resources field, for example, the Corps of Engineers has grown stronger while the Bureau of Reclamation has, since 1950, suffered an organizational decline. Likewise, it has become a common practice to give the Soil Conservation Service the small, upstream projects after the Corps has been granted project authorization for the massive, downstream structures. And the Fish and Wildlife Service is frequently regarded by the Corps and others, including present administration officials, as an organizational gnat. To a less pronounced extent perhaps, the Forest Service performs the role of big brother to the National Park Service and Bureau of Land Management in their common, overlapping policy areas. Imperialism is alive and well in the resource management area.

A second body of research closely related to our findings is modern economic history. Although one does not want to push the analogy too far, given the small sample with which we have worked, nevertheless the processes at work in the bureaucratic environment appear similar to those that economists have observed in the private sector. In *The New Industrial State*, John Kenneth Galbraith makes a distinction between the large corporation and the small business firm:

> The two parts of the economy—the world of the few hundred technically dynamic, massively capitalized and highly organized corporations on the one hand and of the thousands of small and traditional proprietors on the other—are very different. It is not a difference of degree but a difference which invades every aspect of economic organization and behavior, including the motivation to effort itself.[6]

While emphasizing again that we are dealing with a much smaller total population of organizations, nevertheless there appears to be developing within the federal bureaucracy a similar dichotomy between the very large and the small. This is especially in evidence in the data displayed in chapter 5, in which a clear clustering effect is seen: Five agencies—the Park Service, Soil Conservation Service, Bureau of Land Management, Bureau of Reclamation, and the Fish and Wildlife Service—all hover at the bottom of the various figures and tables, while two agencies—the Corps and the Forest Service—are found at the upper extremities.

Furthermore, fifty years ago the differences distinguishing the Corps and the Forest Service from their cohorts could be described as differences of degree, and not of kind. By 1980, however, the differences were much more differences of kind. Comparing the Corps, for example, with the Fish and Wildlife Service or with the then newly reorganized Bureau of Reclamation is like comparing the proverbial apples and oranges. It is no longer a meaningful comparison when one agency has an annual budget of about $3 billion and a work force of 28,000, while the other has to do with a $400 million appropriation and has fewer than 4,000 permanent positions.

We may, then, be witnessing a similar phenomenon operating in both the public and the private sectors—the gradual concentration of power and wealth in fewer hands. Oligopoly and monopoly may be appropriate terms to characterize both sectors. At the very least, in the natural resources policy arena, two types of federal agencies have developed that are roughly comparable to what Galbraith calls the two parts of the economy: the large agencies that more closely resemble the large corporations, and the smaller agencies looking and behaving like specialized small business firms. This is a particularly fertile area for future research, with several implications for the political process suggesting themselves to us—a subject with which we conclude.

A final connection that we wish to make is between this research and what Herbert Kaufman has probed in *Are Government Organizations Immortal?*[7]. This connection concerns agency longevity. The present study is further evidence of what Max Weber as well as more contemporary students of bureaucracy have pointed out—the remarkable stability of the bureaucratic form of organization. Our research into the histories of seven federal agencies shows an unusual ability on their part to survive and to transcend even the most hostile kinds of external environments. We were equally impressed with how some agencies were able to weather a high degree of outright incompetence on their part, thereby managing to stumble through, relatively intact, up to the present day. Once in existence, agencies seldom die; rather, they are reorganized. They may be split up, combined, or subsumed under another agency, but they are rarely phased out of existence altogether. A kernel of their original self persists.

Likewise, we uncovered no evidence to support the proposition that the bureaucracy is on the verge of withering away. On the contrary, this study agrees with Kaufman's sobering conclusion concerning agency survivability:

> one thing is not in much doubt: public officers of the future will have to deal with larger numbers of organizations than do their counterparts today, and many of these abundant organizations— probably an increasing proportion of the total—will be extremely long-lived.[8]

CLOSING THE CIRCLE: APPLYING ECOLOGICAL AND SYSTEM THEORY PRINCIPLES TO ENVIRONMENTAL MANAGERS

The dominant metaphor for this study, introduced in chapter 1, is that organizations behave very much like biological organisms. They have a life history: They are born/are created; they develop an identity; they seek to control their environment; they grow, interact with others, mature, and some, Kaufman observes, eventually succumb to old age and die, or are otherwise dissolved. On the whole, they are much longer lived than we human beings, as is shown in both the present study and Kaufman's recent research. To a very significant degree, then, organizations take on a life of their own, and we mean this in a quite literal sense.

As a group, large organizations such as the seven studied here are characterized by stability, permanence, growth, and independence. In a word, the bureaucracy as an element in our political system is now generally recognized as being powerful indeed; as a result, much attention is currently devoted to finding ways and means to control it. Moreover, the necessity to adequately regulate the bureaucracy is an issue that cuts across partisan lines, institutional allegiances, and traditional academic boundaries. These days, for instance, Democrats are almost as interested in controlling the growth of the executive branch as are Republicans—though the latter admittedly have a longer history of concern on this subject. Likewise, both the Congress and the president now find it in their respective interests to make the bureaucracy toe the line in a more systematic fashion than has occurred in the past. The support given President Reagan by the Congress in his first two years in office to whittle down the size of the bureaucracy is evidence of this generalized concern. Finally, the scholarly interest in such subjects as taxpayers' revolts, sunset legislation, congressional oversight, budgetary reforms, including decremental budgeting, and public interest lobbies as countervailing powers to the iron triangles indicate that academics also have been quick to jump on the anti-bureaucracy bandwagon. The movement is gathering momentum.

Our research suggests that such concern is both timely and appropriate, but, more than than, the hour has come to revitalize the conservation principles that fired the early progressive conservation movement and use these as a strategy designed to control the bureaucracy. We also agree with the advice given recently by David S. Brown in " 'Reforming' the Bureaucracy: Some Suggestions for the New President."[9] Briefly, his argument is that policymakers and policy scholars must get inside the system, so to speak, in order to make meaningful, long-lasting changes in bureaucratic behavior. It is not very useful today for Congress, or the president, or policy scholars to come up with sweeping generalizations regarding the functioning of the federal bureaucracy. The injunction to "abolish the bureaucracy," for example, might generate sympathy from the American public and some short-lived attention by the news media, but it would produce little substantive reform beyond the purely symbolic. As he says,

> those who seek to revitalize federal administration must be selective in what they do. There are many bureaucracies within the federal system, and these are neither equally efficient or inefficient. . . .
> There should, therefore, be an understanding of the *specific bureau-*

cratic behaviors which must be changed, and an effort mounted to modify or eradicate them.[10]

Naturally we find great wisdom in these guidelines because they describe precisely what we have attempted to do with our seven-agency sample in this study.

Specifically, what we propose is that policymakers take seriously the evolutionary/ecological perspective that has been used here to analyze agency power, and then to apply ecological values and some principles emanating from systems theory, along with the usual political ones, to approach the task of evaluating and regulating federal agencies.

These suggestions are not so esoteric as they might appear at first glance, for we believe that the systems approach, and the ecological perspective, are currently being widely applied—though perhaps in some cases they are not identified as such. For example, the science of ecology is the study of the relationships between organisms and their environments. Darwin's formulation of the survival of the fittest came to be widely accepted as an ecological law in the nineteenth century. In a brilliant book on the subject, Richard Hofstadter showed how Darwin's biological law became quickly transformed into social Darwinism in the United States and elsewhere.[11] More recently, Rachel Carson's careful study of the food chain resulted in a fuller recognition of the interdependence of species. This idea, too, became generalized and applied to human societies. Both examples illustrate how laws or theories generated in a quite specialized scientific field quickly gain popular intellectual appeal. Thus, the two ecological principles that we see as particularly appropriate to the issues raised above are: (1) the importance of maintaining diversity, and (2) the desirability of limiting growth.

The history of the growth of the federal bureaucracy suggests that a principle of specialization and increasing diversity has been at work. Throughout the twentieth century, the list of federal organizations has grown absolutely larger; by one recent count approximately eighteen hundred subunits comprised the federal bureaucracy.[12] This growth is seen by many as haphazard, unplanned, uncoordinated, and consequently irrational. Overlap of functions and duplication of effort often are viewed as wasteful, unnecessary, inefficient. Calls for a *systematic* reorganization of the executive branch are made frequently by presidents and commissioners on executive reorganization.

An ecological perspective would question this view. So might a systems approach. Rather than having a single federal agency, for example, in charge of water resources development, it is preferable to have several, as we do today. To be even more concrete, it might appear reasonable at this juncture to phase out altogether the Bureau of Reclamation—given its continuing organizational difficulties—and to transfer its functions to the more successful Army Corps of Engineers. The actions of the former Carter administration vis-à-vis the Bureau came close to doing this, in fact. For both systemic and ecological reasons, we think that such a fusion would be unwise. Interagency competition over water resources development has probably produced greater benefits than it has costs, in the long run. Having three or four agencies in on the act, rather than one superorganization, allows for different points of view, differing approaches, and differing solutions. Moreover, as Martin Landau has observed in a somewhat different context, "redundancy, duplication, and overlap" are essential factors in reducing risks and thus promoting safety in complex systems.[13] The argument is generalized in von Bertalan-ffy's book, *General Systems Theory*, where he discusses conditions of equilibrium and disequilibrium within complex systems (i.e., sets of organizations):

> The important law of oligopoly states that, if there are competing organizations, the instability of their relations and hence the danger of friction and conflicts increases with the decrease of the number of those organizations. Thus, so long as they are relatively small and numerous, they muddle through in some way of coexistence. But if only a few or a competing pair are left, as is the case with the colossal political blocks of the present day, conflicts become devastating to the point of mutual destruction.[14]

Up to a point, then, policymakers should encourage diversity within the executive branch rather than try to reorganize it out of existence. However, they should also give greater consideration to working with already existing organizations rather than creating yet more new ones, as Lowi's important research advocates.[15]

The second ecological principle that has relevance here is the recognition that bigness is not always better. Our study amply documents the rise of two agencies to positions of power and influence within the natural resources policy arena. By our own criteria, they are highly successful organizations. Their growth, however, should not come at the expense of other agencies engaged in similar activities and functions. Whether intentional or not, there are data that suggest that they do. Here the values of diversity and of limiting growth dovetail. Careful attention should be paid to whether the Corps and the Forest Service should continue to be encouraged to grow much larger than they are at present. This is not to suggest a punitive course of action vis-à-vis these agencies, since we believe that their success has been based for the most part on their impressive records of achievement. But we do think that the time has come to examine whether there are, or ought to be, "limits to organizational growth."

This idea is not especially new, but it is one that has been neglected by policymakers and others seeking to find rational ways to control the executive branch. Von Bertalanffy refers to Kenneth Boulding's 1953 book, *The Organizational Revolution*, in discussing certain "iron laws" of organization. Among them are, of course, the question of size:

> Then there is the optimum size of organizations: the larger an organization grows, the longer is the way of communication and this, depending on the nature of the organization, acts as a limiting factor and does not allow an organization to grow beyond a critical size.[16]

Whether these checks to further growth are self-imposed or a product of the organization's environment is an intriguing empirical question, but the primary point, we think, is the recognition that there exists an optimal size, beyond which further growth becomes dysfunctional.

One could engage in an extended discussion of the pros and cons of competition, oligopoly, and monopoly as they pertain (and we argue that they do indeed) to the federal bureaucracy, but we think we have made our position clear on these issues. In our examination of these seven resource managers, we discovered considerable competition and interagency rivalry existing among them. In many instances, what spurred agencies on to better levels of achievement and better service in the public interest was some very realistic assessments of their own self-interest. This included, of course, doing a better job than the "other guy." It would be unwise in the long run to significantly diminish this competitive edge in the interests of other values currently in vogue — efficiency, streamlining, long-range planning, and administrative orderliness. The current situation can be improved upon, of course, but again that should be accomplished, as Brown and others argue, by looking at specific bureaucratic behaviors that operate, in large part, within agencies.

We give the last word to Gifford Pinchot, who observed earlier in this century that monopoly is always to be avoided. It can be as detrimental to democratic values when it appears in the public sector as it is to free enterprise when it is left unchecked in the private sector. Policymakers therefore have a responsibility to recognize the growing power of some federal agencies within the executive establishment, and to discuss possibilities for checking these monopolistic tendencies. Though it might sound gratuitous or trite in an era when public apathy and cynicism about government are so prevalent, nevertheless we urge ordinary citizens to assume a more active role in checking the guardians of our public trust. A revitalization of democratic impulses is very much in order today, and a search for new and more effective ways to secure representative government is imperative. We can learn a lot in this endeavor from the early Progressives.

Appendix

Could you please rank 6 of the 7 agencies listed below according to the criteria at the top of each column of blanks. Omit your own agency from consideration. Place a number one beside the agency that you think best meets the criteria. Number the rest of the agencies in consecutive fashion.

Relative Power within Executive Branch	Close Relationship with Congress	Interest Group Support	Quality of Response to NEPA	
_____	_____	_____	_____	Bureau of Reclamation
_____	_____	_____	_____	Bureau of Land Management
_____	_____	_____	_____	Corps of Engineers
_____	_____	_____	_____	Fish & Wildlife Service
_____	_____	_____	_____	Forest Service
_____	_____	_____	_____	National Park Service
_____	_____	_____	_____	Soil Conservation Service

Notes

CHAPTER 1. DIFFERENTIALS IN AGENCY POWER

1. Anthony Downs, "Up and Down with Ecology: The Issue-Attention Cycle," *Public Interest* (Summer 1972), pp. 38-50.

2. For example, under President Jimmy Carter the Department of Energy came into being; efforts were intensified to decontrol natural gas prices; and laws to conserve fuels, such as the 55-miles-per-hour speed limit, were enacted.

3. For an excellent discussion of the nature of modern legislation and the policy process, see Theodore Lowi, *The End of Liberalism*, 2d ed. (New York: W. W. Norton, 1979), esp. chap. 5.

4. Francis Rourke, "Grappling with the Bureaucracy," in Arnold J. Meltsner, ed., *Politics and the Oval Office* (San Francisco: Institute for Contemporary Studies, 1981), p. 130.

5. Grant McConnell, *The Modern Presidency*, 2d ed. (New York: St. Martin's Press, 1976), p. 65.

6. Francis Rourke, *Bureaucracy, Politics, and Public Policy*, 2d ed. (Boston: Little, Brown, 1976), p. 81.

7. Allan F. Wichelman, "Administrative Agency Implementation of the National Environmental Policy Act of 1969: A Conceptual Framework for Explaining Differential Responses," *Natural Resources Journal* (Apr. 1976), pp. 263-300.

8. Richard N. L. Andrews, *Environmental Policy and Administrative Change* (Lexington, Mass.: D. C. Heath, 1976).

9. Richard A. Liroff, *NEPA and Its Aftermath: The Formation of a National Policy for the Environment* (Bloomington: Indiana University Press, 1976).

10. Herbert Kaufman, *Are Government Organizations Immortal?* (Washington, D.C.: Brookings Institution, 1976).

11. Rourke, *Bureaucracy*, pp. 81-106.

12. Max Weber, "Polictics as a Vocation," in H. H. Gerth and C. W. Mills, eds., *From Max Weber: Essays in Sociology* (New York: Oxford University Press, 1958), pp. 232-33.

13. We are aware of the recent erosion in public confidence in virtually all professions and specializations. However, relative to other occupations, these still maintain their edge.

14. Rourke, *Bureaucracy*, p. 83.

15. Lowi, *End of Liberalism*, p. 120.

16. Kaufman, *Are Government Organizations Immortal?*, p. 4.

17. Rourke, *Bureaucracy*, p. 89.

18. Ibid., p. 90.

19. Arthur Maass, *Muddy Waters: The Army Engineers and the Nation's Rivers* (Cambridge: Harvard University Press, 1951).

20. We are using the concept of type or category here in the sense that Weber used "ideal type"—that is, as a heuristic device not intended to do damage to the idiosyncratic features of each organization. Likewise, no value judgments are necessarily implied by our categories.

21. Charles E. Lindblom, "The Science of 'Muddling Through'," *Public Administration Review* 19 (Spring 1959), pp. 79-88.

CHAPTER 2. BUREAUCRATIC SUPERSTARS

1. Frank E. Smith, *The Politics of Conservation* (New York: Harper Colophon Books, 1966), p. 3.

2. 7th Congress, 1st sess, chap. 9, sec. 26, Mar. 16, 1802. "An Act fixing the military peace establishment of the United States."

3. 18th Congress, 1st sess, chap. 139, sec. 2, May 24, 1824. "An Act to improve the navigation of the Ohio and Mississippi rivers."

4. Smith, *Politics of Conservation*, p. 12.

5. Hearings, House Committee on Appropriations, Subcommittee on Public Works, *Public Works for Water and Power Development and Atomic Energy Commission Appropriation Bill, 1975*, Part 1,93rd Cong., 2d sess., p. 229.

6. Richard N. L. Andrews, *Environmental Policy and Administrative Change* (Lexington, Mass.: D. C. Heath, 1976), pp. 57, 141-43.

7. Smith, *Politics of Conservation*, p. 271.

8. Arthur Maass, *Muddy Waters: The Army Engineers and the Nation's Rivers* (Cambridge: Harvard University Press, 1951).

9. Smith, *Politics of Conservation*, p. 290.

10. Hearings, House Committee on Rivers and Harbors, *Pollution of Navigable Waters*, testimony of Thomas Robins, deputy chief of the Corps of Engineers, 79th Cong., 1st sess., Nov. 13-15, 20, 1945, p. 94.

11. Smith, *Politics of Conservation*, pp. 267-71.

12. See for example: Daniel Mazmanian and Jeanne Nienaber, *Can Organizations Change? Environmental Protection, Citizen Participation, and the Corps of Engineers* (Washington, D. C.: Brookings Institution, 1979); Richard Andrews, *Environmental Policy*; Richard Liroff, *A National Policy for the Environment: NEPA and Its Aftermath* (Bloomington: Indiana University Press, 1976).

13. Mazmanian and Nienaber, *Can Organizations Change?*, p. 194.

14. *Appendix to the U. S. Budget for Fiscal Year 1981*, pp. 337-50, and the *U. S. Budget for FY 1981*, pp. 426-28, 1022.

15. *New York Times*, Feb. 21, 1977, p. 1; Feb. 22, 1977, p. 13; Mar. 7, 1977, p. 1.

16. Quoted in Phillip L. Fradkin, *A River No More* (New York: Alfred A. Knopf, 1981), p. 5.

17. Ibid., p. 9.

18. The letter was ambiguous on this point but could certainly be interpreted to apply to ongoing projects. The letter urges Mr. Carter to "halt the construction of unnecessary and environmentally destructive dams." Quoted in *New York Times*, Mar. 13, 1977, p. 24.

19. These were the Dickey-Lincoln in Maine, Paintsville Lake in Kentucky, and the Freepoint project in Illinois (*New York Times*, Mar. 24, 1977, p. 1).

20. Two projects—the Auburn-Folsom South in California, and the Narrows Unit in Colorado—were left unfunded pending further safety studies (*New York Times*, Apr. 16, 1977. p. 1).

21. *New York Times*, May 3, 1977, p. 34.

22. *New York Times*, Apr. 17, 1977, p. 1; and the *Congressional Quarterly Weekly Report*, Mar. 4, 1978, p. 568.

23. Congressperson Boggs made a very appropriate comment during congressional hearings: "When some of the few projects that were asked to be deleted are within your own state, and within your own district, of course you have an entirely different set of criteria to use." Senator Johnston made a similar comment: "Do I have a parochial interest in [the Atchafalaya project]? You bet I do." See Hearings, House Committee on Appropriations, Subcommittee on Public Works, *Public Works For Water and Power Development and Energy Research Appropriation Bill, 1978*, 95th Cong., 1st sess., part 9, p. 52; *Congressional Quarterly Weekly Report*, July 2, 1977, p. 1338.

24. *Presidential Documents: Jimmy Carter, 1977*, vol. 13, no. 17, Apr. 18, 1977, p. 557.

25. Hearings, House Committee on Appropriations, Subcommittee on Public Works, *Public Works For Water and Power Development and Energy Research Appropriation Bill, 1978*, 95th Cong., 1st sess., part 9, pp. 3-42.

26. Ibid., p. 4; and *National Journal*, Apr. 9, 1977, p. 547.

27. *Presidential Documents: Jimmy Carter, 1977*, vol. 13, no. 17, Apr. 18, 1977, p. 558.

28. *Washington Post*, Dec. 19, 1977, p. 1.

29. Hearings, House Committee on Appropriations, Subcommittee on Public Works, *Public Works For Water and Power Development and Energy Research Appropriation Bill, 1978*, 95th Cong., 1st sess., part 9, pp. 4-5.

30. Ibid., p. 4.

31. Ibid.

32. Ibid., p. 45.

33. *New York Times*, May 17, 1979, p. 16.

34. *Washington Post*, Dec. 19, 1977, pp. 1-4.

35. Ibid., Aug. 5, 1977, p. 5; *New York Times*, Aug. 9, 1977, p. 17.

36. *Los Angeles Times*, June 10, 1978, p. 1.

37. Ibid., June 16, 1978, p. 11.

38. Ibid., Oct. 12, 1978, p. 7.

39. *Hoover Commission Report on Organization of the Executive Branch of Government* (New York: McGraw-Hill, 1949), p. 263.

40. Hearings, House Committee on Government Operations, *Reorganization of Executive Departments*, 91st Cong., 1st sess., June 2, 1971, part 1, p. 8.

41. *New York Times*, Feb. 12, 1979, p. 18.

42. Ibid., July 19, 1979, p. D-18.

43. Hearings, House Committee on Appropriations, *The Federal Budget for 1979*, 95th Cong., 2d sess., p. 109.

44. *New York Times*, July 19, 1979, p. D-18; Hearings, House Committee on Appropriations, *the Federal Budget for 1979*, 95th Cong., 2d sess., pp. 11, 21.

45. *New York Times*, Jan. 24, 1980, p. D-22.

46. Hearings, House Committee on Appropriations, *Supplemental Appropriations and Rescission Bill, 1981*, 97th Cong., 1st sess., part 1, p. 633.

47. Hearings, House Committee on Appropriations, Subcommittee on Energy and Water Development, *Energy And WAter Development Appropriations for 1982*, 97th Cong., 1st sess., part 1, p. 9.

48. Hearings, House Committee on Appropriations, Subcommittee on Public Works, *Public Works For Water And Power Development And Energy Research Appropriation Bill, 1978*, 95th Cong., 1st sess., part 9, p. 2.

49. *Chicago Tribune*, Dec. 29, 1977, sec. 3, p. 2.

50. *New York Times*, Dec. 13, 1977, p. 16.

51. Ibid., Feb. 12, 1979, p. 1.

52. Hearings, House Committee on Appropriations, Subcommittee on Energy and Water Development, *Water And Power Development Appropriations for 1982*, 97th Cong., 1st sess., part 1, pp. 5-7.

53. Ibid., pp. 7-9.

54. Of the $230 million reduction proposed by Reagan, $167 million was in the construction program, and $117 million of that was due to reductions in these three projects. Hearings, House Committee on Appropriations, Subcommittee on Energy and Water Development, *Supplemental Appropriation and Rescission Bill for 1981*, 97th Cong., 1st sess., part 1, pp. 560-62.

55. Ibid., p. 624.

56. Ibid., p. 578.

57. Ibid., pp. 581, 629.

58. Ibid., pp. 565, 610, 611, 639, 656.

59. Ibid., pp. 624-25.

60. Ibid., p. 611.

61. Ibid., pp. 562, 581, 626-27, 637.

62. *Congressional Quarterly Weekly Report*, Nov. 28, 1981, p. 2352.

63. Executive Order 12322, Sept. 17, 1981.

64. *National Journal*, July 23, 1983, p. 1559.

65. *New York Times*, Feb. 12, 1979, p. 18.

66. Ibid., Feb. 6, 1980, p. 17.

67. Hearings, House Committee on Appropriations, Subcommittee on Energy and Water Development, *Water And Power Development Appropriations for 1982*, 97th Cong., 1st sess., part 1, pp. 143-49.

68. *New York Times*, June 16, 1981, p. B-12.

69. See, for example, Robert Reinhold's article in *New York Times*, Aug. 9, 1981, p. 1.

70. Hearings, House Committee on Appropriations, Subcommittee on Energy and Water Development, *Water And Power Development Appropriations for 1982*, 97th Cong., 1st sess., part 1, p. 327.

71. Ibid., part 1, pp. 16, 23.

72. *New York Times*, Jan. 24, 1980, p. D-22.

73. Hearings, House Committee on Appropriations, Subcommittee on Energy and Water Development, *Supplemental Appropriation and Rescission Bill for 1981*, 97th Cong., 1st sess., part 1, p. 663.

74. Hearings, House Committee on Appropriations, Subcommittee on Energy and Water Development, *Water And Power Development Appropriations for 1982*, 97th Cong., 1st sess., part 1, pp. 9-10, 21.

75. *Tucson Citizen*, Jan. 20, 1982, p. A-3.

76. George Sibley, "The Desert Empire," *Harper's* (Oct. 1977), p. 66.

77. *Appendix to the Budget for Fiscal Year 1984*, pp. I-H2 to I-H4.

78. A number of bills have been proposed in the Senate which would have a deleterious effect on the Corps. In 1977, Senator Ribicoff's Committee on Governmental Affairs recommended that the Corps' water resource development program be turned over to the Department of Transportation. See *Chicago Tribune*, Dec. 27, 1977, p. 8. In 1979 Senators Moynihan and Domenici proposed a bill that supported Carter's effort to transfer decision-making power in regard to water projects to the Water Resources Council. See *New York Times*, Oct. 25, 1979, p. 18. In 1981, Senator Metzenbaum proposed that $300 million be deleted from water projects and subtracted from the national debt. He asked, rhetorically: "What's so sacred about water projects?" He found out when the bill went to the floor for a vote. It failed to pass, as did the other bills cited above. See *New York Times*, May 12, 1981, p. D-22.

79. Hearings, House Committee on Appropriations, Subcommittee on Energy and Water Development, *Supplemental Appropriation and Rescission Bill, 1981*, 97th Cong., 1st sess., part 1, p. 668.

80. Smith, *Politics of Conservation*, p. 91.

81. Ibid., pp. 89-91.

82. Ibid., p. 97.

83. Gifford Pinchot, *Breaking New Ground* (New York: Harcourt and Brace, 1947), p. 27.

84. Ibid., p. 85

85. 51st Congress, 2d sess., Chap. 561, Sec. 24, "An act to repeal timber-

culture laws, and for other purposes," Mar. 3, 1891.

86. Pinchot, *Breaking New Ground*, pp. 107-8.

87. Ibid., p. 140.

88. Samuel Trask Dana and Sally K. Fairfax, *Forest and Range Policy* (New York: McGraw Hill, 1980) p. 96.

89. Pinchot, *Breaking New Ground*, pp. 506-7.

90. Dana and Fairfax, *Forest and Range Policy*, p. 121.

91. Hearings, House Committee on Appropriations, Subcommittee on Agriculture, *Department of Agriculture Appropriations for 1960*, 86th Cong., 2d sess., part 1, p. 18.

92. William L. O'Neill, *The Progressive Years: America Comes of Age* (New York: Dodd, Mead, and Co., 1975), p. 30.

93. Pinchot, *Breaking New Ground*, p. 140.

94. *U.S. Budget for FY 1981: Special Analysis*, p. 374.

95. Hearings, House Committee on Appropriations, Subcommittee on Agriculture, *Agriculture Department Appropriation Bill for 1931*, 71st Cong., 2d sess., p. 1.

96. Hearings, House Committee on Appropriations, Subcommittee on Agriculture, *Agriculture Department Appropriation Bill for 1939*, 75th Cong., 3d sess., p. 21.

97. Paul J. Culhane and H. Paul Friesema, "Land Use Planning for the Public Lands," *Natural Resources Journal* 19 (Jan. 1979), pp. 43-74.

98. Hearings, House Committee on Appropriations, Subcommittee on the Department of the Interior and Related Agencies, *Department of the Interior and Related Agencies Appropriations for 1971*, 91st Cong., 2d sess., part 1, p. 3.

99. U. S. Department of Agriculture, Forest Service, *RARE II: Final Environmental Statement, Roadless Area Review and Evaluation* (January 1979), p. iv.

100. Ibid.

101. Forest and Rangeland Renewable Resources Planning Act, 16 U.S.C. 1601 (1974), and the National Forest Management Act, 16 U.S.C. 1600 (1976).

102. Culhane and Friesema, "Land Use Planning," pp. 52-63.

103. For an excellent analysis of the problems and advantages associated with comprehensive planning in the Forest Service, see: Christopher Leman, "Resource Assessment and Program Development: An Evaluation of Forest Service Experience under the Resources Planning Act, with Lessons for other Natural Resource Agencies." Mimeographed, p. 123.

104. Christopher Leman, "Political Dilemmas in Evaluating and Budgeting Soil Conservation Programs: The RCA Process," in Harold G. Halcrow, Earl O. Heady, and Melvin L. Cotner, *Soil Conservation Policies, Institutions, and Incentives* (Ankeny, Iowa: Soil Conservation Society of America, 1982), p. 57.

105. Hearings, House Committee on Appropriations, Subcommittee on the Department of the Interior and Related Agencies, *Department of the Interior and Related Agencies Appropriations for 1982*, 97th Cong., 1st sess., part 10, p. 337.

106. Ibid., part 8, p. 525.

107. Hearings, House Committee on Appropriations, Subcommittee on the Department of Interior and Related Agencies, *Department of the Interior and Related Agencies Appropriations for 1982*, 97th Cong., 1st sess., part 10, p. 314.

108. Ibid., p. 248.

109. Ibid., pp. 243-48.

110. Ibid., p. 243.

111. *Appendix to the Budget for Fiscal Year 1983*, pp. I-E103 to I-E104.

112. *Appendix to the Budget for Fiscal Year 1984*, pp. I-E99 to I-E100.

113. Hearings, House Committee on Appropriations, Subcommittee on the Department of the Interior and Related Agencies, *Department of the Interior and Related Agencies Appropriations for 1982*, 97th Cong., 1st sess., part 10, p. 455. Remarks by Chief Forester Max Peterson.

114. Ibid., p. 310.

115. Ibid.

116. Ibid., part 8, p. 564.

117. Ibid., part 10, p. 454.

118. "Facilities in Many National Parks and Forests Do Not Meet Health and Safety Standards," report by the General Accounting Office, CED-80-115, Oct. 10, 1980.

119. Hearings, House Committee on Appropriations, Subcommittee on the Department of the Interior and Related Agencies, *Department of the Interior and Related Agencies Appropriations for 1982*, 97th Cong., 1st sess., part 10, p. 534.

120. Ibid., p. 413.

121. Ibid., pp. 245, 453-54.

122. *New York Times*, Mar. 29, 1981, p. 32.

123. Hearings, House Committee on Appropriations, Subcommittee on the Department of the Interior and Related Agencies, *Department of the Interior and Related Agencies Appropriations for 1982*, 97th Cong., 1st sess., part 10, pp. 323-37.

124. Sally K. Fairfax, "RPA and the Forest Service", Unpublished paper, Department of Natural Resources, University of California at Berkeley.

125. Kenneth Gold, "A Comparative Analysis of Successful Organizations," U.S. Office of Personnel Management, July 1, 1981. Mimeographed.

126. Paul J. Culhane, *Public Lands Politics: Interest Group Influence on the Forest Service and the Bureau of Land Management* (Baltimore: Johns Hopkins University Press, 1981), p. 68.

127. Ibid.

CHAPTER 3. AGENCIES THAT MUDDLE THROUGH

1. Roderick Nash, *Wilderness and the American Mind* (New Haven: Yale University Press, 1967).

2. 42nd Congress, 2d sess., chap 24, pp. 32-33, Mar. 1, 1872 "An Act to set apart a certain Tract of Land lying near the Head-waters of the Yellowstone River as a Public Park."

3. U. S. Department of the Interior, "Background Material on the National Park Service," document 527-76, Nov. 1976, p. 1.

4. William C. Everhart, *The National Park Service* (New York: Praeger, 1972).

5. "An Act to establish a National Park Service, and for other purposes," Aug. 25, 1916 (39 stat. 535; 16 U.S.C. 1).

6. Department of the Interior, "Background Material," p. 2.

7. Donald Swain, *Wilderness Defender* (Chicago: University of Chicago Press, 1970), p. 2.

8. Gifford Pinchot, *Breaking New Ground* (New York: Harcourt and Brace, 1947), pp. 26-27.

9. Everhart, *National Park Service*, p. 95.

10. Swain, *Wilderness Defender*, p. 319.

11. F. Fraser Darling and Noel D. Eichhorn, *Man and Nature in the National Parks* (Washington, D. C.: Conservation Foundation, 1967), p. 32.

12. Howard Bloomfield, "Quandary in the Campgrounds," *American Forests* 75 (July, 1969), p. 6.

13. Paul J. Culhane, *Public Lands Politics: Interest Group Influence on the Forest Service and the Bureau of Land Management* (Baltimore: Johns Hopkins University Press, 1981), p. 52.

14. Darling and Eichhorn, *Man and Nature*, p. 77.

15. Memorandum from Secretary of the Interior Stewart L. Udall, July 10, 1964. U.S. Department of the Interior, National Park Service. *Administrative Policies for the Historical Areas of the National Park Service*. Washington: Government Printing Office, 1968, Appendix A, p. 73.

16. Department of the Interior, National Park Service, *Management Policies*, 1975 Introduction. Also see: Ronald Foresta, *America's National Parks and Their Keepers* (Washington, D. C.: Resources for the Future, 1984), pp. 93-112.

17. Darling and Eichhorn, *Man and Nature*, p. 36.

18. Department of the Interior, National Park Service, *Park Road Standards*, Mimeograph, 1968.

19. "Detailed Budget Estimate," in *U.S. Budget*, 1956, 1966, 1967, 1968.

20. National Park Service, *Management Policies*, p. V-1.

21. Ibid., pp. I-1, I-9, IV-1.

22. "Detailed Budget Estimate," in *U.S. Budget*, 1964, 1968.

23. House Committee on Government Operations, 24th Report, *The Degradation of Our National Parks*, 94th Cong., 2d sess., June 30, 1976.

24. Joseph Novogrod, Gladys O. Dimock, and Marshall E. Dimock, *Casebook in Public Administration* (New York: Holt, Rinehart and Winston, 1969), p. 96.

25. George B. Hartzog, "Management Considerations for Optimum Development and Protection of National Park Resources," in *World Conference on National Parks*, 2d, 1972 (Lausanne, Switzerland: International Union for Conservation

of Nature and Natural Resources, 1974, p. 158.

26. Bloomfield, "Quandary in the Campgrounds," pp. 38-40.

27. Stewart M. Brandborg, "The Wilderness Law and the National Park System in the U. S.," in J. G. Nelson, ed., *Canadian Parks in Perspective* (Quebec, Canada: Harvest House, 1970), p. 272.

28. Jeanne Nienaber and Aaron Wildavsky, *The Budgeting and Evaluation of Federal Recreation Programs: Or, Money Doesn't Grow on Trees* (New York: Basic Books, 1973), p. 38.

29. Much of the information concerning problems with the reservation system was compiled from interviews with Park Service officials in the Washington headquarters. Also see Hearings, Senate Committee on Interior and Insular Affairs, Subcommittee on Parks and Recreation, *Proposed Reservation System in Selected National Parks*, 93d Cong., 1st sess., Feb. 23, 1973.

30. Hearings, Senate Committee on Interior and Insular Affairs, *Overnight Park Reservation System*, Subcommittee on Parks and Recreation, 93rd Cong., 2d sess., Aug. 21, and Sept. 19, 1974, pp. 2-4, 11, 16.

31. National Parks and Conservation Association, "Park Resource Survey, 1975". *National Parks and Conservation Magazine* (Feb., 1976), pp. 11-16, and (Mar., 1976), pp. 9-14.

32. Nienaber and Wildavsky, *Budgeting and Evaluation*, p. 19.

33. James B. Craig, "Plusses and Minuses in the National Parks," *American Forests* (June 1976), p. 4.

34. "The Crisis in National Park Personnel," *National Parks and Conservation Association Magazine* (Apr. 1975), p. 20.

35. "Budget Plans Starve the National Park Service," *National Parks and Conservation Association Magazine* (June 1975), p. 19.

36. Hearings, House Committee on Government Operations, *Degradation of the National Parks*, 94th Cong., 1st, 2d sess., Dec. 4, 1975 to Apr. 7, 1976, p. 74.

37. "Closing the Door on the National Parks," *National Parks and Conservation Association Magazine* (Jan. 1975), p. 23.

38. "Senate-House Views Expressed on National Parks," *National Wildlife Federation Newsletter*, Aug. 8, 1976, report no. 24, p. 290.

39. In 1975, the Service operated 302 park areas. By the following year that number had dropped to 286. See *Appendix to the Budget Fiscal Year 1976*, p. 546, and *Fiscal Year 1977*, p. 456.

40. Brandborg, "Wilderness Law," p. 271.

41. Theodore Swem, "Planning of National Parks," in *Canadian Parks in Perspective*, p. 253.

42. Nienaber and Wildavsky, *Budgeting and Evaluation*, p. 42.

43. Charles Fraser, "Park Agencies for the Future," *Parks and Recreation* (Aug. 1973), p. 38.

44. Prior to the passage of the 1980 Alaska National Interest Lands Conservation Act, the Forest Service managed about 85 percent of the total acreage in the National Wilderness Preservation System. See Department of Agriculture, Forest

Service, *RARE II: Final Environmental Statement, Roadless Area Review and Evaluation* (January 1979), p. 5.

45. Everhart, *National Park Service*, p. 182.

46. This survey questionnaire was administered by Daniel McCool to a sample of National Park Service employees at the Albright Training Center at Grand Canyon, Arizona.

47. Newton B. Drury, "Former Directors Speak Out," *American Forests* (June 1976), p. 30.

48. Craig, "Plusses and Minuses," p. 14.

49. *Wall Street Journal*, Nov. 11, 1983, p. 1.

50. *Appendix to the Budget for Fiscal Year 1984*, p. I-M28.

51. Richard Ganzel and Dorothy Olkowski, "The Politics of Coalition-Building: The Inholders Reach Out" Paper presented at the Western Social Science Association Meeting, Albuquerque, N.M., April 1983. Also see *Newsweek*, July 25, 1983, pp. 22-31.

52. *Appendix to the Budget for Fiscal Year 1983*, p. I-M38, and *1984*, p. I-M33.

53. Hearings, House Committee on Appropriations, Subcommittee on the Department of the Interior and Related Agencies, *Department of the Interior and Related Agencies Appropriations For 1982*, 97th Cong., 1st sess., part 12, p. 694.

54. *State of the Parks, 1980*, prepared by the Office of Science and Technology for the National Park Service, Department of the Interior, May 1980.

55. General Accounting Office, *Facilities in Many National Parks and Forests Do Not Meet Health and Safety Standards*, CED-80-115, Oct. 10, 1980.

56. Hearings, House Committee on Appropriations, Subcommittee on the Department of the Interior and Related Agencies, *Department of the Interior and Related Agencies Appropriations for 1982*, 97th Cong., 1st sess., part 12, p. 768.

57. Ibid., p. 686.

58. Ibid., p. 687.

59. Hearings, House Committee on Appropriations, Subcommittee on the Department of the Interior and Related Agencies, *Revised Justifications for Fiscal Year 1982*, 97th Cong., 1st sess., part 8, pp. 147-57.

60. Hearings, House Committee on Appropriations, Hearings before the Subcommittee on the Department of the Interior and Related Agencies, *Department of the Interior and Related Agencies Appropriations for 1982*, 97th Cong., 1st sess., part 1, p. 698.

61. Ibid., pp. 708, 715.

62. Ibid., p. 710. Also see pp. 712, 717.

63. Ibid., pp. 716-17.

64. Ibid., p. 1015.

65. *State of the Environment 1982*, report by the Conservation Foundation, Washington, D. C. 1982, p. 318.

66. *Life*, July 1983, pp. 106-112.

67. Hearings, House Committee on Appropriations, Subcommittee on the Department of the Interior and Related Agencies, *Department of the Interior and Related Agencies Appropriations for 1982*, 97th Cong., 1st sess., part 1, p. 763.

68. Frank E. Smith, *Politics of Conservation* (New York: Harper Colophon Books, 1966), p. 248.

69. Ibid., p. 247.

70. Hearings, House Committee on Appropriations, Subcommittee on Agriculture Department Appropriations, *Agriculture Department Appropriation Bill for 1936*, 74th Cong., 1st sess., p. 63.

71. Hearings, House Committee on Appropriations, Subcommittee on Department of Agriculture and Related Agencies Appropriations, *Department of Agriculture Appropriations for 1964*, 88th Cong., 2d sess., part 2, p. 1015. Also see Smith, *Politics of Conservation*, p. 249.

72. "An Act for the protection of land resources against soil erosion, and for other purposes", 74th Cong., 1st sess., Chap. 85, Apr. 27, 1935, p. 163, no. 46.

73. Hearings, House Committee on Appropriations, Subcommittee on Department of Agriculture and Related Agencies Appropriations, *Department of Agriculture Appropriations for 1964*, 88th Cong., 2d sess., part 2, p. 1015.

74. Hearings, House Committee on Appropriations, Subcommittee on Agriculture Appropriations, *Agricultural Department Appropriations Bill for 1936*, 74th Cong., 1st sess., p. 63.

75. Hearings, House Committee on Appropriations, Subcommittee on Agriculture Department Appropriations, *Agricultural Department Appropriations Bill for 1938*, 75th Cong., 1st sess., p. 1039.

76. Hearings, House Committee on Appropriations, Subcommittee on Department of Agriculture Appropriations, *Agriculture Department Appropriation Bill for 1947*, 79th Cong., 2d sess., p. 1001.

77. House, Committee on Appropriations, Subcommittee on Agriculture Department Appropriations, *Agricultural Department Appropriation Bill for 1937*, 74th Song., 2d sess., p. 21.

78. Wayne D. Rasmussen, "History of Soil Conservation, Institutions, and Incentives," in Halcrow, Heady, and Cotner, *Soil Conservation Policies, Institutions, and Incentives* (Ankeny, Iowa: Soil Conservation Society of America, 1982), p. 8.

79. Ibid., p. 16.

80. Robert J. Morgan, *Governing Soil Conservation* (Baltimore: Johns Hopkins University Press, 1962), p. 169.

81. 49 stat. 163, 1935.

82. Rasmussen, "History of Soil Conservation," p. 12.

83. Morgan, *Governing Soil Conservation*, p. 103.

84. Hearings, House Committee on Appropriations, Subcommittee on Agriculture Department Appropriations, *Agriculture Department Appropriation Bill for 1944*, 78th Cong., 1st sess., p. 954.

85. Hearings, House Committee on Appropriations, Subcommittee on Department of Agriculture Appropriations, *Department of Agriculture Appropriations*

for 1951, 81st Cong., 2d sess., part 1, p. 151.

86. Hearings, House Committee on Appropriations, Subcommittee on Department of Agriculture and Related Agencies Appropriations, *Department of Agriculture Appropriations for 1955*, 83d Cong., 2d sess., part 3, p. 1361.

87. Rasmussen, "History of Soil Conservation," p. 11.

88. Ibid., p. 12.

89. See Executive Orders 9060 (Feb. 23, 1942) and 9577 (June 29, 1945).

90. Hearings, House Committee on Appropriations, Subcommittee on Department of Agriculture and Related Agencies Appropriations, *Department of Agriculture Appropriations for 1956*, 84th Cong., 1st sess., part 2, pp. 834-35.

91. Hearings, House Committee on Appropriations, Subcommittee on Department of Agriculture and Related Agencies Appropriations, *Department of Agriculture Appropriations for 1964*, 88th Cong., 1st sess., part 2, p. 1018.

92. Hearings, House Committee on Appropriations, Subcommittee on Agriculture and Related Agencies Appropriations, *Agriculture and Related Agencies Appropriations for 1972*, 94th Cong., 2d sess., part 4, p. 238.

93. Hearings, House Committee on Appropriations, Subcommittee on Department of Agriculture and Related Agencies Appropriations, *Department of Agriculture Appropriations for 1960*, 86th Cong., 1st sess., part 2, p. 1062.

94. Hearings, House Committee on Appropriations, Subcommittee on Agriculture and Related Agencies Appropriations, *Agriculture and Related Agencies Appropriations for 1977*, 94th Cong., 2d sess., part 4, p. 279.

95. Hearings, House Committee on Appropriations, Subcommittee on Department of Agriculture and Related Agencies Appropriations, *Department of Agriculture Appropriations for 1965*, 88th Cong., 2d sess., part 2, p. 504.

96. Hearings, House Committee on Appropriations, Subcommittee on Agriculture and Environmental and Consumer Protection Appropriations, *Agricultural, Environmental and Consumer Protection Appropriations for 1975*, 93d Cong., 2d sess., part 2, p. 338.

97. Christopher Leman, "Political Dilemmas in Evaluating and Budgeting Soil Conservation Programs: The RCA Process," in Halcrow, Heady, and Cotner, *Soil Conservation Policies, Institutions, and Incentives* (Ankeny, Iowa: Soil Conservation Society of America, 1982), p. 52.

98. Pub. L. 83-566, 16 U.S.C. 1001-8.

99. Hearings, House Committee on Government Operations, Subcommittee on Conservation and Natural Resources, *Stream Channelization*, 92d Cong., 1st sess., May 1971, p. 10.

100. Richard N. L. Andrews, *Environmental Policy and Administrative Change* (Lexington, Mass.: D.C. Health, 1976), p. 96.

101. Ibid., p. 99.

102. Helen Ingram, "The Politics of Information: Constraints on New Sources," in John C. Pierce and Harvey R. Doerksen, eds., *Water Politics and Public Involvement* (Ann Arbor: Ann Arbor Science Publishers, 1976), p. 71.

103. Andrews, *Environmental Policy*, pp. 99, 119.

104. Hearings, House Committee on Appropriations, Subcommittee on Agriculture

and Environmental and Consumer Protection Appropriations, *Agriculture, Environmental and Consumer Protection Appropriations for 1975*, 93d Cong., 2d sess., part 2, p. 393.

105. Leman, "Political Dilemmas in Evaluating and Budgeting Soil Conservation Programs," p. 84.

106. *Appendix to the Budget for Fiscal Year 1981*, pp. 167-77.

107. Leman, "Political Dilemmas in Evaluating and Budgeting Soil Conservation Programs," p. 80.

108. Hearings, House Committee on Appropriations, Subcommittee on Agriculture, Rural Development and Related Agencies, *Agriculture Rural Development and Related Agencies Appropriations for 1982*, 97th Cong., 1st sess., part 5, p. 658.

109. Ibid., pp. 660-61, 690.

110. General Accounting Office, "Agriculture's Soil Conservation Programs Miss Full Potential in the Fight Against Soil Erosion," RCED-84-48, Nov. 28, 1983, p. i.

111. *Washington Post*, "HOT Soil-Saving Campaigns Are SOARing," March 4, 1984, p. A-14.

112. Hearings, House Committee on Appropriations, Subcommittee on Agriculture, Rural Development and Related Agencies, *Agriculture, Rural Development and Related Agencies Appropriations for 1982*, 97th Cong., 1st sess., part 5, p. 662.

113. *Appendix to the Budget for Fiscal Year 1984*, pp. I-E68 to I-E76.

114. Leman, "Political Dilemmas for Evaluating and Budgeting Soil Conservation Programs," p. 57.

115. Hearings, House Committee on Appropriations, Subcommittee on Agriculture, Rural Development and Related Agencies, *Agriculture, Rural Development and Related Agencies Appropriations for 1982*, 97th Cong., 1st sess., part 5, p. 726.

116. *New York Times*, Jan. 29, 1980, p. 10.

117. Smith, *Politics of Conservation*, p. 230.

118. Hearings, House Committee on Appropriations (remarks of Chairman Jamie Whitten), Subcommittee on Agriculture and Related Agencies, *Agriculture and Related Agencies Appropriations For 1977*, 94th Cong., 2d sess., part 4, p. 317.

119. 41st Congress, 3d sess., [No. 22] "Joint Resolution for the Protection and Preservation of the Food Fishes of the Coast of the United States," Feb. 9, 1871.

120. Richard A. Cooley, *Politics and Conservation: The Decline and Fall of the Alaska Salmon* (New York: Harper and Row, 1963), p. 73.

121. Ibid.

122. Ibid., p. 78.

123. Ibid., pp. 124-25.

124. Ibid., p. xiv.

125. "An Act to enlarge the powers of the Department of Agriculture, prohibit the transportation by interstate commerce of game killed in violation of local laws, and for other purposes." 56th Congress, 1st sess., chap. 553, 1900, pp. 187-88.

126. "To supplement and support the Migratory Bird Conservation Act by providing funds for the acquisition of areas for use as migratory bird sanctuaries, refuges, and breeding grounds, for developing and administering such areas, for the protection of certain migratory birds, for the enforcement of the Migratory Bird Treaty Act and regulations thereunder, and for other purposes." 73d Cong., 2d sess., Chap. 71, Mar. 16, 1934, p. 451.

127. Public Land Law Review Commission, *One Third of the Nation's Lands* (Washington, D.C.: Government Printing Office, 1970), p. 21.

128. Pub. L. 1024, Aug. 8, 1956, 70 stat., p. 1120.

129. Hearings, House Committee on Merchant Marine and Fisheries, *Reorganization of Fish and Wildlife Service*, 85th Cong., 1st sess., 1957, p. 148.

130. For a discussion of this point see Herbert Kaufman, *The Forest Ranger: A Study in Administrative Behavior* (Baltimore: Johns Hopkins University Press, 1960).

131. Hearings, House Committee on Appropriations, Subcommittee on Department of the Interior and Related Agencies Appropriations, *Department of the Interior and Related Agencies Appropriations For 1973*, 92d Cong., 2d sess., part 2, p. 825.

132. Hearings, House Committee on Appropriations, Subcommittee on Department of the Interior and Related Agencies Appropriations, *Department of the Interior and Related Agencies Appropriations For 1972*, 92d Cong., 1st sess., part 2, p. 220.

133. Hearings, House Committee on Appropriations, Subcommittee on Department of the Interior and Related Agencies Appropriations, *Department of the Interior and Related Agencies Appropriations For 1973*, 92d Cong., 2d sess., part 2, p. 837.

134. *Appendix to the Budget for Fiscal Year 1981*, pp. 569-75.

135. Hearings, House Committee on Appropriations, Subcommittee on Energy and Water Development, *Energy and Water Development Appropriations for 1982*, 97th Cong., 1st sess., part 3, pp. 7-9.

136. Ibid., part 10, pp. 16, 44.

137. Ibid., pp. 41-42, 109.

138. Ibid., pp. 40-41.

139. Ibid., pp. 127-28; part 8, p. 126.

140. Hearings, House Committee on Appropriations, Subcommittee on the Department of the Interior and Related Agencies, *Department of the Interior and Related Agencies Appropriations For 1984*, 98th Cong., 1st sess., part 1, pp. 358-71.

141. Hearings, House Committee on Appropriations, Subcommittee on the Department of the Interior and Related Agencies, *Department of the Interior and Related Agencies Appropriations For 1982*, 97th Cong., 1st sess., part 1, p. 812.

142. Ibid., p. 814.

143. Ibid., part 8, pp. 100-111.

144. Ibid., part 1, p. 836.

145. Ibid., part 8, p. 108.

146. Ibid., part 10, pp. 16-17.

147. Ibid., p. 18.

148. Ibid., p. 44.

149. This report is discussed in an article in *USA Today*, Oct. 6, 1983, p. 11A.

150. Hearings, House Committee on Appropriations, Subcommittee on the Department of the Interior and Related Agencies, *Department of the Interior and Related Agencies Appropriations For 1983*, 97th Cong., 2d sess., part 1, p. 361.

151. K. William Easter and Melvin L. Cotner, "Evaluation of Current Soil Conservation Strategies," in Halcrow, Heady, and Cotner, *Soil Conservation Policies, Institutions, and Incentives* (Ankeny, Iowa: Soil Conservation Society of America, 1982), p. 286.

Chapter 4. Organizational Shooting Stars

1. Bernard DeVoto, The Year of Decision: 1846 (Boston: Houghton Mifflin, 1942), p. viii.

2. George Sibley, "The Desert Empire," *Harpers* (Oct. 1977), p. 53.

3. Frank E. Smith, *Politics of Conservation* (New York: Harper Colophon Books, 1966), p. 50.

4. Sibley, "Desert Empire," p. 54.

5. "An Act Appropriating the receipts from the sale and disposal of public lands in certain States and Territories to the construction of irrigation works for the reclamation of arid lands," 1902 (43 U.S.C. 391), p. 388 (known as the Reclamation Act).

6. Hearings, House Committee on Appropriations, Subcommittee on Public Works Appropriations, *Public Works for Water, Pollution Control and Power Development and AEC Appropriation Bill, 1971*, 91st Cong., 2d sess., part 3, pp. 28-46.

7. Reclamation Act of 1902 (43 U.S.C. 391), p. 389.

8. Hearings, House Committee on Appropriations, Subcommittee on Department of Interior Appropriations, *Department of Interior Appropriations for 1923*, 67th Cong., 2d sess., p. 619.

9. Sibley, "Desert Empire," p. 56.

10. Hearings, House Committee on Appropriations, Subcommittee on Department of Interior, Interior Department Appropriation Bill For 1940, 76th Cong., 1st sess., p. 250.

11. Owen Stratton and Phillip Sirotkin, *The Echo Park Controversy* (University: University of Alabama Press, 1959), p. 10.

12. Arthur Maass, *The Kings River Project: Case Studies in Public Administration and Policy Formation* (University: University of Alabama Press, 1950).

13. Hearings, House Committee on Appropriations, Subcommittee on the Department of the Interior, *Interior Department Appropriation Bill For 1946*, 79th Cong., 1st sess., p. 1377.

14. Elmo Richardson, *Dams, Parks, and Politics* (Lexington: University Press of Kentucky, 1973), p. 48.

15. Hearings, House Committee on Appropriations, Subcommittee on Department of the Interior and Related Agencies Appropriations, *Department of the Interior and Related Agencies Appropriations For 1966*, 89th Cong., 1st sess., part 1, p. 13.

16. Hearings, House Committee on Appropriations, Subcommittee on Department of Interior and Related Agencies Appropriations, *Department of the Interior and Related Agencies Appropriations For 1975*, 93d Cong., 1st sess., part 2, p. 154.

17. Richard L. Berkman and W. Kip Viscusi, *Damning the West* (New York: Grossman Publishers, 1973).

18. Hearings, House Committee on Appropriations, Subcommittee on Public Works, *Public Works For Water and Power Development and Energy Research Appropriation Bill, 1978*, 95th Cong., 1st sess., part 3, p. 225.

19. Ibid., p. 220.

20. *New York Times*, Mar. 12, 1977, p. 11.

21. Ibid., Mar. 7, 1977, p. 20.

22. *Congressional Quarterly Weekly Reports*, July 1, 1977, p. 1338.

23. Ibid., July 30, 1977, p. 1585.

24. Ibid., July 2, 1977, p. 1338.

25. *Los Angeles Times*, June 10, 1978, p. 1.

26. Hearings, House Committee on Appropriations, Subcommittee on Public Works, *Public Works For Water and Power Development and Energy Research Appropriation Bill For 1979*, 95th Cong., 2d sess., part 3, pp. 2-3.

27. 438 U.S. 645 (1978).

28. Ibid., pp. 655-67.

29. Executive Order 12113, Jan. 4, 1979.

30. *New York Times*, Feb. 12, 1979, p. 5. Also see Hearings, House Committee on Appropriations, Subcommittee on Energy and Water Development, *Energy and Water Development Appropriations For 1980*, 96th Cong., 1st sess., part 1, p. 46.

31. Department of the Interior news release, Nov. 6, 1979.

32. Ibid.

33. *U.S. Budget*, fiscal years 1979, 1982.

34. Hearings, House Committee on Appropriations, Subcommittee on Energy and Water Development, *Energy and Water Development Appropriations For 1980*, 96th Cong., 1st sess., part 1, pp. 193-95.

35. R. Keith Higginson, speech before the American Water Resources Association, Denver, Colo., Nov. 6, 1979.

36. *Arizona Daily Star*, Nov. 15, 1981, p. 1.

37. *New York Times*, Sept. 18, 1981, p. 15.

38. Christopher Leman, "Political Dilemmas in Evaluating and Budgeting Soil Conservation Policies: The RCA Process," in Halcrow, Heady, and Cotner, *Soil*

Conservation Policies, Institutions, and Incentives (Ankeny, Iowa: Soil Conservation Society of America, 1982), p. 54.

39. Hearings, House Committee on Appropriations, Subcommittee on Energy and Water Development, *Energy and Water Development Appropriations For 1982*, 97th Cong., 1st sess., part 3, p. 27.

40. Ibid., pp. 11-12.

41. Ibid., p. 26.

42. Ibid., pp. 26-27.

43. *Congressional Quarterly Weekly Report*, June 19, 1982, p. 1461.

44. General Accounting Office, "Federal Charges for Irrigation Projects Reviewed Do Not Cover Costs," PAD-81-07, Mar. 3, 1981.

45. Hearings, House Committee on Appropriations, Subcommittee on Energy and Water Development, *Energy and Water Development Appropriations For 1984*, 98th Cong., 1st sess., part 3, p. 71.

46. General Accounting Office, "Impact Uncertain from Reorganization of the Water and Power Service," CED-81-80, Apr. 29, 1981.

47. *Congressional Quarterly Weekly Report*, May 8, 1982, p. 1072.

48. *National Journal*, Aug. 8, 1982, p. 1423.

49. Wesley Calef, *Private Grazing and Public Lands* (Chicago: University of Chicago Press, 1960), p. 250.

50. Roy M. Robbins, *Our Landed Heritage: The Public Domain, 1776-1936* (Lincoln: University of Nebraska Press, 1962), p. 257.

51. Samuel P. Hays, *Conservation and the Gospel of Efficiency* (Cambridge: Harvard University Press, 1959), pp. 49-50.

52. Ibid., pp. 63-65.

53. Robbins, *Landed Heritage*, p. 411.

54. Ibid., pp. 413-15.

55. Quoted in Ibid., p. 416.

56. Ibid., p. 417.

57. Ibid., p. 418.

58. Ibid., p. 421.

59. Paul J. Culhane, *Public Lands Politics: Interest Group Influence on the Forest Service and the Bureau of Land Management* (Baltimore: Johns Hopkins University Press, 1981), p. 83.

60. Robbins, *Landed Heritage*, p. 423.

61. Culhane, *Public Lands Politics*, p. 88.

62. Robbins, *Landed Heritage*, p. 413.

63. Public Land Law Review Commission, *One Third of the Nation's Land* (Washington, D.C.: Government Printing Office, 1970), p. 105.

64. Phillip Foss, *Politics and Grass* (Seattle: University of Washington Press, 1960), p. 202.

65. Paul J. Culhane and H. Paul Friesema, "Land use Planning for the Public Lands," *Natural Resources Journal* 19 (Jan. 1979) pp. 43-74.

66. Calef, *Private Grazing*, p. 261.

67. Samuel Trask Dana and Sally K. Fairfax, *Forest and Range Policy* (New York: McGraw-Hill, 1980), p. 342.

68. Culhane, *Public Lands Politics,* pp. 86-88.

69. Dorotha M. Bradley and Helen M. Ingram, "Science vs. the Grassroots: Representation in the Bureau of Land Management" Unpublished paper, Department of Political Science, University of Arizona, p. 12.

70. Calef, *Private Grazing,* p. 262.

71. Ibid., p. 265.

72. Dana and Fairfax, *Forest and Range Policy,* p. 229.

73. Ibid.

74. Culhane and Friesema, "Land Use Planning," p. 45.

75. Culhane, *Public Lands Politics,* p. 105.

76. Public Land Law Review Commission, *One Third of the Nation's Land,* p. ix.

77. Hearings, House Committee on Appropriations, Subcommittee on the Department of Interior and Related Agencies, *Department of Interior and Related Agencies Appropriations for 1982,* 97th Cong., 1st sess., part 9, pp. 268-69.

78. Ibid., part 5, p. 190.

79. Ibid., part 9, p. 441.

80. Ibid., part 5, p. 175.

81. Jim Zumbo, "Rebellion Rationale," *American Forests* 87 (Mar. 1981), p. 25.

82. Ibid.

83. *Natural Resources Defense Council v. Morton,* 458 F.2d 827 (D.C. Cir., 1972).

84. Hearings, House Committee on Appropriations, Subcommittee on the Department of Interior and Related Agencies, *Department of Interior and Related Agencies Appropriations For 1982,* 97th Cong., 1st sess., part 9, p. 175.

85. John Francis, "The West and the Prospects for Rebellion: An Analysis of State Legislative Responses to the Public Lands Question," in Richard Ganzel, ed. *Resource Conflicts in the West* (Reno: Nevada Public Affairs Institute, 1983), p. 25.

86. Hearings, House Committee on Appropriations, Subcommittee on the Department of the Interior and Related Agencies, *Department of the Interior and Related Agencies Appropriations For 1982,* 97th Cong., 1st sess., part 9, p. 191.

87. Burford has a permit to graze livestock on 33,614 acres of public lands. In order to meet conflict-of-interest laws Burford was required to dispose of his grazing permits. He transferred his permits to his son. Ibid., pp. 151-52.

88. Ibid., part 8, pp. 2, 13.

89. Ibid., pp. 8-11.

90. Ibid., part 9, pp. 293-96.

91. Ibid., pp. 402-4, and part 8, pp. 4-5.

92. Ibid., pp. 22-23; and *NRDC v. Morton,* 458 F.2d 827 (D.C. Cir., 1972).

93. Hearings, House Committee on Appropriations, Subcommittee on the Department of the Interior and Related Agencies, *Department of the Interior and Related Agencies Appropriations For 1982*, 97th Cong., 1st sess., part 9, p. 399.

94. Ibid.

95. Ibid.

96. Ibid., part 3, p. 10.

97. Ibid., part 8, p. 38.

98. Ibid., part 9, pp. 355-56.

99. Ibid., pp. 358-59.

100. General Accounting Office, "Analysis of the Powder River Basin Federal Coal Lease Sale: Economic Valuation Improvements and Legislative Changes Needed," RCED-83-119, May 11, 1983.

101. *Congressional Quarterly Weekly Report*, June 25, 1983, p. 1306.

102. James Watt, Secretary of the Interior, Secretarial Order No. 3087, December 3, 1982.

103. Secretary Clark may also abandon Watt's plan to lease the entire Outer Continental Shelf. See *Wall Street Journal*, Jan. 11, 1984, p. 6.

104. Telephone interview with Paul Herndon, Information Specialist, Bureau of Land Management, Apr. 5, 1984.

105. Telephone interview with Bob Johns, Information Specialist, Bureau of Land Management, Apr. 5, 1984. A *Wall Street Journal* article claimed 399 leases were made illegally, but this included 143 leases still under study to determine how they should be leased. The program is currently suspended. See *Wall Street Journal*, Apr. 4, 1984, p. 2.

106. A recent article in the *National Journal* concluded that "Watt will leave an entrenched ideological team that will attempt to carry on his pro-development policies regardless of the mounting opposition" (Nov. 5, 1983, p. 2306).

107. Hearings, House Committee on Appropriations, Subcommittee on the Department of Interior and Related Agencies, *Department of the Interior and Related Agencies Appropriations For 1984*, 98th Cong., 1st sess., part 1, p. 11.

Chapter 5. A Cross Validation of Agency Power

1. Eugene J. Webb, Donald T. Campbell, Richard D. Schwartz, and Lee Sechrest, *Unobtrusive Measures: Nonreactive Research in the Social Sciences* (Chicago: Rand McNally, 1966), pp. 1-2.

2. See appendix for the questionnaire schedule.

3. Hearings, House Committee on Appropriations, Subcommittee on the Department of Interior and Related Agencies, *Department of Interior and Related Agencies Appropriations For 1973*, 92d Cong., 2d sess., part 2, p. 837.

4. Hearings, House Committee on Appropriations, Subcommittee on Public Works, *Public Works for Water and Power Development and Atomic Energy Commission Appropriation Bill, 1974*, 93d Cong., 1st sess., part 1, p. 26.

5. Jeanne Nienaber and Aaron Wildavsky, *The Budgeting and Evaluation of Federal Recreation Programs: Or, Money Doesn't Grow on Trees* (New York:

Basic Books, 1973).

6. In 1950 there was an annual visitation of 33 million to the national park system. In 1976 there was an annual visitation of 240 million, plus the additional responsibility for executing the bicentennial program. U.S. Budget, 1950-76.

7. A deficit was mentioned again in 1971. Hearings, House Committee on Appropriations, Subcommittee on the Department of the Interior and Related Agencies, *Department of the Interior and Related Agencies Appropriations For 1972,* 91st Cong., 2d sess., part 3, p. 455.

8. Nienaber and Wildavsky, *Budgeting and Evaluation of Federal Recreation Programs,* pp. 107-8.

9. For a concise statement of this proposition, see Matthew Holden, Jr., " 'Imperialism' in Bureaucracy," *American Political Science Review* 60 (Dec. 1966), pp. 943-51.

10. Richard Fenno, *The Power of the Purse* (Boston: Little, Brown, 1966), p. 412. His study did not include the Corps of Engineers.

11. Fenno, *Power of the Purse;* Ira Sharkansky, "Agency Requests, Gubernatorial Support, and Budget Success in State Legislatures," *American Political Science Review* 62 (Dec. 1968), pp. 1223-35; Otto Davis, M. A. H. Dempster, Aaron Wildavsky, "On the Process of Budgeting II: An Empirical Study of Congressional Appropriations," in R. F. Byrne, A. Charles, W. W. Cooper, O. A. Davis, and Dorothy Gifford, eds., *Studies in Budgeting* (New York: American Elsevier Pub., 1971) pp. 292-391; Harvey Tucker, "Budgeting Strategy: Cross-Sectional Versus Longitudinal Models," *Public Administration Review* 41 (Nov. /Dec. 1981), no. 6, pp. 644-49.

12. Anthony Downs, "Up and Down with Ecology: The Issue-Attention Cycle," *Public Interest* 28 (Summer 1972), pp. 38-50.

13. Holden, " 'Imperialism' in Bureaucracy," pp. 943-51.

14. *The State of the Environment 1982* (Washington, D. C.: Conservation Foundation, 1982).

15. Bureau of Labor Statistics, *Current Wage Developments* (Washington, D. C.:Government Printing Office, 1975), table 1, p. 47.

16. Burt Schorr and Andy Pasztor, "In Command: Reaganites Make Sure That the Bureaucracy Toes the Line on Policy," *Wall Street Journal,* Feb. 10, 1982, pp. 1, 6.

CHAPTER 6. RESOURCE MANAGEMENT IN THE 1980S

1. Gifford Pinchot, *Breaking New Ground* (New York: Harcourt and Brace, 1947), p. 507.

2. Frederick Lewis Allen, *The Lords of Creation* (Chicago: Quadrangle Books, 1966).

3. Hugh Heclo, *A Government of Strangers: Executive Politics in Washington* (Washington, D.C.: Brookings Institution, 1977), p. 15.

4. Charles C. Alexander, *Holding the Line: The Eisenhower Era, 1952-1961* (Bloomington: Indiana University Press, 1975).

5. Matthew Holden, Jr., " 'Imperialism' in Bureaucracy," in Francis E. Rourke,

ed., *Bureaucratic Power in National Politics*, 3d ed. (Boston: Little, Brown, 1978), pp. 164-81.

ed., *Bureaucratic Power in National Politics*, 3d ed. (Boston: Little, Brown, 1978), pp. 164-81.

6. John Kenneth Galbraith, *The New Industrial State* (New York: Signet Books, 1967), p. 21.

7. Herbert Kaufman, *Are Government Organizations Immortal?* (Washington, D.C.: Brookings Institution, 1976).

8. Ibid., p. 70.

9. David S. Brown, " 'Reforming' the Bureaucracy: Some Suggestions for the New President," in Francis E. Rourke, ed., *Bureaucratic Power in National Politics*, pp. 377-89.

10. Ibid., p. 380.

11. Richard Hofstadter, *Social Darwinism in American Thought* (Boston: Beacon Press, 1955).

12. Grant McConnell, *The Modern Presidency*, 2d ed. (New York: St. Martin's Press, 1976), p. 65.

13. Martin Landau, "Redundancy, Rationality, and the Problem of Duplication and Overlap," in Francis E. Rourke, ed., *Bureaucratic Power in National Politics*, pp. 422-36.

14. Ludwig von Bertalanffy, *General System Theory* (New York: George Braziller, 1968), p. 48.

15. Theodore J. Lowi, *The End of Liberalism: The Second Republic of the United States*, 2d ed. (New York: W.W. Norton, 1979).

16. Von Bertalanffy, *General System Theory*, p. 48.

Bibliography

Alexander, Charles C. *Holding the Line: The Eisenhower Era, 1952-1961.* Bloomington: Indiana University Press, 1975.

Allen, Frederick Lewis. *The Lords of Creation.* Chicago: Quadrangle Books, 1966.

Andrews, Richard N. L. *Environmental Policy and Administrative Change.* Lexington, Mass.: D. C. Heath, 1976.

Arizona Daily Star. Nov. 15, 1981, p. 1.

Berkman, Richard L., and W. Kip Viscusi. *Damning the West.* New York: Grossman Publishers, 1973.

Bloomfield, Howard. "Quandary in the Campgrounds," *American Forests* 75 (July 1969): 6, 39-40.

Bradley, Dorotha M., and Helen M. Ingram, "Science vs. the Grassroots: Representation in the Bureau of Land Management." Paper presented at the Public Lands Conference, Politics vs. Policy: The Public Lands Dilemma, Utah State University, Logan, Utah, Apr. 21-23, 1982.

Brandborg, Stewart. "The Wilderness Law and the National Park System in the U.S." In *Canadian Parks in Perspective,* edited by J. G. Nelson, pp. 264-83. Quebec, Canada: Harvest House, 1970.

Brown, David S. " 'Reforming' the Bureaucracy: Some Suggestions for the New President." In *Bureaucratic Power in National Politics,* edited by Francis E. Rourke. Boston: Little, Brown, 1978: 377-89.

"Budget Plans Starve the National Park Service." *National Parks and Conservation Association Magazine* (June 1975): 19-20.

U. S. Bureau of Labor Statistics. *Current Wage Developments.* Washington, D.C.: Government Printing Office, 1975.

Calef, Wesley. *Private Grazing and Public Lands.* Chicago: University of Chicago Press, 1960.

Chicago Tribune. Dec. 27, 1977, p. 8; Dec. 29, 1977, p. III-2.

"Closing the Door on the National Parks." *National Parks and Conservation Association Magazine* (Jan. 1975): 23-4.

Congressional Quarterly Weekly Reports. July 2, 1977, p. 1338; July 30, 1977, p. 1585; Mar. 4, 1978, p. 568; Nov. 28, 1981, p. 2352; May 8, 1982; June 19, 1982, p. 1461; June 25, 1983, p. 1306.

175

Cooley, Richard A. *Politics and Conservation: The Decline and Fall of The Alaskan Salmon.* New York: Harper and Row, 1963.

Craig, James B. "Plusses and Minuses in the National Parks." *American Forests* (June 1976): 4.

"The Crisis in National Park Personnel." *National Parks and Conservation Association Magazine* (Apr. 1975): 20.

Culhane, Paul J. *Public Lands Politics: Interest Group Influence on the Forest Service and the Bureau of Land Management.* Baltimore: Johns Hopkins University Press, 1981.

Culhane, Paul J., and H. Paul Friesema. "Land Use Planning for the Public Lands." *Natural Resources Journal* 19 (Jan. 1979): 43-74.

Dana, Samuel T., and Sally K. Fairfax. *Forest and Range Policy.* New York: McGraw-Hill, 1980.

Darling, F. Fraser,. and Noel D. Eichhorn. *Man and Nature in the National Parks.* Washington, D.C.: Conservation Foundation, 1967.

Davis, Otto, M. A. H. Dempster, and Aaron Wildavsky. "On the Process of Budgeting II: An Empirical Study of Congressional Appropriations." *Studies in Budgeting,* edited by R. F. Byrne, A. Charles, W. W. Cooper, O. A. Davis, and Dorothy Gifford. New York: American Elsevier Publishing, 1971: 292-392.

Devoto, Bernard. *The Year of Decision: 1846.* Boston: Houghton Mifflin, 1942.

Downs, Anthony. "Up and Down With Ecology: The Issue-Attention Cycle." *Public Interest* 28 (Summer 1972): 38-50.

Drury, Newton B. "Former Directors Speak Out." *American Forests* (June 1976): 28.

Easter, K. William, and Melvin L. Cotner. "Evaluation of Current Soil Conservation Strategies." In *Soil Conservation Policies, Institutions, and Incentives,* edited by Harold G. Halcrow, Earl O. Heady, and Melvin L. Cotner. Ankeny, Iowa: Soil Conservation Society of America, 1982: 283-301.

Everhart, William C. *The National Park Service.* New York: Praeger Pub., 1972.

Fairfax, Sally. "RPA and the Forest Service." University of California, Berkeley. Typescript.

Fenno, Richard. *The Power of the Purse.* Boston: Little, Brown, 1966.

Foss, Phillip. *Politics and Grass.* Seattle: University of Washington Press, 1960.

Foresta, Ronald A. *America's National Parks And Their Keepers.* Washington, D.C.: Resources For the Future, 1984.

Fradkin, Phillip L. *A River No More.* New York: Alfred A. Knopf, 1981.

Francis, John. "The West and the Prospects for Rebellion: An Analysis of State Legislative Responses to the Public Lands Question." In *Resource Conflicts in the West,* edited by Richard Ganzel. Reno: Nevada Public Affairs Institute, 1983: 4-29.

Fraser, Charles. "Park Agencies for the Future." *Parks and Recreation* (Aug. 1973): 21, 23, 35, 37-8.

Galbraith, John Kenneth. *The New Industrial State.* New York: Signet Books, 1967.

Ganzel, Richard, and Dorothy Olkowski. "The Politics of Coalition-Building: The Inholders Reach Out." Paper presented at the Western Social Science Association Meeting, Albuquerque, New Mexico, Apr. 1983.

Gold, Kenneth. "A Comparative Analysis of Successful Organizations." U.S. Office of Personnel Management, July 1, 1981. Mimeographed.

Hays, Samuel P. *Conservation and the Gospel of Efficiency.* Cambridge: Harvard University Press, 1959.

Hartzog, George B. "Management Considerations for Optimum Development and Protection of National Park Resources." In *World Conference on National Parks 2d.* Lausanne, Switzerland: International Union for Conservation of Nature and Natural Resources, pp. 155-161.

Heclo, Hugh. *A Government of Strangers: Executive Politics in Washington.* Washington, D.C.: Brookings Institution, 1977.

Hofstadter, Richard. *Social Darwinism in American Thought.* Boston: Beacon Press, 1955.

Holden, Matthew, Jr. " 'Imperialism' in Bureaucracy." *American Political Science Review* 60 (Dec. 1966): 943-51.

Hoover Commission. *Report on Organization of the Executive Branch of Government.* New York: McGraw-Hill, 1949.

Ingram, Helen. "The Politics of Information: Constraints on New Sources." In *Water Politics and Public Involvement,* edited by John C. Pierce and Harvey R. Doerksen. Ann Arbor, Mich.: Ann Arbor Science Publishers, 1976: 63-73.

Kaufman, Herbert. *The Forest Ranger: A Study in Administrative Behavior.* Baltimore: Johns Hopkins University Press, 1960.

————. *Are Government Organizations Immortal?* Washington, D.C.: Brookings Institution, 1976.

Landau, Martin. "Redundancy, Rationality, and the Problem of Duplication and Overlap." In *Bureaucratic Power in National Politics,* edited by Francis Rourke. Boston: Little, Brown, 1978: 422-36

Leman, Christopher. "Resource Assessment and Program Development: An Evaluation of Forest Service Experience under the Resources Planning Act, with Lessons for Other Natural Resource Agencies." Mimeographed.

————. "Political Dilemmas in Evaluating and Budgeting Soil Conservation Programs: The RCA Process." In *Soil Conservation Policies, Institutions, and Incentives,* edited by Halcrow, Heady, and Cotner. Ankeny, Iowa: Soil Conservation Society of America, 1982: 47-88.

Lindblom, Charles E. "The Science of ' 'Muddling Through' '." *Public Administration Review* 19 (Spring 1959): 79-88.

Liroff, Richard. *A National Policy for the Environment: NEPA and Its Aftermath.* Bloomington: Indiana University Press, 1976.

Los Angeles Times. June 10, 1978, p. 1; June 16, 1978, p. 11; Oct. 12, 1978, p. 7.

Lowi, Theodore. *The End of Liberalism,* 2d ed. New York: W.W. Norton, 1979.

Maass, Arthur. *The Kings River Project: Case Studies in Public Administration and Policy Formulation.* University: University of Alabama Press, 1950.

————. *Muddy Waters: The Army Engineers and the Nation's Rivers.* Cambridge: Harvard University Press, 1951.

McConnell, Grant. *The Modern Presidency,* 2d ed. New York: St. Martin's Press, 1976.

Mazmanian, Daniel, and Jeanne Nienaber. *Can Organizations Change? Environmental Protection, Citizen Participation, and the Corps of Engineers.* Washington, D.C.: Brookings Institution, 1979.

Morgan, Robert J. *Governing Soil Conservation.* Baltimore: Johns Hopkins University Press, 1962.

Nash, Roderick. *Wilderness and the American Mind.* New Haven: Yale University Press, 1967.

National Journal Apr. 9, 1977, p. 547; Aug. 8, 1982, p. 1423; July 23, 1983, p. 1559; Nov. 5, 1983, p. 2306.

National Parks and Conservation Association. "Park Resource Survey, 1975." *National Parks and Conservation Magazine* (Feb. 1976): 11-16, and (Mar. 1976): 9-14.

"National Parks in Peril." *Life,* July 1983, pp. 106-112.

Natural Resources Defense Council v. Morton. 458 F.2d. 827 D.C. Cir., 1972.

New York Times. 1977: Feb. 21, p. 1; Feb. 22, p. 13; Mar. 7, pp. 1, 20; Mar. 12, p. 11; Mar. 13, p. 24; Mar. 24, p. 1; Apr. 16, p. 1; May 3, p. 34; Aug. 9, p. 17; Dec. 13, p. 16. 1979: Feb. 12, pp. 1, 5, 18; July 19, p. 18; Oct. 25, p. 18. 1980: Jan. 24, p. D-22; Jan. 29, p. 10; Feb. 6, p. 17. 1981: Mar. 29, p. 32; May 12, p. D-22; June 16, p. D-12; Aug. 9, p. 1.

Nienaber, Jeanne, and Aaron Wildavsky. *The Budgeting and Evaluation of Federal Recreation Programs: Or, Money Doesn't Grow on Trees.* New York: Basic Boks, 1973.

Novogrod, Joseph, Gladys O. Dimock, Marshall E. Dimock. *Casebook in Public Administration.* New York: Holt, Rinehart and Winston, 1969.

O'Neill, William. *The Progressive Years: America Comes of Age.* New York: Dodd, Mead and Co., 1975.

Pinchot, Gifford. *Breaking New Ground.* New York: Harcourt and Brace, 1947.

Rasmussen, Wayne D. "History of Soil Conservation, Institutions, and Incentives." In *Soil Conservation Policies, Institutions, and Incentives,* edited by Halcrow, Heady, and Cotner. Ankeny, Iowa: Soil Conservation Society of America, 1982: 3-18.

Richardson, Elmo. *Dams, Parks, and Politics.* Lexington: University of Kentucky Press, 1973.

Robbins, Roy M. *Our Landed Heritage: The Public Domain, 1776-1936.* Lincoln: University of Nebraska Press, 1962.

Rourke, Francis. *Bureaucracy, Politics, and Public Policy.* Boston: Little, Brown, 1976.

―――. "Grappling with the Bureaucracy." In *Politics and the Oval Office,* edited by Arnold J. Meltsner. San Francisco: Institute for Contemporary Studies, 1981.

Schorr, Burt, and Andy Pasztor. "In Command: Reaganites Make Sure That the Bureaucracy Toes the Line on Policy." *Wall Street Journal,* Feb. 10, 1982, 1.

"Senate-House Views Expressed on National Parks." *National Wildlife Federation Newsletter,* report no. 24, Aug. 8, 1976, p. 290.

Sharkansky, Ira. "Agency Requests, Gubernatorial Support, and Budget Success in State Legislatures." *American Political Science Review* 62 (Dec. 1968): 1223-37.

Sibley, George. "The Desert Empire." *Harper's* (Oct. 1977): 49-68.

Smith, Frank E. *The Politics of Conservation.* New York: Harper Colophon Books, 1966.

State of the Environment 1982. Washington, D.C.: Conservation Foundation, 1982.

Stratton, Owen, and Phillip Sirotkin. *The Echo Park Controversy*. University: University of Alabama Press, 1959.

Swain, Donald. *Wilderness Defender*. Chicago: University of Chicago Press, 1970.

Swem, Theodore. "Planning of National Parks." In *Canadian Parks in Perspective*, edited by J. G. Nelson. Quebec, Canada: Harvest House, 1970. pp. 249-63.

Tucker, Harvey. "Budgeting Strategy: Cross-Sectional versus Longitudinal Models." *Public Administration Review* 41, no. 6 (Nov/Dec. 1981): 644-49.

Tucson Citizen. Jan. 20, 1982, p. A-3.

USA Today, Oct. 6, 1983, p. 11-A.

von Bertalanffy, Ludwig. *General System Theory*. New York: George Braziller, 1968.

Wall Street Journal. Nov. 11, 1983, p. 1; Jan. 11, 1984, p. 6; Apr. 4, 1984, p. 2.

Washington Post. Aug. 5, 1977, p. 5; Dec. 19, 1977, p. 1-4; "HOT Soil Saving Campaigns are SOARing," Mar. 4, 1984, p. A14.

Webb, Eugene J., Donald T. Campbell, Richard D. Schwartz, Lee Sechrest. *Unobtrusive Measures: Nonreactive Research in the Social Sciences*. Chicago: Rand McNally, 1966.

Weber, Max. "Politics as a Vocation." In *From Max Weber: Essays In Sociology*, edited by H. H. Gerth and C. W. Mills, pp. 232-33. New York: Oxford University Press, 1958.

Wichelman, Allan F. "Administrative Agency Implementation of the National Environmental Policy Act of 1969: A Conceptual Framework for Explaining Differential Responses." *Natural Resources Journal* 16, no. 2 (Apr. 1976): 263-300.

GOVERNMENT DOCUMENTS

Army Corps of Engineers

Executive Order 12322. Sep. 17, 1981.

Presidential Documents: Jimmy Carter, 1977. Vol. 13, no. 17, Apr. 18, 1977, pp. 557-58.

U.S. Congress. 7th Cong., 1st sess., chap 9, sec. 26, Mar. 16, 1802. "An Act fixing the military peace establishment of the United States."

———. 18th Cong., 1st sess., chap. 139, sec. 2, May 24, 1824. "An Act to improve the navigation of the Ohio and Mississippi rivers."

———. House. Committee on Appropriations. Subcommittee on Public Works. Hearings on Appropriations for 1975. 93rd Cong., 2d sess., part 1.

———. Appropriations for 1978. 95th Cong., 1st sess., part 9.

———. Subcommittee on Energy and Water Development. Appropriations for 1982. 97th Cong., 1st sess., part 1.

———. House. Committee on Appropriations. Hearings on the Budget for 1979. 95th Cong., 2d sess., part 1.

———. Supplemental Appropriations and Rescission Bill, 1981. 97th Cong., 1st sess., part 1.

_____. Committee on Government Operations. Hearings on H.R. 6959, Reorganization of Executive Departments. 91st Cong., 1st sess., June 2, 1971, part 1.

_____. Committee on Rivers and Harbors. Pollution of Navigable Waters. Testimony of Thomas Robins, Deputy Chief of the Corps of Engineers. 79th Cong., 1st sess., 1945.

U.S. Department of the Treasury. *Appendix to the Budget for Fiscal Year 1981*, pp. 337-50.

_____. *Appendix to the Budget for Fiscal Year 1984*, pp. I-H2 to I-H4.

_____. *U.S. Budget, 1981*, pp. 426-28, 1022.

Bureau of Land Management

Public Land Law Review Commission. *One Third of the Nation's Land*. Washington, D.C.: Government Printing Office, 1970.

U.S. Congress. House. Committee on Appropriations. Subcommittee on the Department of Interior and Related Agencies. Appropriations for 1982. 97th Cong., 1st sess., part 9.

_____. Appropriations for 1984. 98th Cong., 1st sess., part 1.

U.S. Department of the Interior. Secretarial Order no. 3087, Dec. 3, 1982.

U.S. Department of the Treasury. *U.S. Budget, 1981*, pp. 539-49.

_____. General Accounting Office. "Analysis of the Powder River Basin Federal Coal Lease Sale: Economic Valuation Improvements and Legislative Changes Needed." RCED-83-119, May 11, 1983.

Bureau of Reclamation

Higginson, R. Keith. Speech before the American Water Resources Association, Denver, Colo. Nov. 6, 1979.

U.S. Congress. 438 U.S.C. 645 (1978).

_____. House. Committee on Appropriations. Subcommittee on the Department of Interior. Hearings on Appropriations for 1923, 67th Cong., 2d sess.

_____. Appropriations for 1940. 76th Cong., 1st sess.

_____. Appropriations for 1946. 79th Cong., 1st sess.

_____. Subcommittee on the Department of Interior and Related Agencies. Appropriations for 1966. 89th Cong., 1st sess., part 1.

_____. Subcommittee on Public Works. Appropriations for 1971. 91st Cong., 2d sess., part 3.

_____. Subcommittee on the Department of Interior and Related Agencies. Appropriations for 1975. 93rd Cong., 1st sess., part 2.

_____. Subcommittee on Public Works. Appropriations for 1978. 95th Cong., 1st sess., part 3.

_____. Appropriations for 1979. 95th Cong., 2d sess., part 3.

_____. Subcommittee on Energy and Water Development. Appropriations for 1980. 96th Cong., 1st sess., part 1.

_____. Appropriations for 1982. 97th Cong., 1st sess., part 3.

_____. Appropriations for 1984. 98th Cong., 1st sess., part 3.

U.S. Department of the Interior. News release, Nov. 6, 1979.

U.S. Department of the Treasury. *Appendix to the U.S. Budget for Fiscal Year 1981*, pp. 549-62.

———. General Accounting Office. "Federal Charges for Irrigation Projects Reviewed Do Not Cover Costs." PAD-81-07, Mar. 3, 1981.

———. "Impact Uncertain from Reorganization of the Water and Power Service." CED-81-80, Apr. 29, 1981.

Fish and Wildlife Service

Public Land Law Review Commission. *One Third of the Nation's Land.* Washington, D.C.: Government Printing Office, 1970.

U.S. Congress. 41st Cong., 3d sess., [no. 22] "Joint Resolution for the Protection and Preservation of the Food Fishes of the Coast of the United States." Feb. 9, 1871.

———. "An Act to enlarge the powers of the Department of Agriculture, prohibit the transportation by interstate commerce of game killed in violation of local laws, and for other purposes." 56th Cong., 1st sess., chap. 553, 1900, pp. 187-88.

———. "An Act to supplement and support the Migratory Bird Conservation Act by providing funds for the acquisition of areas for use as migratory bird sanctuaries, refuges, and breeding grounds, for developing and administering such areas, for the protection of certain migratory birds, for the enforcement of the Migratory Bird Treaty Act and regulations thereunder, and for other purposes", 73rd Congress, 2d sess., Chap. 71, Mar. 16, 1934, p. 451.

———. House. Committee on Merchant Marine and Fisheries. *Reorganization of the Fish and Wildlife Service.* 85th Cong., 1st sess., 1957.

———. Committee on Appropriations. Subcommittee on the Department of Interior and Related Agencies. Appropriations for 1972. 92nd Cong., 1st sess., part 2.

———. Appropriations for 1973. 92nd Cong., 2d sess., part 2.

———. Subcommittee on Energy and Water Development. 97th Cong., 1st sess., part 3.

———. Subcommittee on the Department of Interior and Related Agencies. Appropriations for 1983. 97th Cong., 2d sess., part 1.

———. Appropriations for 1984. 98th Cong., 1st sess., part 1.

U.S. Department of Interior. "Resource Problems." Fish and Wildlife Service report, July 1983.

U.S. Department of the Treasury. *Appendix to the U.S. Budget for Fiscal Year 1981,* pp. 569-75.

Forest Service

U.S. Department of Agriculture. Forest Service. RARE II: Final Environmental Statement, Roadless Area Review and Evaluation. (January 1979)

U.S. Congress. Act of Mar. 3, 1891. 51st Cong., 2d sess., chap. 561, sec. 24, "An Act to repeal timber-culture laws, and for other purposes."

———. Forest and Rangeland Renewable Resources Planning Act. 16 U.S.C. 1601 (1974).

———. National Forest Management Act. 16 U.S.C. 1600 (1976).

———. House. Committee on Appropriations. Subcommittee on Agriculture. Appropriations for 1931. 71st Cong., 2d sess.

————. Appropriations for 1939. 75th Cong., 3rd sess.

————. Appropriations for 1960. 86th Cong., 2d sess., part 1.

————. Subcommittee on the Department of Interior and Related Agencies. Appropriations for 1971. 91st Cong., 2d sess., part 1.

————. Appropriations for 1982. 97th Cong., 1st sess., part 10.

U.S. Department of the Treasury. *Appendix to the U.S. Budget for Fiscal Year 1981*, pp. 197-200.

————. *Appendix to the U.S. Budget for Fiscal Year 1983*, pp. I-E103 to I-E104.

————. *Appendix to the U.S. Budget for Fiscal Year 1984*, pp. I-E99 to I-E100.

General Accounting Office. "Facilities in Many National Parks and Forests Do Not Meet Health and Safety Standards." CED-80-115, Oct. 10, 1980.

National Park Service

U.S. Congress. "An Act to set apart a certain Tract of Land lying near the Head-waters of the Yellowstone River as a Public Park," Mar. 1, 1872, 42d Cong., 2d sess., Chap. 24, pp. 32-33.

————. "An Act to establish a National Park Service, and for other purposes," Aug. 25, 1916 (39 stat.535;16 U.S.C. 1).

————. Senate. Committee on Interior and Insular Affairs. Subcommittee on Parks and Recreation. *Proposed Reservation System in Selected National Parks*. 93rd Cong., 1st sess., 1973.

————. *Overnight Park Reservation System*. 93rd Cong., 2d sess., 1974.

————. House. Committee on Government Operations. *Degradation of Our National Parks*. 94th Cong., 1st sess., 1975, and 2d sess., 1976.

————. "The Degradation of the National Parks." 24th report, June 30, 1976.

————. Committee on Appropriations. Subcommittee on the Department of Interior and Related Agencies. Appropriations for 1982. 97th Cong., 1st sess., parts 1 and 12.

————. *Revised Justifications for Fiscal Year 1982*. 97th Cong., 1st sess., part 8.

U.S. Department of the Interior. "Background Material on the National Park Service." Document 527-76.

————. Memorandum from Secretary Stewart L. Udall. July 10, 1964. U.S. Department of Interior, National Park Service, *Administrative Policies For the Historical Areas of the National Park Service*. Washington: Government Printing Office, 1968, Appendix A, pp. 72-76.

————. National Park Service. *Management Policies*. Washington, D.C.: Government Printing Office, 1975.

————. National Park Service. *Park Road Standards*. Washington, D.C. Government Printing Office, 1968.

U.S. Department of the Treasury. "Detailed Budget Estimate." In *U.S. Budget*, 1956, 1964, 1966, 1967, 1968.

————. Office of U.S. Annual Budget. *State of the Parks 1980*. Special analysis, p. 373.

Soil Conservation Service

Executive Order 9060. Feb. 23, 1942.

Executive Order 9577. June 29, 1945.

U.S. Congress. Soil Conservation Act of 1935. 49 stat. 163.

———. House. Committee on Appropriations. Subcommittee on the Agriculture Department. Appropriations for 1936. 74th Cong., 1st sess.

———. Appropriations for 1937. 74th Cong., 2d sess.

———. Appropriations for 1938. 75th Cong., 1st sess.

———. Appropriations for 1944. 78th Cong., 1st sess.

———. Appropriations for 1947. 79th Cong., 2d sess.

———. Appropriations for 1951. 81st Cong., 2d sess., part 1.

———. Subcommittee on the Department of Agriculture and Related Agencies. Appropriations for 1955. 83rd Cong., 2d sess., part 3.

———. Appropriations for 1956. 84th Cong., 1st sess., part 2.

———. Appropriations for 1960. 86th Cong., 1st sess., part 2.

———. Appropriations for 1964. 88th Cong., 1st sess., part 2.

———. Appropriations for 1965. 88th Cong., 2d sess., part 2.

———. Subcommittee on Agriculture, Environment, and Consumer Protection. Appropriations for 1975. 93rd Cong., 2d sess., part 2.

———. Subcommittee on the Department of Agriculture and Related Agencies. Appropriations for 1977. 94th Cong., 2d sess., part 4.

———. Subcommittee on Agriculture, Rural Development and Related Agencies. Appropriations for 1982. 97th Cong., 1st sess., part 5.

———. Committee on Government Operations. Subcommittee on Conservation and Natural Resources. *Stream Channelization.* 92nd Cong., 1st sess.

U.S. Department of Treasury. *Appendix to the U.S. Budget for Fiscal Year 1981*, pp. 167-77.

———. *U.S. Budget, 1981*, Special analysis, p. 376.

Index

Abourezk, James, 100
An Act to repeal timber-culture laws, and for other purposes, 35
Agencies, *See* Environmental agencies
Agricultural Conservation and Adjustment Administration, 70
Agricultural Stabilization and Conservation Service (ASCS), 67-68
Alaska, 84, 85, 107
 national park expansion, 57, 59, 61, 63, 64
 salmon industry, 78, 79, 90
 water projects, 33, 98
Alaska National Interest Lands Conservation Act of 1980 (ANILCA), 86, 88
American Bicentennial Program, 54
American Express, 56
American Forest Congress, 38
American Forestry Association, 38
American Forests, 116
Andrews, Richard, 4, 16, 73, 74
Andrus, Cecil, 24, 102
Antiquities Act of 1906, 48, 53
Applegate Lake project, 24
Are Government Organizations Immortal?, 146
Army Corps of Engineers, 13-33, 39, 64, 79, 101-2, 125, 148
 budget, 18, 25, 28-30, 127, 129, 131, 132, 133
 constituency support, 19, 33
 creation of, 13-14
 criticism of, 31-32
 dam inspections, 18
 Environmental Effects Laboratory, 27
 exploration by, 14
 flood control, 16, 69-70
 hydroelectric power studies, 16
 minority hiring by, 32-33
 mission of, 7, 15-16, 68

navigational improvements by, 14-15
 NEPA, response to, 4, 16, 18, 139
 pollution control, 17
 power perceptions of personnel, 139-41
 recreational facility development, 17
 water projects, 18-26, 30, 31, 144-45
 work force, 135, 137
Atchafalaya project, 23
Atomic Energy Commission, 80
Auburn Dam project (Colo.), 99, 100, 103
Bankhead-Jones Farm Tenant Act, 68
Bayou Bodcau project, 23, 26
Bennett, Hugh, 64-65
Bevill, Tom, 26, 29, 33
Big South Fork National River and Recreation Area project, 28
Bitterroot National Forest controversy, 40
Bonneville Unit project (Utah), 99, 101
Boulder Dam. *See* Hoover Dam
Boulding, Kenneth, 150
Bradley, Dorotha M., 113
Breaking New Ground, 143
Brown, David S., 147-48, 150
Bureau of Agricultural Economics, 68
Bureau of Agricultural Engineering, 68
Bureau of Biological Survey, 79-80, 81
Bureau of Commercial Fisheries, 83
Bureau of Fisheries, 78, 79
Bureau of Indian Affairs, 87
Bureau of Land Management, 42, 45, 87, 107-22
 budget, 115, 118-21, 127, 129, 132
 constituency support, 112, 113
 creation of, 107, 111
 mission of, 114-15
 power perceptions of personnel, 140-41
 problems within, 121
 public land sale, 120
 Sagebrush Rebellion, 115-18

Wilderness Inventory, 115, 119-20
Wilderness Study Areas (WSAs), 120
work force, 135, 137
Bureau of Outdoor Recreation, 83
Bureau of Reclamation, 19, 23, 24, 25,
27-28, 34, 39, 69, 92-107,144-45, 148-49
budget, 96-97, 100, 101, 102-3, 104-5,
127, 129, 131-32
constituency support, 105
creation of, 92
criticism of, 106
dam construction, 98
hydroelectrical power development,
96-97, 98
Indian water rights and, 103-4
irrigation projects, 105
limitations of, 10, 30
mission of, 98, 106
NEPA, response to, 4
power perceptions of personnel, 141
Public Involvement and Environmental
Education programs, 103
reclamation fund, 94-95, 96
recreation program, 98
responsibility, reduction of, 101
work force, 135
"Bureau of Reclamation Faces the 1980's,
The," 103
Bureau of Sports Fisheries and Wildlife, 83
Bureaucracy, Politics, and Public Policy, 5
Burford, Robert, 118, 121
Calef, Wesley, 113
Califano, Joseph, 11
California et al v. United States, 101
California State Water Resources Control
Board, 101
Carson, Rachel, 148
Carter, Jimmy, 19-28, 30, 99-100, 101, 102,
104, 117, 132, 133, 149
Case-Wheeler Act of 1939, 69
Central Arizona Project (CAP), 100, 102
see also Orme Dam project
Channelization projects, 15, 73
Citizens Concerned About the Project, 101
Civilian Conservation Corps, 65, 110
Clark, William, 117, 121
Clarke-McNary Act of 1924, 39
Classification and Multiple Use Act of 1964,
114
Cleveland, Grover, 35
Coal leasing, 118-19, 120, 121
Coalition for Water Project Review, 21-22
Colorado River Basin Bill of 1968, 97-98
Common Cause, 22
Congress, U.S., 25, 35-36, 40, 48, 109
committee membership effect on water
projects, 19, 21, 22
creation of agencies, 8, 13, 26, 49, 65,
78, 92, 114
support for agencies, 11-12, 20, 33, 45,

50, 60-61, 63, 81, 96, 98, 129
see also House of Representatives, U.S.;
specific Acts; specific Bills
Conservation
description of, 36-37
history of, 107-8
public expenditures for, 90
Conservation Foundation, 63
Conservationists, 48-50, 97
Constituency support for agencies, 5, 6, 9-12
see also under specific agencies
Consumer Protection Agency (proposed), 10
Consumers' movement, 10
Cooley, Richard, 77, 78
Corps of Engineers. See Army Corps of
Engineers
Cotner, Melvin L., 89-90
Council of Environmental Quality, 74
Crowell, John, 44
Culhane, Paul J., 45, 51, 112
Cultural centers, 54
Dam safety, 18, 27-28
Damning the West, 99
"Dams and Other Disasters," 31
Dana, Samuel T., 36, 37, 112, 113
Darling, 51
Darwin, Charles, 148
"Degradation of Our National Parks, The,"
51
Department of Agriculture, 4, 35, 43, 44,
64, 65
Department of Commerce, 79, 81, 83
Department of Commerce and Labor, 78
Department of Defense, 11
Department of Energy, 101
Department of Health and Human Services,
104
Department of the Interior, 17, 25, 56, 65,
79, 81, 83-84, 86, 104, 106, 107, 121
Department of Justice, Civil Rights Division,
11
Department of Natural Resources (pro-
posed), 25, 236
Department of the Treasury, 78
Desert Land Act of 1877, 93
Desert settlement, 92-94
DeVoto, Bernard, 92
Dickenson, Russell, 60, 64
"Dilemma of Our Parks, The," 50-51
Dinosaur National Monument, 97
Downs, Anthony, 133
Drury, Newton B., 50
Duck Stamp Act of 1934, 80
Duck stamps, 81, 82
Dust Bowl of the 1930's, 64-65, 110
Easter, K. William, 89-90
Echo Park controversy, 97
Eichhorn, 51
EIS. See Environmental Impact statements
Eisenhower, Dwight D., 144

Elliott, A.J., 97
Endangered Species Act of 1973, 85
Endangered Species Program, 87
Energy crisis, 2, 4, 132
Environmental agencies
    budgets, 126-27, 128, 129, 130, 131-35
    bureaucratic behavior, 147-48
    competition, 141-42, 149, 150
    coordination, 85, 88
    creation of, 7-8, 9
    ecological perspective on, 146-50
    economic dichotomy, 145-46
    incremental model of development, 89-91
    leadership of, 9
    longevity, 146
    NEPA, response to, 3-4, 133
    organizational change in, 3, 18
    personnel rotation, 112
    political appointments to, 45
    power perceptions of personnel, 137, 138, 139-42
    regulatory agencies, 9-10
    research on, methods of, 125-26, 137, 139, 151
    resources of, 5, 6
    service agencies, 9
    size and success, 149-50
    work forces, 135, 136, 137
    see also Research methods; specific agencies
Environmental crisis, 1, 132-33
Environmental movement, 83, 84-85
Environmental Defense Fund, 22
Environmental Effects Laboratory, 27
Environmental impact statements (EIS), 4, 85-86, 99, 116, 121
Environmental Policy and Administration Change, 4
Environmental Protection Agency, 7, 10
Environmentalists, 55, 73, 90, 99, 103
Erosion. See Soil erosion
Eufaula Lake project (Okla.), 32
Fairfax, Sally F., 36, 37, 45, 112, 113
Farm Security Administration, 69
Federal Bureau of Investigation, 9
Federal Land Policy and Management Act of 1976 (FLPMA), 114, 115, 116, 122, 132
Federal Trade Commission, 10
Fenno, Richard, 129
Field Operations Study Team (FOST), 54
Fish and Wildlife Act of 1946, 17-18
Fish and Wildlife Act of 1956, 83
Fish and Wildlife Coordination Act of 1934, 80
Fish and Wildlife Service, U.S., 18, 77-89
    budget, 86-88, 126, 127, 129, 132, 133
    constituency support, 82, 90
    creation of, 80-81
    criticism of, 83-84
    Endangered Species Program, 87

    mission of, 7, 77-78, 89
    NEPA, response to, 4, 85-86
    origins of, 77-80
    power perceptions of personnel, 141
    reorganization, 82-83
    rodent and pest control program, 84
    technical assistance program, 88
    work force, 135
    workload, 85
Fish Commission, U.S., 78
Fish hatcheries, 82, 87
Fisheries, 43
Flood control, 16, 29, 69-70, 71, 98
Flood Control Act of 1936, 16, 69-70
Flood Control Act of 1944, 69-70
Flood Control Act of 1948, 98
"Flooding America in Order to Save It,", 31
FLPMA. See Federal Land Policy and Management Act of 1976
Food and Agriculture Act of 1962, 72
Food Production Administration, 70
Ford, Gerald, 100
Forest and Rangeland Renewable Resources Planning Act of 1974,(RPA), 41-42, 44-45
Forest Ranger, The, 112
Forest Service, U.S., 33-46, 51, 58, 64, 76, 79
    budget, 41-45, 127, 131, 132, 133
    constituency support, 38, 42
    creation of, 34
    fire fighting, 38
    forest management, 37-38
    mission, 7, 38-40, 68
    NEPA, response to, 4, 40, 139
    Operation Outdoors, 40
    personnel rotation, 112
    power perceptions of personnel, 139-41
    recreation areas, 40, 43-44
    research by, 38-39
    Roadless Area Review and Evaluation (RARE I, RARE II), 41
    soil conservation project, 39-40
    timber sales, 43
    work force, 135, 137
Fort McDowell Indian Reservation (Ariz.), 104
Foss, Phillip, 111
Frodkin, Phillip, 19-20
Frémont, John C., 14
Fruitland Mesa project (Colo.), 99, 100
Galbraith, John Kenneth, 145
Garfield Commission, 109
Garrison Division project, 99, 101, 103
Gas leasing, 118
Gateway Park (New York City), 54
General Accounting Office (GAO), 56, 60, 75, 106
General Land Office, 35, 107, 108, 115
General Systems Theory, 149

Geological Survey, U.S., 93, 118
Glen Canyon Dam, 98
Golden Eagle Pass, 54
Golden Gate Park (San Francisco), 54
Grand Canyon, 98
Grazing land, 108-12, 121
Grazing Service, 107, 110
Great Plains Conservation Project, 71-72, 75, 76
Great Plains Shelterbelt project, 40
Gregg, Frank, 123
Gruening, Ernest, 79
Hartzog, George, 52, 53, 54, 55
Hastey, Edward, 116
Hays, Samuel P., 34, 36, 108
Heclo, Hugh, 144
Heiberg, 32
Heritage Conservation and Recreation Service, 61
Hetch Hetchy reservoir project, 49
Higginson, 102, 103
Historic resource preservation, 53
Hofstadter, Richard, 148
Holden, Matthew, 133, 144
Homestead Act of 1862, 93
Homesteading, 107-8
Hoover, Herbert, 109, 110
Hoover, J. Edgar, 9
Hoover, Commission, 25
Hoover Dam, 96
Hornblower, Margot, 24
House of Representatives, U.S.,
    Appropriations Committee, Public Works Subcommittee, 15, 20-21, 22
    Committee on Irrigation of Arid Lands, 95
Hunting licenses, 81
    see also Duck Stamp Act; Duck stamps
Hurricane Allen, 28
Hydroelectric power, 16, 32, 96-97, 98
Ickes, Harold, 65, 79, 109
Indian water rights, 103-4
Ingram, Helen, 74, 113
Interest groups, 10, 19, 31, 100, 139
    see also specific interest groups
Interest rates and project economics, 23
Irrigation, 68-69, 71, 93, 95, 105
Johnson, Lyndon B., 11
Kaufman, Herbert, 112, 146-47
Kennedy, John F., 11
Kennedy Center for the Performing Arts (Washington, D.C.), 54
Kings River project (Calif.), 97
Lacey Act of 1900, 79-80
Lamm, Richard, 100
Land and Water Conservation Fund, 42, 45, 53, 60, 61
Landau, Martin, 149
League of Kentucky Sportsmen, 31
League of Women Voters, 22

Leman, Christopher, 41-42, 74-75, 76, 104
Lewis and Clark expedition, 14
Life, 63
Lindblom, Charles E., 12, 89
Liroff, Richard, 4
Lobbies, 11, 22
Lowi, Theodore J., 149
Maass, Arthur, 11, 16, 97
McCarran, Pat, 110
Mather, Stephen, 50
Meramec Lake project, 23
Migratory Bird Treaty Act of 1918, 80
Mineral resources, 96, 115
    see also Coal leasing; Gas leasing; Oil drilling and exploration
Minerals Management Service, 120-21, 122
Minority contractors, 32-33
Mission '66 program, 51-52
Mississippi River, 16
Missouri River, 33
Monopoly, description of, 36-37, 146, 150
Mt. St. Helens eruption, 28
Mountain States Legal Foundation, 117
Moynihan, Daniel Patrick, 30
Muir, John, 50
Multiple Use-Sustained Yield Act of 1960, 37
Nader, Ralph, 99
Narrows Unit project (Colo.), 99, 100-2
National Agricultural Lands Study, 76
National Association of Conservation Districts, 72
National Audubon Society, 73, 101
National Board of Trade, 38
National Emergency Preparedness Planning Activities, 33
National Environmental Policy Act of 1969. *See* NEPA
National Forest Management Act of 1976, 40, 41
National Industrial Recovery Act program, 65
National Inholders Association, 59
National Oceanographic and Atmospheric Administration, 83
National park land categories, 52
National Park Service, 34, 39, 40, 45, 48-64, 82, 97
    budget, 50, 53, 54, 56-57, 60-61, 63, 127, 129,132, 133
    constituency support, 54-55, 90
    creation of, 49-50
    criticism of, 56-58
    Field Operations Study Team (FOST), 54
    mission of, 49-50, 89
    Mission '66 program, 51-52
    NEPA, response to, 4
    park expansion, 59-60
    power perceptions of personel, 139
    recreation facility visitors, 17

research on, 57-58
reservation system, 55-56
survey of personnel, 58-59
work force, 135, 137
National Park Service Organic Act of 1916,
   49, 52
National Parks and Conservation
   Association, 56
National Parks and Recreation Act of 1978,
   59
National Resources Defense Council, 116,
   121
National Taxpayers Union, 22, 31
National Visitor Center (Washington, D.C.),
   61
National Water Quality Commission, 17
National Water Resources Association, 19,
   100, 103
National Wilderness Preservation System,
   58, 120
National Wildlife Refuge System, 86
Natural areas, 52-53
   see also Preservation
NEPA (National Environmental Policy Act
   of 1969), 1, 2, 3-4, 16, 18, 40, 53, 57,
   73, 74, 85-86, 139
New Industrial State, The, 145
Nixon, Richard, 25, 55, 126
North American Water and Power Alliance,
   33
North Loup Division project (Neb.), 105
Oahe Unit project (S.D.), 99, 100, 103
Occupational Safety and Health Adminis-
   tration, 10
Office of Economic Opportunity (OEO), 10,
   11
Office of Management and Budget (OMB),
   29, 57, 75, 86, 126
Office of Science and Technology, 60
Office of Water Policy, 29
Ohio River, 17
Oil drilling and exploration, 87, 96, 118-
   19, 120, 121
Oligopoly, description of, 146, 149
Omnibus Flood Control Act of 1936, 69
One Third of the Nation's Land, 114
O'Neill Unit project (Neb.), 105
Operation Outdoors, 40
Organizational Revolution, The, 150
Orme Dam project (Ariz.), 104
Oroville-Tonasket Unit of the Chief Joseph
   Dam (Wash.), 101
Park rangers, 53
Park Service. See National Park Service
Peace Corps, 11
Pesticides, 84
Pike, Zebulon M., 14
Pinchot, Gifford, 34-37, 38, 39, 48, 50,
   143-44, 150
Politics and Grass, 111

Pope-Jones Act of 1937, 69
Powell, John Wesley, 93
Prairie States Forestry Project, 69
Preservation, 55, 89
   see also Wilderness preservation;
   Wildlife preservation
Preservationists, 48-50, 81
Presidential powers, 14, 48, 77
   see also specific presidents
Price, Waterhouse and Company, 31
Progressive conservation movement, 34, 36,
   147
Progressive movement, 144
Public Health Service, 17
Public Land Law Review Commission, 114
Public lands, 62, 96, 107-9, 120
Public Law 95-507, 302
Public Law 96-487, 59
Public relations programs, 42
Public Reservation Systems (PRS), 56
Public use facilities. See Recreation areas
Public works, 4, 25, 31
Reagan, Ronald, 11, 28-30, 42-45, 58,
   59-63, 75-76, 82, 104, 105, 115, 117-
   21, 132, 133-35
Reclamation Act of 1902, 92, 93, 101, 102,
   103, 105
Recreation, 38, 40, 52, 58, 71, 98, 113, 114
   budget cuts regarding, 29, 42, 43-44,
   119-20
Recreation areas
   automobiles in, 50
   health and safety problems in, 44, 60, 120
   urban, 53, 54, 62
Red River Waterway project, 28
" 'Reforming' the Bureaucracy: Some Sug-
   gestions for the New President," 147-48
Refuse Act of 1899, 17
River Killers, The, 31
Rivers-and-harbors bill, 14-15, 16
Roadless Area Review and Evaluation
   (RARE I,RARE II), 41
Robbins, Roy, 108-9
Rocky Mountain National Park, 57
Roosevelt, Franklin D., 17, 65, 67, 79, 96,
   97, 109
Roosevelt, Theodore, 1, 34, 108
Rourke, Francis, 2, 5, 7, 8, 10-11
Sagebrush Rebellion, 59, 115-18
Salmon industry, 77-78, 79, 90
Save Our Red River, 31
Save Our Sound Fisheries, 31
Savory Pot Hook project (Colo.), 99, 100
Sirotkin, 97
Smith, Virginia, 105
Soil and Water Resource Conservation Act
   of 1977 (RCA), 74, 76
Soil Conservation Act of 1935, 65
Soil Conservation Service, 19, 39, 40, 64-77
   budget, 70, 75-76, 127, 129, 132

conservation programs, 75
constituency support, 72-73, 90
creation of, 65
criticism of, 73, 74
demonstration projects, 66
erosion prevention projects, 71
flood control programs, 69-70, 71, 75
irrigation programs, 68-69, 71
mission of, 65-66
NEPA, response to, 73, 74
power perceptions of personnel, 141
reorganization, 70
resource conservation and development
program, 72, 75
soil conservation districts, 66-67, 72
work force, 135, 137
Soil erosion, 39-40, 64-67, 71
"Soil Erosion, A Natural Menace," 64
"State of the Parks 1980," 60
Stratton, 97
"Streamlining" of budgets, 119
Taylor Grazing Act of 1934, 197, 109-10,
111, 112, 114
Tennessee-Tombigbee Waterway, 22, 26,
30, 31, 33
Tennessee Valley Authority, 19, 23
Teton Dam disaster, 18, 99
Ticketron, 56
Timber and Stone Act of 1878, 35
Timber Culture Act of 1873, 93
Trans-Alaska pipeline, 85
Truman, Harry S, 17
Udall, Stewart, 52, 98
Uncompahgre project (Colo.), 96
Unobtrusive Measures, 125
Urban recreation areas, 53, 54, 62
von Bertalanffy, Ludwig, 149, 150
Walker, Ron, 55-56
Wallop, Malcolm, 106
War Food Administration, 70
Washington Post, 24
Water and Power Resources Service, 93
  see also Bureau of Reclamation
Water pollution, 16-17
Water projects, 18-26
  Congressional committee membership
  and, 21, 22
  economics of, 22-24
  see also Dam safety; Flood control;
  Hydroelectric power; Irrigation; specific
  projects
Water Resources Council, 26, 102, 104
Water treatment plants, 32
Watershed Protection and Flood Protection
  Act of 1954, 70, 71, 73
Watt, James, 59-63, 86, 87, 104, 105, 115-
  17, 119, 120, 121
Weber, Max, 3, 5, 7, 146
Western States Water Council, 19, 100
White Act of 1924, 78-79

Wichelman, Allen F., 4
Wildavsky, 126
Wilderness Act of 1964, 53, 57, 113
Wilderness Inventory, 115, 119-20
Wilderness preservation, 114, 121
Wilderness Study Areas (WSAs), 120
Wildlife preservation, 43, 81
  refuges, 81, 82, 85, 86, 88
Wolf Trap Park (Va.), 54
Yates, Sidney, 62, 115-16, 117, 119
Yatesville Lake project, 28
Yatesville, Dam project, 26
Yellowstone Valley, 48
Yosemite National Park, 49, 50, 63
Young Adult Conservation Corps (YACC),
  42, 43
Youth Conservation Corps (YCC), 42, 43